D0766930

WAR OF WORDS

Born in England, Elizabeth Mapstone lived in Montreal for ten years, working as a journalist and translator. She returned to Britain with her three children and worked as a public relations executive before going on to study experimental psychology at Oxford University, and completing a doctorate in the psychology of interpersonal communication. She was founding editor of *The Psychologist: Bulletin of the British Psychological Society*, from 1987 to 1993. Dr Mapstone is now a chartered psychologist practising in Cornwall and is married to John Tyerman Williams, author of *Pooh and the Philosophers*.

Elizabeth Mapstone

WAR OF WORDS

Women and Men Arguing

V

VINTAGE

Published by Vintage 1999

2 4 6 8 10 9 7 5 3 1

First published in Great Britain in 1998 by
Chatto & Windus

Vintage
Random House, 20 Vauxhall Bridge Road,
London SW1V 2SA

Random House Australia (Pty) Limited
20 Alfred Street, Milsons Point, Sydney
New South Wales 2061, Australia

Random House New Zealand Limited
18 Poland Road, Glenfield,
Auckland 10, New Zealand

Random House South Africa (Pty) Limited
Endulini, 5A Jubilee Road, Parktown 2193,
South Africa

Random House UK Limited Reg. No. 954009

A CIP catalogue record for this book
is available from the British Library

ISBN 0 09 976361 3

Papers used by Random House UK Ltd are natural, recyclable products made from wood grown in sustainable forests. The manufacturing processes conform to the environmental regulations of the country of origin

Printed and bound in Great Britain by
Mackays of Chatham plc, Chatham, Kent

To John Tyerman Williams,
who proves it is possible
to resolve the Porcupine's Dilemma

Contents

What This Book Is About

Where viewpoints clashed and arguments began...
(P.G. Wodehouse, 1933)[1]

There are no mere facts, only interpretations.
(Friedrich Nietzsche, 1901)[2]

This book is about the psychology of argument, and more especially, it is about how the meaning of an argument changes depending on who you are and whether the other person is a woman or a man. It looks at how we interpret all those everyday discussions, debates, disagreements we all get involved in, and shows that central to their meaning is gender.

It is not about the words we exchange, it is not about how we argue. There are lots of books about conversational style and linguistic studies. It is about what happens after the words are over and we take stock.

In everyday life, contrary to what is generally supposed, what really matters is not so much what people actually say but *how people remember what was said.*

Think about it. While you are actually engaged in arguing, you are busy: monitoring the other person's words, sorting out the hidden from the overt implications, seeking weak points, marshalling your own defences, ransacking your memory for useful information, constructing as unassailable a position as you can from the material at hand; or when agreement is important, you may be actively seeking points of contact, sometimes even demolishing part of your own argument to incorporate the best bits of the other's, monitoring the other's body language and tone of voice, adjusting your own responses to make sense of both your interpretation of the other person's intentions and meanings and to convey your own. You are busy, and the other person is busy.

It is only afterwards, when the argument is over, that its importance and meaning can be assessed. At that stage, it is rare for anyone to remember more than a few selected verbal exchanges. Outrageous statements may be hung on to and repeated to interested third parties ('Would you believe, he actually said . . .'). You may remember those warming words, 'I entirely agree with you', or a key exchange which focused the debate. But generally speaking, you are unlikely to be able to recall the sequence of words, the body language, the non-verbal signals we all pick up. What you remember is the overall sense of what happened, why the argument arose in the first place and how successful you were in getting your own views across. It is this interpretation which remains with you and which affects your subsequent actions.

So this book is not about logic or what makes a rational argument, nor does it set out to tell you how to win an argument – though once you understand what is going on when people argue, you may well find it helps, and I do give a few tips on how one might use this knowledge. This book looks at, not *how* people argue and the words they use – there are lots of books on that topic – but how people *interpret* an argument after it has occurred, how they reconstruct its meaning.

Arguments in real life do not occur in a vacuum. They arise between people, and people are social beings with roles, expectations, relationships. It is impossible to conceive of two people arguing and not being in some kind of relationship, even if only that of strangers. And even strangers are gendered. I will show that relationships are central to how people interpret disagreements with each other. Not only does it matter how well you know the other person, how intimate you are, whether you like or dislike her or him, or which of you has the higher status; gender turns out to be one of the most important factors of all.

It is widely accepted in our society that there is a fundamental incompatibility between the desire to defend a point of view and care of people's feelings. On the one hand, people generally believe in principle that argument as rational debate and exchange of views

2

cruel light of a late twentieth-century day. My book is a serious attempt to expose these hidden beliefs that undermine and even destroy relations between women and men – and by exposing, end them.

The Research

This book is based on research begun in 1984 into how people *remember and interpret* arguments in different relationships. Investigations involved more than 600 people (mainly in Britain and the USA) in interviews, keeping diaries, completing questionnaires and some experimentation.

A brief explanation of how I analysed what people say (qualitative analysis) may be found in the Notes[1].

1. **Interviews** were of three kinds:
(a) Informal, in which I talked casually about my research and invited comments. Argument being a universal phenomenon, people were usually very willing to talk about their views, attitudes and experience. More than 200 people provided anecdotes and other details which contributed to this book.
(b) Formal: I constructed a set of questions, both closed and open-ended, to be able to make comparisons and draw conclusions. People were asked to recall a specific argument in a series of different relationships, and to answer questions about these specific arguments. 49 women and 40 men have been involved in the full interview, and 119 people provided incomplete data.
(c) Taped: I also tape-recorded longer interviews with 23 people. This includes those whose story I give in the book, but also a number of others whose views enriched my investigations but who may not have been quoted.

2. Diaries

In my doctoral thesis[2] I reported on 54 diaries sent in by 38 women and 26 men. Diaries from a further 146 people are included in this book.

Diarists were asked to keep a record of every argument they had for a week, argument being defined as 'any situation in which two people disagree about an issue, and each wishes to convince the other of her/his point of view'. Some people kept diaries for 2 weeks. Keeping a diary turned out to be difficult, and people frequently mentioned that they forgot, and that many arguments were not recorded. It was also particularly interesting to note that people who lived together (husband and wife, parent and adult child) usually did not record the same argument. Thus no conclusions about frequency can be drawn from these data. In addition, many who volunteered found the task too difficult, especially if they were very busy people or else involved in a difficult relationship in which there were 'just too many arguments all on the same topic'. Diaries therefore come from a self-selected group, and do need to be supplemented by data from interviews and other sources to give a generalised picture.

Statistical analyses quoted in this book are taken from the first set of 54 diaries analysed. To avoid distortions caused by individuals with idiosyncratic patterns of behaviour, comparisons are made by taking a single argument only for each person in any given relationship (the first with complete data). Full details may be found in Mapstone (1992a).

3. Experimental Investigations

An experimental situation was devised which led to argument between pairs, and established measures of how far each influenced the other. Questionnaires also asked for participants' attitudes to their partner after the argument session. The experiment was run with strangers matched for age and education level: 12 all male pairs, 12 all female pairs and 12 mixed; or 72 people in all. A further 72 people took part in pairs as friends.

4. Questionnaire
The Mapstone Attitude to Argument Questionnaire (MAQ) was administered to 152 members of the Oxford Subject Panel (81 women, 71 men) as well as 54 contributors to the diary study (38 women, 26 men).

Acknowledgements

I now understand why so many books include a section acknowledging the help and encouragement of others. It is impossible to complete a book based on research without becoming indebted to many people, and I would like to take this opportunity to thank publicly some of those who helped me.

First, I must thank all those more than 600 people who contributed to this research. Most of those who sent in diaries did so anonymously, and even if they made themselves known to me, I promised I would not reveal identities. So I can thank the majority of those to whom I am indebted only in the most general terms. Thank you for being willing to share your experiences of argument, and to many, thank you also for passing on my request for diarists to friends and relations, and so enabling me to include people of all ages, from all parts of the country and all walks of life.

Many people shared more, sending me long letters, ideas, suggestions, newspaper cuttings, books, proving beyond a shadow of doubt that the psychology of argument is important to lots of us. Others responded generously to my enquiries, some by seeking out relevant material, others by being willing to be interviewed at length on tape. Acknowledging most publicly is difficult because anonymity was promised, but I must thank specially: Lesley Riddoch and Clare Short for taking time out of their busy schedules to talk to me at length; Margaret Godel for doing computer searches on my behalf, sending lots of useful data, as well as for commenting on several chapters; Mary Boyle and Maryon Tysoe for their helpful comments on several chapters; Adrian

Coyle for sending printed papers and a taped discussion; David Wilcox for sending lots of information over many years, and for preparing the graphs in Part Three, Ian Norwell for all his comments and clippings; Margaret and Malcolm Yee for their support and long hours of friendly argument; my American friends Gertrude Rieger, Pit Lucking, Stephan Garnett, Lyn Carver, Phyllis and Bill Stigall, Polly Beck and Stephanie May, for sending letters, stories, clippings; and to Chuck McKee and all those on the Odyssey to Oxford who offered friendship and help in ensuring I had an American perspective on argument.

Discussion is so much a part of psychological research, it would be impossible to remember everyone who contributed over the past twelve years. Nevertheless, I wish to record my thanks to: the late Jos Jaspars and Donald Broadbent; Bob Abelson, Michael Argyle, Mick Billig, Peter Collett, Muriel Egerton, Ralph Exline, Gillian Finchilescu, Paul Harris, Olle Hogberg, Phil Johnson-Laird, Celia Kitzinger, Sonia Livingstone, Patrick McGee, John Medcof, Don Mixon, Ben Slugoski, Tim Smithin, Maria Yapp, for their interest and suggestions; to Rom Harré who gave so generously of his time and restored my belief in my work; and to Michael Lockwood for comments on my Power–Gender model in Part Five. Statistics being my Achilles' heel, I am particularly grateful to Francis Marriot, who checked all my calculations, and to Phil Levy, James Reason, Les Prince and Peter Lunt, who generously shared their own knowledge and experience.

One's family inevitably becomes involved in a project of this kind, and everyone at some stage cheerfully contributed to this investigation. Particular thanks are due to my son Michael Abbott, who created a computer program to help with data analysis; to my daughters Lise Kelly and Akita Grinnall, who read and criticised numerous drafts, discussed ideas and provided lots of useful information; and to my mother Renée Norris, my sister Penny Manders, and my nieces Dinah Loasby and Sarah Knafler, for their contributions, interest and support.

Finally, I want to say a heartfelt thank you to the two most important people in a writer's life: to Michael Thomas, my agent, for believing in me when others didn't; and to Alison Samuel, my editor, who encouraged, supported and cajoled through the nine-month gestation period, literary midwife to my late-life baby.

This book records many instances of men who treat the women in their lives as incomprehensible, irrational and unimportant. I am glad to have the opportunity to note that the men I thank here showed few signs of subscribing to such stereotypes – further evidence that statistics tell you nothing about the individual.

Part One

Argument and Humpty Dumpty

'But "glory" doesn't mean "a nice knock-down argument",'
Alice objected.

'When I use a word,' said Humpty Dumpty in rather a scornful
tone, 'it means just what I choose it to mean – neither more nor
less.'

(Lewis Carroll, *Through the Looking Glass*)

Everybody argues. We all see things from our own perspective,
and this inevitably means that other people will say things with
which we disagree. It might be something very simple, like getting
their facts wrong: Laura, for example, had an argument with
Sandra in the office about which road the laundromat was in. It
was very low key and perfectly friendly, and they sorted it out
eventually by looking in the telephone directory, so you might
wonder why they bothered to argue about a matter of fact in the
first place. But as Laura said: 'When you *know* you're right, you
just have to convince the other person.'

Lots of everyday arguments are like this – disagreements about
matters of fact, such as what time the post goes or the significance
of a landmark or even the name of a chocolate bar. Lots more are
about practical matters. When people all over Britain were asked to
keep diaries of their arguments, more than half of all arguments
reported were about practical issues, whether with family or at
work or with various officials, tradespeople, professionals. The list
of topics is endless: who should do the washing up, or get the
dinner, which television programme to watch, where to park the

car, how to cut down production costs, the feasibility of a project, the relevance of certain statistics, how to run a meeting, whether library books could be renewed, what time the plumber would call, 'neighbour's complaints about my cat'.[1] Some of these arguments can be of great practical importance to the people involved, which is why even the most peace-loving among us find ourselves involved in argument from time to time.

Note that this list does not include those notoriously upsetting topics like politics, religion and sex. People do argue about these things, but perhaps because they can be so distressing, some people go out of their way to avoid getting involved in discussing such issues, unless they can be fairly sure that they are with friends who share their values. As the American psychologist Fritz Heider put it:

> We tend to like people who have the same beliefs and attitudes we have, and when we like people, we want them to have the same attitudes we have.[2]

Heider believed that this would inevitably lead to conflict, as each person would try to persuade the other to 'see reality as he sees it'. For this reason, many of us may find ourselves trying to persuade someone important – a friend, a lover, a spouse, a child – to see things the way we do.

The trouble is that when someone disagrees with us, we do tend to see them as distancing themselves from us, and the further away from us they appear to be, the less inclined we feel to enjoy their company. Arguments about important values can lead to bad feelings precisely because they show that the other person sees the world differently, and this seems to suggest that our own view of reality must be wrong. This can be so infuriating that sometimes people do not dare say what they think for fear of going too far. Anger is not far from the surface when people dispute about values.

> We want other people to have the same values that we ourselves have. If [the other person] flouts my values he is a thorn in my flesh, he does not recognize what is reality for me.[3]

In some parts of the world, arguments about politics and religion can, as we know, be deadly. As one woman from South Africa said to me, the year before Nelson Mandela was released from prison:

> 'In South Africa ... there is no such thing as a superficial argument. You get very sensitively attuned to underlying meanings. Shared values and assumptions give you a means of communication, and allow you to agree to differ because it doesn't matter.'

You may, of course, be feeling that this is not about you at all. You may believe that 'Nice people don't argue', and that you yourself never do. But in an important sense you are arguing with me, even though your disagreement may remain silent. Even if you would never *express* your opposing views, your own thoughts are a part of what is meant by that opening statement 'Everybody argues'. When you disagree, however silently, with another person, you are arguing in your head with that person, because you *think* what you think.

Arguing is part of thinking. It is a part of human nature to hear a statement and disagree, to look for contradictions, to seek exceptions to every rule. Indeed, some psychologists believe that thinking is essentially a dialogue with oneself, an internal debate.[4] We have all seen those cartoons which show a person confronting temptation, with an angel saying 'Don't do it!' in one ear and a devil urging 'Go for it!' in the other. We recognise the situation because all of us at one time or another have had to deal with inner conflict, where one part of us wanted something that another part of us thought was wrong. But internal arguments are not always about serious questions of right or wrong. Anything can trigger an internal debate because that is how we think about the world.

Everybody argues, but not everyone argues out loud. Or perhaps I should say that everyone argues inside their head and everyone has the potential to express contradictory views to others. I have been investigating argument for twelve years now, and I have never come across anyone who has not found themselves involved in argument at some time or other. Disagreement, discussion, discord are part of our everyday lives, and anything some other person says can trigger an argument. Whether the argument remains internal or whether it is expressed seems to depend very much on how the different people involved react to the fact that they are disagreeing, whether they actually care what the other person thinks and how they feel about argument itself. Most important of all, it seems to depend on whether the person is a woman or a man, and on which the other person is.

1

Debate or Battle: Men Define Argument

Argument is a word that carries an enormous baggage of emotion. You may feel that I am behaving a bit like Humpty Dumpty, insisting that a word means what I say it means, and it is true that I am trying to use the word in its very broadest sense. People vary enormously in how they interpret the word, and often they behave like Humpty Dumpty too.

Early on in my investigations into the psychology of argument, I asked people what they thought about argument, and whether it is a good way to get people to see your point of view. Their replies made it clear that women and men don't see argument in the same way.

Most men I have interviewed think of argument as *debate* in which people exchange views and affect each others' opinions.

'An argument to me is an exchange of ideas, debating back and forth.' (Steve)

'Discussion and debate are good ways to get people to understand.' (Ben)

'Argument means trying to persuade the other person to see your point of view, and the other guy does the same.' (Jon)

'Argument is a process of bargaining. You need to understand the other's aims, and you have to be prepared to give up your own point of view in the face of a good argument.' (Mark)

Some men have a more aggressive approach, though:

'Argument is about winning and losing. I'm always out to win.' (Hank)

'An argument is a battle you have to win. To be made angry is a sign of weakness. Basically you have to sell yourself, tear down the other's argument. Don't give him any credit for his point of view. Otherwise you're lost.' (Homer)

'I find I become more aggressive when the opposition is both strong and intransigent. I don't like being beaten. I ... would feel cruel satisfaction at smashing someone's argument if it had annoyed me. ... If you get into arguments, you must be a fighter.' (Henry)

and more disturbing:

'An argument's a difference of opinion which leads to an exchange, whether it be verbal or physical.' (Grant)

(Talking about arguments that lead to blows is unusual, though one man did say that in his experience it was liable to happen in groups of men who had been drinking. Disagreements that escalated into violence were never reported in diaries.)

Whether or not they see it as a verbal battle, many men say they enjoy argument:

'I find argument stimulating. Gets the adrenalin going and helps you think.' (Bill)

'I enjoy playing the devil's advocate, even if I agree.' (Les)

'I enjoy the cut and thrust of a good argument.' (Stewart)

Some men are willing to acknowledge that the other person's point of view must be given its due, and that the relationship between protagonists can be important if either is to be persuaded to change his or her mind:

'Rapport is very important. The other person needs time and space.' (Dhuleep)

'The meaning of the relationship is as important as the rational evidence for being convinced. Depends whether you are committed to the relationship or to the argument itself.' (Leslie)

'I argue with anyone who expresses a different opinion to my own, but when no common ground can be reached, I will suggest that we agree to disagree. I would never jeopardise a relationship or friendship for the sake of an argument.' (Jack)

However, as Mark put it,

'I don't think you can put a relationship ahead of everything because sooner or later your views will come out. Argument is the only way to deal with polarised situations.'

The general attitude of most men appears to be that, given rapport and a willingness to listen to the other, argument is not something they would fear or avoid.

A minority of men is less happy about arguing. David, for example, is worried about antagonising a friend. He explained that arguing is not necessary to change people's minds:

'I've found that my thinking has changed over time, because of my friends, because I valued their friendship and needed to change. You're not likely to be changed by someone you don't like. It's best not to antagonise a friend, but I don't worry about other people.'

Darren goes further and avoids argument:

'If a situation arises where I feel my remarks might be inflammatory, I sit silent. I never risk an argument by being contrary. If I need to get it off my chest, I'll go to a third party. I only try to persuade in calm debate, usually with a casual acquaintance, not a friend. I like to keep good relationships.'

Darren is unusual. Though he was among the first men I interviewed, I very rarely found any other man talking of remaining silent so as to protect relationships. Other men may be less articulate about such concerns, and yet still be cautious, but the expressed attitude of the vast majority of men is that argument is inevitable, useful and even enjoyable.

2

Friendship, Fear and Anger: Women Talk about Quarrels

Even more striking is the fact that these words from a man ('I like to keep good relationships') provide a good summary of the attitudes of many women. Indeed, all the women I have interviewed over the past twelve years, without exception, have expressed concern at some point about the damage disagreement might cause to important relationships.

Women have a strongly ambivalent attitude to argument. On the one hand, they want to be able to express their opinion without causing problems:

> 'If I accept the other person has a genuine point of view, then she or he should be prepared to hear mine without feeling under attack.' (Sarah)

and many women talk of shared values or of relationships in which it is safe to argue.

> 'It makes a lot of difference in a friendship if you have got the same underlying value system. It's safe to argue then.' (Beryl)

> 'If you share the same kind of values, you can usually defend your beliefs without ending up hating each other. But when values are really different, there's no point in arguing. Friendships are difficult if you dare not disagree, I'm not sure I think they're worth the effort.' (Irene)

'You need common ground. When you have similar value systems, differences can be negotiated. Where you don't, disagreements can tear the very fabric of a relationship. If I can't express my opinion, I wouldn't have the friendship.' (Valerie)

On the other hand, many women say they prefer to avoid argument: there is an implication, nothing more explicit, that argument is hostility. This is at least in part because women try to restrain themselves until they get angry.

'I don't often argue, not until forced into it by a real challenge to my opinions, when I get worked up. If it's something that means a lot, like religion, I would have to walk away. There are certain points where it is "no go".' (Jane)

'I really dislike confrontation, so I try to avoid it by backing down. I have never felt it was right for me to argue with others as they may know better. Unless it's about really important things like injustice. I feel it is not wrong to argue about justice.' (Rena)

'I only ever argue when I have really thought about things deeply, and it is something really important. I can get really angry when I try to say something I have really thought about, and the other person just won't listen. Why don't my views count too?' (Kathy)

Why do many women feel they should restrain themselves from speaking out? Why do some women feel it is 'not right' for them to argue, but that 'really important things' make arguing 'not wrong'? Why do most men see argument as debate and most women tend to interpret the word as conflict, even quarrel? Many women agree with Rebecca that 'Relationships are more important than any issue.'

'I don't argue'

Everyone who was interviewed knew, of course, that I was investigating attitudes to argument and that I would ask them about their memories of arguments in different relationships.[5] Very early on it became clear that I had to find a way of establishing that I was not just interested in rows or quarrels, but wanted to know about all disagreements, whether friendly or hostile. For this reason I established the following definition of an argument:

> An argument is taken to mean a verbal disagreement between two people, each of whom wishes to convince the other of the validity of her/his point of view.

Since everyone involved was presented with this definition, and everyone had agreed to talk about their recall of argument, it was particularly interesting to find some women arguing that they never argue.

Kathleen said very quietly, 'I don't like arguing, it upsets people. I don't argue.' When reminded this was an investigation into people's recall of argument, she went on:

> 'I'll ask for other people's opinion and give mine – that can lead to lots of interchange of opinion. Not real argument. I might make a good analogy which the other is happy with, you know, recasting it into a formula they can understand. That's a good way to persuade people, adapting your argument to a different framework. It has to fit into their own motivations.'

So Kathleen suggests that exchanging opinions and trying to convince the other person is not argument, even though that is part of the given definition.

Patricia also redefines argument, and provides a witty variant on the 'official' definition:

> 'An argument is a heated disagreement between two people who don't want to agree.'

She agreed that she was disagreeing with me, but suggested that this was not an argument but

> 'a gentle process of talking about differences. I think that once you have got the other person to see your point of view there ceases to be an argument. It's a matter of morality and respect.'

Marion, a teacher I met at a party and who expressed great interest in the research, told me: 'I never argue.' To the amusement of everyone listening, she then proceeded to undermine her position by arguing with me that my definition of argument was quite wrong, because 'an argument is a quarrel'. I explained why I wanted to define the topic in the broadest possible way. She said I could not do this. I suggested that since it was my research, I should be able to define my own topic and asked how she thought I could do it better. She insisted I was quite wrong because argument could not be thought of in that way. I pointed out that we were having an argument, but it didn't feel like a quarrel. 'No,' she said. 'I never argue.' And she was genuinely bewildered when other people standing round started to laugh.

We then drew apart to talk it over, for we were both somewhat upset that what had started out as a pleasant exchange had led to deadlock, and I certainly did not want her to feel she had been mocked. She acknowledged that she felt very uncomfortable at the suggestion she had been arguing, because that did not fit in with her self-image. She sees herself as a reasonable and capable person, well able to hold her own in company, but does not think that she would ever argue if she did not know she could prevail.

'I never allow children to argue with me at school. My own daughter knows better too.'

'Do you really not enjoy exchanging views with people as equals?' I asked. She looked at me, startled, and suddenly laughed, the tension broken.

'I know, it's true, I do put my own views across strongly when I disagree with someone. Just like I did just now. But I don't like to think of myself as argumentative. We'll have to find another word, or we could go on like this all night.'

Kathleen, Patricia and Marion all appear to agree that 'nice people don't argue'. Marion never did come up with a description of what she was doing, but Kathleen and Patricia both said that when they disagreed, they were not arguing but 'talking about differences'.

3

Humpty Dumpty and the Search for Truth

If it had been possible to accommodate Marion by finding another word, I would have done so, as *argument* carries a burden of negative meanings for many women. But I chose to stick with the word for several reasons.

First, *argument* is the most general of all terms available, since its meanings include discussion, debate, negotiation, presentation of evidence, disagreement, dispute, quarrel. The very multiplicity of meanings has led to the interesting fact that even dictionaries of the English language differ markedly in which meaning they give primary place.[6]

Second, Western culture has developed several ideologies of argument, and these ideologies intervene when people find they disagree about – well, anything. And argument has a peculiar status, in that it both governs how people argue and interpret the argument behaviour of others, depending on which ideology each person subscribes to, and can be a topic of argument in its own right. People can argue about the meaning of argument and whether or not what they are doing is really arguing at all.

Third, argument is a central element in how women and men communicate, or mis-communicate. My own theory is that ideologies of argument have been a key cultural factor in ensuring that women and men have different attitudes to argument and different conversational styles. Now that roles of women and men are changing, these differences are frequently unproductive, and can lead to misunderstanding and even misery. A great deal has been written recently about how women and men have different ways of talking. I will suggest that examining how we deal with disagreement and argument is indispensable if we are to understand how women and men differ in their attitudes to communication and what purpose these differences have served in the past. Until we look at how people think as well as how they speak, needed changes in our attitudes are unlikely to occur.

How we hear what others say is crucially dependent on our mind-set, and this in turn depends on our past experiences and our expectations. Expectations and interpretations of others arise out of what we have learned, both in our personal lives and from what we are taught at school, in books, on TV and films and radio. All societies have ideologies which govern how people talk and think about key issues, and the ideology of argument is no exception. We all learn about argument from earliest childhood, and all of us learn certain ideas about it, even if we are not aware of doing so.

Understanding how people may adopt different aspects of the ideology of argument depending on circumstances is an important step towards understanding why it is that women and men very often have difficulty communicating. I must therefore first give a brief outline of what I mean by this. The ideology of argument may be analysed into three categories: argument as a rational means of reaching the truth, argument as adversarial confrontation, and argument as rhetoric. This last is conceptually separate but linked to both others.

Argument as a Rational Means of Reaching the Truth

Greek philosophers may well be responsible for the widespread belief that argument is a rational means of reaching the truth.[7] Western thinkers have long held that Aristotle's analysis of the forms of logical thought provided a means of testing the rationality of an assertion, and argument as pursuit of the truth through logic became part of the accepted thought of all well-educated men.[8]

In this view, where two people disagree, there is a right and a wrong conclusion: evidence is presented, and the logical consequences and entailments of this evidence may be debated, but in the end, these can be logically deduced by application of established laws of cause and effect and by reference to external reality. Truth is seen as free from logical contradiction: in the words of philosopher Anthony Flew,

> If contradiction is tolerated, then, in a very literal sense, anything goes. This situation must itself be totally intolerable to anyone who has any concern at all to know what is in fact true.[9]

Argument as constructive cognitive conflict is a central part of the developmental theories of the Swiss psychologist, Jean Piaget. He explained the individual's capacity to apply abstract principles of logic to all aspects of social activity and abstract thought as a consequence of a regular process of accommodation to cognitive conflicts and assimilation of the meaning of their resolution.

> The social need to share the thought of others and to communicate our own with success is at the root of our need for verification. Proof is the outcome of argument.[10]

A similar view is taken by philosopher Stephen Toulmin, who likens argument to presentation of a case in a judicial setting, and takes as his model the discipline of jurisprudence. Arguments are then compared to lawsuits, and his analysis attempts to characterise what he calls 'the rational process' by detailing the procedures and categories by which claims can be argued for and settled.

Toulmin's analysis of the judicial model of argument demands that logicians take account of the real world, and the different kinds of argument which are appropriate in different fields of enquiry. His conclusion that 'logic and epistemology ... will become not two subjects but one only' suggests an assumption that an objective judgement of the arguments is capable of leading to discovery of real-world truth.[11]

Argument as Adversarial Confrontation

However, legal arguments are not intended to discover 'the truth'. A court of law (under the English system of common law at least) is:

an arena in which different versions of reality compete. Legal truth is not a discoverable entity, existing outside the trial process: it is, and only is a product of the trial process itself.[12]

This gladiatorial approach to argument is an intrinsic part of our ideology, operating not only in the courtroom, but in politics, parliament, on the hustings, in newspapers, on television and radio. But, as psychologist Roger Brown points out, those arguments staged for our entertainment are never resolved:

> The result is a conflict between persons but not a conflict within persons. Somehow we know that ... neither participant will change his [sic] opinion nor even feel any strong pressure in the direction of change.[13]

Worse still, one's opponent's position may be sharpened by argument.[14] Indeed, one of the intriguing aspects of argument as a field of study is that it is a widespread phenomenon, and yet is widely believed *not* to be a good way of persuading people to change their minds. Humorist Miles Kington included in a Christmas quiz the question:

> Why do we have arguments at all, knowing from experience that nobody's mind ever gets changed in an argument?[15]

In this view, arguments are rhetorical battles between irreconcilable opponents. There is no way of deducing the correct view if two people disagree, and the outcome depends on what the majority thinks. Critics have called this way of deciding issues 'a matter of mob psychology'.[16] Or the argument may be resolved through application of power.

Argument as Rhetoric

Argument as rhetoric is ideologically linked to both views of argument, as rational seeking after truth and as gladiatorial conflict.

Rhetoric has in recent years become a focus of psychological study, thanks principally to Professor Michael Billig at Loughborough University, and it was he who first made clear the argumentative nature of thinking.[17] Our ability to argue, to contradict, to redefine and create new distinctions is the positive aspect of rhetoric. It enables us to defend a position by presenting evidence in a rational and logical manner, and by pointing out the flaws in the logical position of our opponent.

However, rhetoric is more often seen by the lay person as an unfair device to get the listener 'on your side', especially used by those whose job is persuasion, like politicians, salespeople and barristers. Here arguments are seen as taking place between partisans of 'camps'.

Analysts have found that all social groups tend to develop 'in-group' jargon (i.e. words, categories, ways of talking) which allows them both to negotiate a shared position and to establish as 'out-groups' those who do not share this language.[18] Here rhetoric is used as a persuasive and separatist device rather than as an aid in seeking the truth.

Let me give a rather frivolous example. Journalist Polly Toynbee has a weekly column in the *Radio Times*, and it is usually well worth reading. Just occasionally she shows signs of having had a struggle to fill it, and this is an example.[19] She writes:

> You can place food sociologically by class and pretension, just as you can with dress. Start at the bottom and ready-made cook-in sauces are in the same pigeon-hole as shell suits. Iced fairy cakes belong with Fanny Cradock afternoon frocks, balti dishes with beer bellies in tight trousers, and Japanese sushi with upper-class anorexic models in tiny skirts.

Did you know that? No, nor did anyone else. But now, for everyone who has read her column, eating balti dishes, iced fairy cakes and cook-in sauces is going to be a problem if they don't like the company she said they keep. If enough people read, remember and react, what Polly Toynbee wrote as a joke may become a social fact. The rhetorical power of words to divide and rule is great.

4

Argument and the Division of Labour

> 'The question is,' said Alice, 'whether you can make words mean
> so many different things.'
> 'The question is,' said Humpty Dumpty, 'which is to be master
> – that's all.'
>
> (Lewis Carroll, *Through the Looking Glass*)

These different views of argument – as rational means of obtaining
the truth and as gladiatorial confrontation – are part of the
ideology with which we grew up. Some families and some schools
may, of course, emphasise one aspect more than another. We can
see, therefore, why the men quoted earlier say they see argument as
debate or as a battle.

What is not so clear is why the women should have such
problems with the concept of arguing that they either need to feel
'safe' or they deny that 'talking about differences' is actually
arguing at all.

To explain this we need to contrast the ideology of argument
with the ideology of affiliation. This is essentially the belief that
everyone in a given society should live in harmony. The United
States, in particular, has a strong cultural pull towards creating a
peaceful harmonious society, with its constitutionally endorsed
right to 'the pursuit of happiness' and socially sanctioned pressures
to conformity. But the desire to live in peace with one's family,
one's neighbours and a broader society is not limited to the States,
or even to the Western world. However much it may conflict with
the ambitions of demagogues and dictators, most people throughout the world would prefer to live in peace.

There is a real conflict here between two opposing elements in the human psyche. On the one hand, we want the pleasures of peace and harmony with others. On the other, we have a deep instinct to feel hostile to anyone who is not 'one of us', not a member of our 'in-group'.

Psychologist Henri Tajfel discovered that we do not even need to know who the people are in 'our group' – a label will do. In experiments which have been repeated innumerable times, women and men, girls and boys, will deliberately act to benefit those anonymous others who 'belong' and to undermine those who do not. Where, for example, the individual is asked to decide how much each of the others will be paid for taking part in the experiment, even where it would be to the individual's own benefit to give everyone the same, because in this case all would get, say £2, most people choose the option that makes the greatest difference between the 'in-group' and the 'out-group'. So they would choose to give their own group £1 if the 'out-group' only got 50p, rather than £2 all round.[20] This has its real-world reflection in union pay negotiations, where unions are sometimes more concerned to maintain their 'differential' with other unions than to get the maximum possible.

So what has this to do with argument? It is this.

Because there is a deep conflict between two opposing elements in our psyche, Western society has tried to solve the problem by a Division of Labour, assigning the task of dealing with one element to men and the task of dealing with the other element to women. Men's task is to deal with the external world, to decide when hostilities with other groups are appropriate, and how to run the broader society. Women's task is to create peace and harmony among people: relationships within the family are obviously the woman's responsibility, but as society has developed, so the in-group has grown larger, and women are expected to care for people's well-being within society as a whole. This is why women are easily accepted as nurse and infant schoolteacher, secretary and personal assistant, but resisted when they try to move into positions of power where they would be making decisions society expects should be made by men.

This Division of Labour holds that women's task is to be caring and nurturing and to safeguard relationships in the in-group; their special qualities are that they are warm, emotional, and good at feelings. Men's task is to be practical and strong, to protect the weak (women and children) and to provide leadership and decision-making; men's special qualities are that they are cool, rational, and good at thinking.

These qualities are directly relevant to argument.

Men who argue are exercising their rational faculties, it is part of their task to debate with others as to the proper way to run society; because power is involved, both within society itself and in relation to out-groups, it is not surprising that many men should see argument as a battle which they must win. Argument in Western society has long been held to be the proper job of men, and indeed, a man who does not 'stand up for himself' may be characterised as weak, wet, a wimp or a jellyfish.

Because their task is nurturing, women are not expected to argue: if they do, they demonstrate that they are inadequate women by failing to be caring and concerned for feelings. Women know they are not expected to risk damage to relationships by disagreement, which is why they need to feel 'safe' in order to express their own opinions. As we have seen, the impulse we all have to argue with other people leads some women to find a new description for what they are doing. 'Nice people don't argue' and it is quintessentially women's job to be 'nice'. They therefore cannot be arguing when they express disagreement, and redefine what they are doing as 'talking about differences'.

This Division of Labour is widely held to be based upon innate, immutable differences between the sexes, and thus any person who tries to act outside these expectations is liable to be judged aberrant. Each sex is held to be poor at what the other excels in. This means that women's supposed inability to follow logic allows others to dismiss their expressions of opinion as unreasonable, irrational and illogical; women's supposed special knowledge of feelings allows them to be dismissed as emotional; and their failure in their primary task of caring opens the door to accusations of disagreeableness, of being a shrew, a bitch, a harridan, or perhaps even more revealing, a strident castrating ball-breaker.

Furthermore, because women are not supposed to argue, the negative aspects of the ideologies of argument are marshalled to explain their failure in a specially masculine activity. Thus women are frequently accused of unfair rhetoric: 'they never say what they mean', 'they use emotional blackmail', even 'they'll use tears if it gets them their way'. In work situations, in particular, where cool rationality seems called for, women who try to adopt a debating style will frequently be accused of aggression and hostility: the negative aspects of gladiatorial style are invoked as a means of undermining a woman's contributions. Never mind that many men use just this style in the same situation without criticism. Women are not supposed to argue at all, and it appears to be an effective attack on a woman trying to present a different view to say she is being aggressive. All these statements come from my research and will be illustrated in the chapters to come.

Bearing this Division of Labour in mind will help in understanding the conflicts that arise in women's and men's accounts of argument. This analysis is, of course, another way of looking at the well-known stereotypes about women and men. It is intended to provide a productive way of examining why women and men have so many difficulties in communicating with each other. In Part Five, the Division of Labour will be re-examined, and issues of power brought into the analysis. Only when we have been able to see what is happening when we try to communicate and exchange opinions will we be able to build a golden bridge between us.

Part Two

The Porcupine's Dilemma

But when two people are at one in their inmost hearts,
They shatter even the strength of iron or of bronze.
And when two people understand each other in their inmost
  hearts,
Their words are sweet and strong, like the fragrance of orchids.

(Confucius)[1]

The sharp quills of the porcupine are notoriously painful, a fact
which has led generations of youthful naturalists to speculate on
their sex lives. Porcupines in love provide a perfect symbol of
human psychology. Imagine two porcupines attempting to make
love, and you have an image of the eternal conflict between our
desire for closeness and its inevitable pain.

The pain arises, of course, from the 'otherness' of the other
person, the sharp jabs of the reality of that person's thoughts and
desires that bear so little resemblance to our fantasies. The trouble
with the Other is that she or he also has fantasies in which we are
supposed to play a part, so that misunderstandings and disagreements can arise apparently out of the blue, at any time. Each of us
has dreams of closeness and love that cannot bear too sharp a jab
from reality.

The Greeks, we are told, thought of the human psyche as split in
two, so that each of us spends our lifetime seeking for our other
missing half. However little this may accord with other aspects of
Greek classical life as we know it (men of ancient Greece did not
value women nearly as much as they valued other men), the myth
of Unity Through One Great Love does seem to govern our
dreams. Many of us believe that there is a 'Miss' or 'Mr Right'

waiting somewhere, and that once we have found her or him, loneliness and heartache will be things of the past. Miss or Mr Right will understand us completely without crucial details even needing to be said, and will never have needs and thoughts and opinions that conflict with our own.

Great lovers never argue. Great lovers have their problems, but not with each other. Their problems arise because the greatness of their love creates conflict with other people – authoritarian parents, jealous rivals, cruel tyrants – or they find their love has bloomed where no love should, and they must resist the demands of family, of duty, of honour. Romeo and Juliet did not have time to discover any incompatibility of thought before they killed themselves for love in the full bloom of youth. Dante, it is true, continued to write of his love for Beatrice into a ripe old age: but he scarcely even spoke to her before her early death, nursed his hopeless love for the beautiful maiden without ever running the slightest risk that she might damage his image by saying the wrong thing. Even Lancelot and Guinevere spent very little time actually together: most of their doomed and sinful love affair was spent yearningly apart, aching for each other and then repenting their wickedness. The great love stories of the world never allow lovers time to explore each other's hearts and minds. Shakespeare's Beatrice and Benedick, whose love grows out of their verbal sparring, are *comic* lovers, not to be taken seriously.

To quote psychologist Maryon Tysoe: 'Myth has endowed mutual love with the power of a psychological superglue.'[2] Love is that powerful, magical bond that just *happens* to you out of the blue, and which lasts for ever. And if it does not last, well it must have been that the lovers were not true lovers, they did not love each other enough. Love is basic, perhaps even primeval in its powers, demanding that we be ready to sacrifice our all in its service.

For centuries, the sacrifice demanded has been principally of woman: that she offer her virginity and her independence of mind on the altar of love. D. H. Lawrence expresses clearly the consequences of this view: the only way to get on with a woman, in his opinion, is to restrict the relationship to the primitive animal, purely sexual intercourse, reserving all intellectual exchange for one's male friends.

> I'm not sure if a mental relation with a woman doesn't make it impossible to love her. To know the *mind* of a woman is to end in hating her. Love means the pre-cognitive flow ... it is the honest state before the apple.[3]

D. H. Lawrence was about as far from being a New Man as it is possible to get, and still be admired as a writer. He did, after all, conclude in *The Plumed Serpent* that a woman's fulfilment could only be achieved through worshipping the great male phallus. But when Erich Segal decided deliberately to put his theories of what might make a bestselling novel to the test, he was not concerned with the mind of a woman either. In that memorably titled book *Love Story*, his lovers are in conflict, not with each other, but with fate. They are doomed to fight a losing battle against her life-threatening illness, transcending death as all true lovers do by the power of their love for and understanding of each other. Segal set out to write a wish-fulfilment novel, and his success was summed up memorably by that lie: 'Love is never having to say you are sorry.'

As most of us know only too well, Love is having to say you are sorry rather too often. But love is the time you really mean it.

Women today are less inclined to sacrifice their independence of mind on the altar of true love, so that when differences arise between them and their lovers they are more likely to say what they think. Men too would like to believe they can talk to their beloved about important things. The main difference between happy and unhappy long-term love relationships, we are told by experts, is that 'hurt' can be transformed and even the most painful exchanges can be negotiated so that they become 'positive communication'. Both women and men then *want* to be able to talk to each other and negotiate differences.

The problem is, of course, that when you talk about differences, those differences exist, out there, and cannot any longer be ignored or wished away. If talking about differences leads to pain and alienation, sometimes it does not seem worth it, especially when such differences seem to prove that love is not true love after all. That new cultural demand to 'communicate' leads to even more unexpected difficulties and discomforts when combined with the old expectations, which may operate unconsciously, that women and men behave differently. Deep down many of us believe that women and men are not human in the same way.

The sharp quills of the porcupine can jab as painfully in friendship as in love. That human desire for closeness to another person can jar against the reality of the other, whether that other is of the same or different gender, whether or not the relationship has, as one dimension, sexual love. Woman daring to disagree with woman, man disputing with man, man and woman in argument, parent and child in dispute: our ideas about the meaning of these situations are very different, and go to the heart of how we expect our relationships to be.

Argument in all intimate relationships will be examined here in Part Two, and we will begin with friendship before venturing into the minefield of heterosexual love and marriage, and ending with family.

Friendship can pose special problems for speaking one's mind. Many people believe that disagreements can damage a relationship by revealing differences that wound. Others claim that frankness is essential in any truly warm and close relationship, and that understanding can be achieved only by talking about differences. What is one to do with such contradictions, if getting it wrong can lead to devastating consequences?

5

Friendship: Woman to Woman

'Relationships are more important than any issue. I think some things should never be said.'

These words were spoken by Rebecca, a 22-year-old laboratory technician.[4] She told me:

'I tend not to have arguments with a woman friend. It's only possible when you are incredibly close and can spend lots of time together. Sometimes I have felt an issue is so important I must argue, but when I tried to give my point of view, she was hurt. Because we were so opposite. I do the same – I'll accept what she says, or if I'm hurt I won't say anything. Somehow I don't feel the same necessity to tell her when I'm upset that I feel when I'm with my boyfriend.'

This was surprising, and not at all what I had expected. After all, there is a widespread view that young women avoid arguing with *men*, especially those they are intimate with: it is supposed to be harmful to a man's ego to argue with him, whereas young women can say anything to their close female friends because they will understand. Perhaps Rebecca is unusual? But no. If anything she has more experience of argument than many of those I talked with, for she comes from a Jewish family where friendly argument is traditionally a form of sociability.[5] Of her family, she said, 'We are very close which means we argue a lot.' However, she is quite clear that discussing really serious matters like religion and politics can lead to painful feelings, and that preserving relationships is more important than any issue.

Arguing with women friends does turn out to be problematic for many of the women I interviewed, and indeed, it is the only relationship in which many of them could not actually recall an argument. This was not always because of avoidance: some women said, 'I just can't think of one' or 'We never seem to argue'. Nevertheless, there was a widespread discomfort at the idea of arguing with a close woman friend, whereas nearly all the women had no difficulty at all in recalling an argument with a close man friend, or with members of their family. Wendy, a 33-year-old psychologist, said: 'I don't have a woman friend close enough to argue with. I would fear spoiling the friendship.'

Fear of spoiling a friendship was a recurrent theme. Jan, a 23-year-old secretary, is like many others who say they avoid expressing differences of opinion:

'I don't like to argue. Sometimes I'll try to make the peace, but people don't often listen. It makes me really sad and uncomfortable when people can't get on.'

Ann, a 27-year-old mother of three, is not really sure that argument is a sign that 'people can't get on'. Sometimes she enjoys argument: she grew up in a family where arguing was a matter of course, and finds exchanging points of view stimulating. But she found this put her at a disadvantage with other women:

'I'd go around, shooting my mouth off, saying just what I thought and expecting other people to say when they didn't agree. And I found myself without any friends. Nobody wanted to know. So when we moved here four years ago, I decided to change. They didn't want to hear my opinions? OK, I wouldn't bother to say anything when I disagree, just let them talk. And now everyone in this neighbourhood thinks I'm wonderful! The problem is, they all think I'm a wonderful listener, so they all come and dump all their problems on me. I'll have to do something about that – it's really exhausting. But I like having friends, and I am learning to say things quietly when I think it's really important. But it's difficult. I don't want to lose the warmth – I can remember what it was like.'

Ann's experience does appear to justify the fears expressed by nearly every woman I interviewed. Young women arguing with other young women leads to problems because they seem to believe they should never cause each other, or be caused, any pain. In the words of Valerie, a 25-year-old academic, 'disagreements can tear the very fabric of a relationship' of woman with woman.

Silence, Not Consent

And why is this? I believe that these young women are caught in what I call 'the tenderness trap'. In their different ways, they have all internalised the belief that women must nurture others and be good at relationships. It follows from this that each must then prove her skills by getting on with people; and if she can't even get on with another woman, who herself is bound to be nurturing, then there must be something very wrong with her. Her self-esteem becomes inextricably bound up with her ability to make friends.

Self-esteem is yet another problem area for women, and one closely linked to their fears about speaking out. The American Association of University Women studied 3,000 adolescents in a national survey, and found an enormous gap in self-confidence between males and females.[6] In 1991, only 29 per cent of American high-school girls felt positive about themselves, a precipitous drop from a high level in primary school. *Women & Self-Esteem: Understanding and Improving the Way We Think and Feel About Ourselves* is the title of a self-help book which has been in print in the US since 1984, and which starts from the premise that 'millions of women ... come to see themselves as less able, less bright, less valuable than they really are'.[7]

Adolescent girls in Sue Lees's study of London schoolgirls interpret disagreement as a possible indication that the friendship is not strong anyway.[8] As one girl puts it, 'You can't argue with a friend.' They emphasise the need to be able to trust each other and the demands of loyalty, and Lees herself points out that

> Where to draw the line and risk a severe disagreement with a friend is a problem that fortunately does not arise very

frequently, as friendship usually rests on a high level of consensus.[9]

But fear of argument seems to be very strong, and Lees suggests that this is in part a fear of being betrayed. She found that girls lose confidence in early adolescence because their identity comes to depend on their sexual reputation, which is both precarious and crucial: girls want to be attractive to boys, and yet, in some schools, being labelled a slag or a slut is an ever-present threat, for any girl at any time. Girls therefore avoid talking about sexual desire. She also found that, because there is no equivalent vocabulary with which to abuse boys, the girls could not raise their morale by their own sexist talk: on the contrary, 'Criticising the sexism of boys labels a girl a man-hater or a lesbian. It in no way enhances femininity.'[10]

Similarly, American psychologists Lyn Mikel Brown and Carol Gilligan find that 'adolescent and adult women silence themselves or are silenced in relationships rather than risk open conflict and disagreements that might lead to isolation.'[11] Indeed, they suggest that this loss of voice can be so serious that girls learn to hide their feelings from themselves, undergoing 'a sort of psychological foot-binding':

> Open conflict and free speaking ... gave way to more covert forms of responding to hurt feelings or disagreements within relationships, so that some girls came to ignore or not know signs of emotional or physical abuse.

This is indeed serious. But if, for the sake of this argument, we set aside the extreme cases of abuse, and examine the standard experiences of those who had a 'normal' childhood and adolescence, we still find that girls and young women learn to mask their thoughts and feelings. In my own studies, those arguments with close friends that young women did recall were unhappy, and they confessed to having felt considerable anger which they were unable to express. Doreen, a 25-year-old engineer, admitted:

> 'I had to live with her, so I didn't dare say what I felt. But I was terribly angry, and it took me all day to get over it.'

When I suggested this might be a bit unfair to both of them, as her friend couldn't know how much she had upset Doreen unless she told her, and so might do it (criticising parents who divorce as selfish) again, Doreen replied, 'But I don't want to hurt her feelings.' Her own feelings had been hurt, because her own parents had divorced in her teens, and she thought her friend should know that and not say such things.

Mind-reading is not a very widely distributed talent, and yet many young women expect their closest friends to be adept at it, as though their closeness can be measured by the extent to which they need never say what they think.

These same young women had little difficulty in talking about arguments with close men friends. Some of them were painful of course, but they rarely talked of *avoiding* disagreement just to preserve the relationship. Explaining this difference was no problem for 29-year-old Rosemary, who is a well-liked office administrator. She told me:

> 'Friendship is based on mutual agreement, that's what it grows from with women. So if you disagree about important things, you would never have pursued the friendship in the first place. But sexual friendship is different. It grows from sexual attraction, and then you just hope you have things in common.'

Growing Older, Growing Bolder

I have been emphasising the youth of these women and this does seem to be significant. A strange fact emerged from my further investigations: women over 35 start to give a different picture, saying they appreciate being able to argue with their women friends; women in their forties and fifties talk of positive pleasure in exchanging views with other women.

Margie, a teacher in her forties, wrote in her diary:

> 'We had a really good argument, though unfortunately neither of us knew enough in the end to come to a conclusion. Fun!'

Ellen, a librarian in her fifties, wrote:

I would suggest that older women in Western society today find they need each other for much the same reason. They have learned that they *can* say what they think to another woman who loves them, and she will listen. Men are often disinclined to listen to a woman.

Third, women of all ages have the same human desire to express their ideas, to say what they think, and to have their opinions treated with respect. They will express disagreement with a close friend if it feels safe to do so. Sometimes, simply redefining this disagreement as 'talking about differences' makes it safe enough. Women learn that they are not supposed to argue, because it is their task to be 'nice'.

As far as I am aware, there is little research into disagreement and conflict between women who become sexual partners, but what there is shows that in this context they may have an advantage over heterosexual partners.[17] Whereas heterosexual lovers find that stereotypical expectations of male rationality and dominance and female conciliation can cut across their attempts at resolving differences, lesbian couples do not start with a skewed relationship. In so far as they are caught in the tenderness trap, the pressure to be warm and nurturing remains, and initially will have the same effects on both as it does in close friendships. Indeed, lesbian psychotherapists talk of the dangers of 'merger' and 'fusion' in lesbian love affairs, and the need for each partner to learn how to separate herself from the other.[18] Love affairs, though, usually demand greater efforts at communication than do ordinary friendships, and both partners will experience conflicts between nurturing and the need to make their own views clear. Though many couples find disagreement and argument 'very scary', much like women who set up in business together, when they do disagree and argue, it is as equals. The intimacy of their relationship means they *need* to hear each other and understand.

6

Friendship: Man to Man

Young men seem to have almost the opposite attitude to young women: they *enjoy* arguing with close men friends, but many are disinclined to get involved in disagreements with close women friends.

The vast majority of the men I talked to think that argument and debate are essentially a Good Thing with a man friend. Sometimes this is because they think in similar ways.

> 'We think along the same lines, have the same basic assumptions.' (Charles)

Or argument can help resolve differences and develop new ideas. As Alan, a 26-year-old computer programmer, put it:

> 'I think that arguing about ideas lets you both work out the best solution. We'll always debate if we find we're on different sides. Usually we end up agreeing in the end. Except about politics, he's a bit bigoted in that area, I'm afraid.'

And Ian, a 30-year-old psychologist, said:

> 'People enjoy arguing. ... You don't necessarily have to have opposing goals, it's part of the real psychology of relationships.'

Enjoyment is an important theme for many men, especially young ones who seem to take pleasure in pitting their wits against each other. Radio broadcaster Mike Dickin Shaw declares that he deliberately takes an extreme stand just to provoke argument with friends 'because it's fun': for example, he will argue that the earth is flat, marshalling all the logical entailments of this premise to support his (admittedly absurd) contention. 'It drives people wild,' he says with glee.[19]

While not everyone goes this far, many men report that they argue with other men with pleasure, even if the issues are important. This report from Winston, a 30-year-old teacher, is quite typical:

'Many discussions start out as some kind of disagreement; but then we explore the topic and something mutually satisfying is achieved. In a sense a win-win situation, except there are no competitors.'

And Ewen, a marketing manager, wrote:

'We both wanted to explore and understand the point at issue ... the further it was explored the better, for shared understanding.'

Men talk of increased understanding of each other and do not find it upsetting that at the end they still strongly disagree.

'We have totally different perspectives and argue all the time, that's part of our relationship.' (Jim)

'We hacked away at why we have different frameworks, and we both gained in understanding each other even if we do still passionately disagree.' (Paul)

Nevertheless, a small number of young men is worried about the effects of disagreement on friendship, though 22-year-old David commented that this special friendship made argument safe:

'I wasn't worried about antagonising him, so was able to express myself clearly.'

Darren, who was quoted in Part One, avoids argument where possible. He would 'never' argue with a close man friend (though he does report arguing with a close woman friend): 'If a situation arises where I feel my remarks might be inflammatory, I sit silent.' Darren explained that he had learned that argument could be devastating when he had a blazing row with his father at the age of 16.

'He was ready to throw me out of the house, and I felt like hitting him. It really shocked me. I realised then that it wasn't worth insisting on my point of view if it was going to destroy my relationship with my parents. They are too important. And friends are too important to risk losing them over a difference of opinion.'

Darren is unusual though, both in his attitude to argument and in his reactions to his father's blazing anger. Men and their teenage sons do tend to have furious confrontations, but the wider tendency is for neither to back down. Darren did back down, and in this he is more like the young women I talked to who found that arguing with loved ones could have painful repercussions that they would rather avoid.

Older men, on the other hand, appear to enjoy argument less and less, and in my first report on the Diary Study,[20] I found no reports at all of men over 35 years of age arguing with a close man friend. However, interviews and later diaries did produce some reports of argument between older men friends. Argumentativeness seems to become established as a trait in some men, as both they and their spouses report them as willing to argue with anyone about anything at the drop of a comment. But the older they are, the less they seem to enjoy the sparring, and report getting angry at the 'absurd' and 'bigoted' views of men friends. Ashley, who lived in Africa for twenty years and is now in his late fifties, explained why he argues so much, and so aggressively:

'If you challenge my position I'm ready at any time to take up the challenge. ... If you get into arguments, you must be a fighter. My feelings don't get hurt, I just get bloody angry and try and contain it.'

Acknowledging he is 'a person with strong views' who 'can be aggressive', he does not believe that this is ever a problem:

'I have some interesting friends who would disagree with many of my attitudes, but they are still friends.'

Older men lay great emphasis on being 'justified' in their views, and state in their diaries that 'any reasonable person' would be bound to agree with them. They want their own views to be heard and understood, but seem less willing than when younger to listen to the views of others. But as Henry put it: 'It is the subject rather than the individual that is under scrutiny. One argues with friends and remains a friend.'

'. . . A Win-Win Situation'

Overall, it seems that men do not find the quills of the porcupine stab too painfully when they exchange views with a friend. Older men may get angry with the 'absurd' or 'bigoted' ideas the other puts forward, but nearly all make a clear separation between arguing about a topic, however important to their world view, and attacking a friend.

Younger men, in particular, confirm what we found in Part One: they know that argument is their domain and they are happy there. Indeed, many of them emphasise that friendship is about being able to exchange ideas, debate and explore even dangerous territory like religion and politics. When two men argue about issues that divide strangers and lead to wars between nations, and they know their friendship is not threatened, this creates a positive sense of well-being and affirmation of their worth. It is, indeed, a win-win situation.

The ability to think out loud with another man reaffirms to both their sense of ownership of the field of argument. Thinking *is* debating, arguing, exploring ideas, playing with possibilities, seeking contradictions, and seeking contradictions to contradictions. Having fun, joking, arguing 'that the earth is flat', 'playing the devil's advocate' are all ways in which men recreate their own sense of control over the elements of debate. They can know that they are rational beings, able to marshal logical arguments to support any position, however absurd.

A further key point is that men arguing with men friends know that arguments are not about feelings, whereas friendship is. Because men know they are rational and have control over their feelings, they do not usually allow any emotional response to cloud their knowledge that to argue with a friend is not to attack the friend.

Again, I know of very little research into arguments between men who become sexual partners, but I consulted Adrian Coyle and Martin Milton at the University of Surrey, whose research and writing address a range of topics within lesbian and gay psychology, including relationship issues.[21] Discussing their knowledge and experience of argument among gay men, they agreed that men who become sexual partners tend to negotiate rules about the relationship itself so that arguments on this topic are mainly pre-empted. However, those everyday practical issues that can cause friction between any two people who live together are not covered by these rules: while some men try to avoid conflict, back off or sulk, others struggle for power, and 'neither would give an inch'. Both agree that there seems to be no particular pattern characteristic of a gay relationship, 'simply two men in close contact' negotiating rules and structure for their liaison.

There are differences, though, between what men and women say about close friends. Women never talk of power and negotiating rules or structure with intimate friends; while both women and men would agree with Martin Milton that 'what upsets anybody is lack of respect or not being taken seriously', women talk of *listening* and *being heard*, while men talk of *negotiation* and *challenge*, and of *who wins*.

7

Lovers' Tiffs

Love's a harbinger of pain –
Would it were not so!

(Dorothy Parker)[22]

So men in general see argument as enhancing friendship with
another man, and women fear that argument might damage
friendship with another woman. What happens when these two
very different attitudes meet and a woman and a man in love find
they disagree?

Inevitably, what happens is conflict and the porcupine quills jab
painfully. Unless they are very remarkable people and exceptionally well informed, both start their love affair with deeply ingrained
beliefs about the relative abilities and functions of each other. Both
'know' that argument is masculine and rational; both 'know' that
women are caring and nurturing. These are well-established
cultural stereotypes, internalised effectively by both when arguing
with their same-sex friends.

Vivian is nearly 30 and a senior secretary in a university
department. She and Simon are in a long-term love affair. On
Tuesday morning they woke in the same bed, and she told him of
her plans to go to a concert with a woman friend on Wednesday,
which led to a 'heated' argument:

> 'He reacted in anger due to feeling excluded. When I reasoned
> with him, he calmed down and saw that he was being over-
> possessive.'

She felt 'very angry, but only for two minutes or so', and blamed
herself for the argument because 'I'm generally more argumentative first thing in the morning.'

However, her diary for the rest of the week shows that this disagreement does not end there, and they have a series of arguments about trivia, such as her borrowing a pint of milk without asking (which she acknowledges could not be justified). On Thursday evening, she reports a progressively more angry and more heated argument that went on and on:

'Everything I did or had ever done was being criticised, or so it seemed. I put up with the criticisms at first, because I knew he was in a bad mood and thought it would blow over. But it didn't and I grew angry because it wasn't justified.'

Then on Friday, they have a 'blazing row' because he asks her to meet him for lunch and she insists on sticking to her earlier arrangements with work colleagues.

'I had not realised how important it was for him that I met him for lunch on this particular occasion – had I known, I would have gone.'

Their annoyance and irritation with each other continue over the weekend, and Vivian blames herself for her own 'impatience' and 'nagging'.

What is going on here? Vivian and Simon are clearly not communicating, and an outsider can see that he is feeling taken for granted and not valued enough. But why is it that Vivian cannot see what we can see? And why is it that she blames herself for being irritable and argumentative? Why does she not hear that Simon is upset? Why is it that Simon cannot tell her how he feels?

There are three main factors involved here. First, the difficulties women and men experience in important relationships have as much to do with their conflicting beliefs about each other and about argument as they do with the differing conversational styles that linguists have documented.

Second, both probably know that couples who want to stay together happily must learn to communicate. This is new in terms of our cultural mythology, but has been written about so frequently in newspapers, magazines and self-help books on relationships since the 1980s that those who start a new love affair today may be expected to 'know' that love means communication. And communication means saying what you think and feel when you disagree. To quote psychologist Maryon Tysoe again, in her book *Love Isn't Quite Enough*:

> It's not disagreement itself that's destructive, it's failing to resolve it in a way satisfactory to both of you without treading heavily on each other's egos on the way.[23]

So it is probable that both *want* to be able to talk to each other and negotiate differences. But talking about differences can be extraordinarily painful, and even when we are willing to go along with the idea that we 'must work at relationships', few of us really know how to go about this.

Third, and crucial for young lovers, are our cultural myths about love. As we saw at the beginning of this section, the 'superglue' of love is supposed to keep two lovers together and transform conflict into understanding by some magical osmosis.

Vivian believes that men are fundamentally cool, rational and logical, because that is what our culture teaches. So when Simon tried to express his hurt feelings that she was planning to take a woman friend to a concert and not him, Vivian 'reasoned with him'. Whereas with a woman she might very well have acknowledged her friend's hurt by saying, 'I'm really sorry you're feeling left out', Vivian tells us she argued with Simon so as to persuade him he was wrong to be 'over-possessive'.

Simon, by the same token, believes women are 'good at feelings', and so Vivian should 'know' when he is hurt. The argument continues for days, because Simon finds she ignores his hurt feelings even though she says she cares for him, and Vivian finds that the man who is supposed to be cool, calm and rational is being irrational and unreasonable. The widespread myth that men are 'no good at feelings' is particularly damaging when feelings are the issue, because men like Simon may find it very difficult to say – or sometimes even to be aware of – how they feel, so hurt comes out as anger; and women like Vivian assume that men don't have problems with feelings in the way women do, because men are cool and unemotional. If he did get upset momentarily about her concert arrangements, this was quickly dealt with on a rational basis. She 'reasoned with him' and he saw the error of his ways.

Yet Vivian knows it is her task to protect their relationship, so she decides to 'put up with his bad mood' on the evening following the concert, 'because it will blow over'. Other women in similar circumstances write 'He was tired', 'He had a bad day at work', 'He was frustrated', explanations designed to show how understanding they are of the outside pressures which could interfere with their relationship. It does not occur to Vivian, as it probably would if she were dealing with a woman friend, that Simon's bad mood is linked to her treatment of him, for she feels that she has shown him unmistakably that she loves him, and continues to show love to him by being willing to put up with bad temper. The offering women make to men is to take responsibility for bad feelings between them, which is why she blames herself when they both get angry. 'I am irritable in the morning,' she writes (Wednesday); 'I was being impatient and he was right to get annoyed' (Saturday); 'I was just nagging' (also Saturday).

Some readers may ask, can Vivian really not be aware of Simon's unhappiness? If we can pick it up quite clearly from these very short extracts from her argument diary, how is it that she can mishear the situation so badly that they have a blazing row about going out to lunch on Friday? She writes 'if I had realised how important it was to him...' she would have changed her arrangements. So why didn't she realise how important it was?

Without knowing more about the individuals, I suggest there were several factors. First, Vivian was herself feeling annoyed with Simon for what she experienced as possessiveness, and resented his assumption that he could phone her and expect her to drop everything to be with him. Psychologists Toni Falbo and Letitia Peplau found that keeping other friends and being able to go out without their love partners is of great importance to women today.[24]

Second, Simon's own impulsive idea that lunch together would be a pleasure felt to him like one of those things that lovers do – most of us would like sometimes to feel like great lovers, and great lovers want to be together. The fact that Vivian did not respond in the right way only confirmed his growing feeling that something was radically wrong between them. Her anger when he tried to express his feelings almost certainly left him with a sense of betrayal (she was not a true lover) and a growing desire to escape: his resistance to her over the following weekend and her interpretation of it simply as a reaction to her own irritability and nagging mean that communication between them is seriously breaking down.

So what could they have done? Vivian is right to explain that his resentment of her taking a woman friend to the concert feels like possessiveness to her, if that is how it feels. Simon is right to explain that this makes him feel unwanted and upset, if that is how he feels. Emotions are the issue here, not logic and rationality. Lovers need to be able to say how they feel, and have these feelings acknowledged. Unfortunately, this diary seems to suggest that though both did express their feelings, Simon's were not acknowledged as feelings in their own right. Because he is a man, he is expected to be able to deal with his feelings rationally: therefore, when Vivian reasons with him that he is being possessive, this is supposed to make the feelings go away. Reason does not have that kind of power.

This may look like blaming the woman. But it is not. It is blaming – if blame is relevant – our myths.

It is a myth that men are rational and not emotional: if lovers can only acknowledge each other as emotional, they will at least be confronting what is really distressing one or both of them. When lovers have opposing feelings about a situation, as here with Simon and Vivian, then they do have a difficulty which needs to be resolved together. And this can be done more easily by expressing the feelings that each has, rather than by arguing supposedly rationally *about* feelings. As psychologist John Rowan has said, there is nothing irrational about expressing differences in feelings, for they are vital to our relationships with other people and to our own well-being.[25] The point I wish to make is that no one person's feelings should be considered more important than the other's, that Simon's feelings of hurt are as important as Vivian's feeling that he was being possessive. The magic of being able to acknowledge each other's feelings *as* feelings, and therefore important, seems to be that this opens the door to a solution. When both have been acknowledged, people really do find it easier to negotiate a way through the conflict which leaves both feeling in balance.

Reasonable Men and Conciliatory Women

Not all conflicts between lovers are about feelings, of course, though very often arguments can *become* conflicts about feelings. When an argument is about a topic that can be treated rationally, myths require that the woman be conciliatory. And she will try, especially if she really cares about the man (and especially if she is young, or the relationship is new). She will be cautious and hedge her comments about with phrases like 'I don't really know' or 'I might be wrong'.

But, and this is an important but, she does not expect her lover to accept this self-deprecation at face value, because their special relationship means he should know better. He should recognise the hedges as what they are – signals that she does not want to fight with him, but does want recognition of her differing point of view.

When her lover does acknowledge her point of view, she is very willing to pay tribute to his good qualities. Wendy, the 33-year-old psychologist who never dares argue with a close woman friend, said of her husband: 'I have confidence in him, so I'm not intimidated, and can express my opinion. He always respects my opinion, he's always willing to listen.'

In interviews and diaries of arguments with close men friends, women who believe the man heard what they said, explain:

'He's a reasonable person.' (Mary)

'He's usually willing to listen.' (Vicky)

'He's interested in my opinion.' (Valerie)

If the issue is something very difficult, the woman attributes his willingness to listen to the seriousness of their relationship. Irene, talking about a recent argument with a new lover, said: 'It's important to both of us to understand each other and resolve conflicts.' And Nan, in her argument diary about her lover's attitude to childbirth, writes: 'We are both working hard at communicating/hearing our differences at the moment and don't want to fall out – especially over approaching shared labour!'

However, when a woman's lover does not acknowledge her point of view, this is frequently explained in terms of 'values':

'We had different value systems, different ideas of right and wrong.' (Beryl)

'We have a different set of values.' (Kathleen)

'We had different goals, couldn't get it together. Some people can tolerate different values, but somehow it was linked up with his self-esteem.' (Judy)

What are these values? Remember, we are talking all the time of people's recall of real-life arguments. People involved are asked 'Did the other person hear what you said, even if they disagreed?' They are not asked if they 'won' the argument, only if they had succeeded in 'getting their point of view across'. Very often, the rest of the report makes clear that the disagreement continued, but the woman felt her lover had 'heard'. When she says he did not hear, this to her is a betrayal of their special relationship. It is as though there is something fundamentally wrong if her lover fails to 'hear' and so does not acknowledge the validity of her point of view. He may disagree, but he is expected to listen. Though women rarely write about 'values' in their diaries, women in all English-speaking countries talk about 'having different values' when anyone important and intimate ignores what they say. I suggest that the values referred to are the values attached to the relationship itself.

Women talking of values are trying to cope with the conflict between needing to put their own point of view across and the value to them of the relationship, which they fear the man does not value as much.

The man, however, is usually not thinking of the relationship while arguing. When a woman disagrees with him, he is very likely to believe she is being emotional and illogical, because he believes that she knows all about emotions, but that he knows about logic and she does not. Her self-deprecating phrases, designed to signal to him that she is caring about his feelings, only reinforce his belief that she should not get involved in argument. Why is she arguing if she 'doesn't really know'? Obviously it is up to him to set her straight – which he proceeds to do in kindly but firm terms. The woman then feels belittled, for he has clearly not recognised her point of view as valid. If the issue matters, she may find it impossible to deal with coolly, as his attitude seems to deny her value to him – and any escalation of the argument will merely reinforce the man's belief in her essential unreasonable emotionality.

Self-deprecatory remarks may be useful signals that the woman does not intend to be threatening, as we shall see in Part Four, but most men interpret them literally, as incompetence rather than concern. A woman who wants her lover to listen is more likely to achieve this by remembering he thinks argument is his domain, and expects her to be emotional: she must avoid raising her voice, keep to calm expression of her point of view, and give him plenty of space to say what he thinks. If a woman wants her partner to hear what she says, she wants him to think of arguments with her in the way these men are recalling arguments with their lovers:

'She's a reasonable person, willing to listen and understand.' (Ian)

'She understood on a logical level. She was just defending another person.' (Mark)

'Her willingness to be reasonable and accept the merit of my points, though she can be stubborn.' (Charles)

Note that 'stubborn', even in a positive context. Men do find it difficult to accept that if they work at persuading the woman to see things their way, she will continue to see things differently. This is almost invariably explained by some failing in the woman, unless he can find a better reason for her not changing her mind, as Mark did. Even men like David and Darren, whom we met earlier, who would otherwise avoid arguments, do get into tangles with lovers, and they explain their failure to get their views across like this:

'Her emotions were riding high and she just didn't want to understand.' (Darren)

'She was being unreasonable. I didn't want to push it.' (David)

Many men say they 'back off' in an argument with a lover. Many husbands say they will 'give in' to their wives. Recently, I came to the conclusion that this might be another version of men not taking what a woman says seriously. As will become very clear in discussion of arguments outside the special intimate relationships we are dealing with here, men tend to dismiss women's arguments as unimportant (see Parts Three and Four). Could it be that lovers and husbands have a similar attitude even with the central woman in their lives? So whenever a man told me he 'let her [wife or lover] win', I started to ask: 'Could it be that you didn't really care? That the issue was not important to you?' The answer was almost invariably a laugh, and 'Yes.' Some further comments I heard:

'It makes for a quieter life to let her have her way.' (Geoff)

'No point in having an argument about things I really don't mind about. She minds more than I do about things, so I don't insist if I think we disagree.' (William)

'She gets much more bothered than I do. I'll usually back off.' (Bob)

This suggests that when a woman persists in trying to get her partner to 'hear' what she is saying, he becomes more and more convinced she is getting emotional and backs off. He too does not want an argument to damage their relationship, and does not know what to do when she gets – as he sees it – emotional.

Muddled Emotions

Clear communication between lovers is an ideal. We know, alas, that it is rare, and that when the issue really matters to one of us, this ideal falls before the onslaught of a tide of muddled emotions.

Tony, a 28-year-old accountant, tells of an argument over the telephone with his 25-year-old lover Cathy 'about whether to open a bottle of champagne I gave her for Xmas'. For Cathy, the champagne was a symbol of their love: when she suggested opening the bottle that night, he surely must have understood she did not want to drink it alone. His reaction 'well go ahead if you want to' was hurtful. He, on the other hand, thought she should *say* what she meant. He writes:

> 'Bottle opening was a secondary issue. I thought she was teasing, but she really just wanted to come over to my place that evening. Unfortunately, I didn't realise it until it was too late. While I suspected the "real" reason, I wanted an *explicit* statement and "played the game" instead.'

Each is expecting the other to 'mind-read'. He refuses to acknowledge the hints he does in fact pick up because he finds the 'fact that women never say what they mean' tiresome, and expects her to realise that he wants her to state explicitly what is on her mind. She believes he should *know* what the champagne means to her, and that anyway she has given enough hints, and if he ignores them it is because he does not care enough about her. If she had come out clearly with the statement, 'I want to come over and open the champagne with you tonight', she could not then know whether his agreement was compliance for the sake of peace or what he really wanted too. They do not trust each other.

Tony's diary of arguments shows that this has long-term effects, which leave him feeling 'more confused than angry'. Cathy accuses him of being moody over the next week, and they argue about trivial practical matters (using pancake mix, the inadequacy of his kitchen), which leaves them both upset. They are not communicating and this is at least partly because of the myth that love should bind them without effort on their part, and each should be able to read the other's mind.

In her popular book *You Just Don't Understand*, linguist Deborah Tannen suggests that men focus on the simple 'message' of the argument, whereas women focus on the 'metamessage': what does this argument mean to our relationship? Was this the case here? It is true that an outside listener might have thought that Tony was focusing on the immediate question 'should she open the bottle now?' whereas Cathy was more concerned with what his answer to that question *meant*, i.e. did he really not care? However, Tony's diary account makes it clear that he was aware of the metamessage, and was deliberately refusing to hear it unless she chose to express it clearly. Why was this?

Part of the reason has already been suggested: the myth of love tells us that communication should never pose problems, and if it does then love is faulty. Another part of the reason is that men expect to be able to dominate a woman, and one way to wield power is to manipulate her feelings. Women foster this belief by being willing to conciliate, until confronted with a conflict that seems to put the relationship in question.

Doing Dominance

This desire to dominate is usually most clear in impermanent love affairs, or in unhappy marriages, and the issues that bring the conflict to a head can range from the crucial to the trivial.

Debbie, for example, found that starting to share a house with her boyfriend of six years led to arguments about trivia like doing the crossword. She explains:

'We wish to do the crossword together, but I felt patronised. He, being quicker than I, doesn't say the words but tries to give clues on the answers. I would rather the answers were put straight in, even if I would then not be able to do much; but of course, he said that that didn't give me a chance. This being the case, I would rather not be given clues as well.'

This looks like a perfect example of a man parading his superiority while masquerading as 'helpful'. She writes, 'We could both understand the other person's feelings', but there is little evidence that he did in fact take any account of hers. His desire to dominate in a field where he is clearly better is emphasised by his claim that if he did do as she asked, this would 'not give [her] a chance'. Both believed that they were 'liberated' and that he was a New Man; but when living together, they found their long-term friendship could not withstand the assaults of these and similar attempts by him to establish his dominance by stealth.

An otherwise happy relationship can founder on arguments about just one issue if it is important to both partners. For example, Sandra and Wilf are both social scientists involved in research. Their love affair happily flourishes until they get on to the subject of research methods, when Wilf attempts to control Sandra's work by insisting that his approach is the only way for her to carry out her research. That he has recently moved to another university, and so they can only get together at weekends, seems to have exacerbated Wilf's attempts at dominance. Sandra told me:

'We have a lot of arguments about his idea that account analysis is the be all and end all. It's important because it relates to work, and I want to get him to admit there are other ways. OK his way is one way, I agree it's a good idea to look at accounts. But it's not the only way . . . . I think it is his arrogance. His assumption that he really knows. And he just won't listen. It makes me really upset. That's the way our arguments usually end. Either I say, let's leave it, it really upsets me. Or he'll see I'm upset and say, let's drop it, we're not getting anywhere.'

Dropping an argument because it is upsetting and agreeing to differ are not quite the same thing. Sandra gets upset because she feels that Wilf has not 'heard' what she said: he is not accepting her equal right to an opinion when it is not the same as his own.

Wilf believes he is a modern man, and dismisses any suggestion that his attitude to his lover's work is a consequence of old-fashioned sexist attitudes. But conversation with him reveals an unconscious assumption that he knows better, and he confided in a low voice: 'Sandra does get emotionally involved with her work, which makes it a bit tricky to talk about it sometimes.'

Wilf appears to be doing what so many men do, even in a relationship with a woman who is important – he is explaining her reluctance to accept his view as 'emotional', not as an intellectual equal's rational choice.

Some men maintain their dominance by turning the belief that a man cannot express feelings to their advantage. Stella's husband sits silent while she tries to talk to him about her needs in their marriage, struggling in vain to get through to him: and when she is utterly exhausted with talking and then shouting and then bursting into tears, he points out that she is being impossibly demanding, and how is he to cope with such outbursts? She told me:

'Men don't seem to want to talk about feelings. It really upsets him if I start to cry, and I try not to.'

And she makes amends for her 'unreasonable' outbursts by being extra loving.

A Canadian writer of my acquaintance is even more devious. He discovered that he could provoke his young wife Betty, by criticising her appearance or her care of the children, and she would fight back. Unoriginally, but with obvious pleasure, he said: 'She's like a tigress. Never met such a woman for giving as good as she gets.'

He would goad her until she spectacularly lost her temper, whereupon he would march off to his study shouting at her that she was a bitch, a slut and a fucking whore who didn't give a shit for her kids. He would then bash away at his word processor, inspired as he said 'by a good fight'. Meanwhile she recovered from her temper, accepted his criticisms – she *had* exploded, maybe broken a dish or slammed a door – took the children out for the day to give him peace, cooked a special meal for him in the evening to make amends. He won every way. Until Betty started listening to what was happening, stopped reacting to his criticisms, and his dominance faded. He found he had come to depend on the stimulus of a fight, for when Betty stopped being manipulated, his muse dried up. It is now her fault that he cannot write.

This is not an isolated example. Many husbands appear to try to maintain their dominance by belittling their wives. A contributory factor is the widespread belief that a woman arguing with a man is failing as a woman. Then all those stereotypical epithets come flying out.

One anonymous woman is quoted in the Sanford and Donovan book as saying:

'I think the problem is that he can't handle the idea of a woman being angry. But even though I know that his calling me names is just a defense for him against his own feelings, the names sometimes can really get me doubting myself. If you get called something enough times, you end up believing it.'[26]

Fiona writes:

'My husband keeps telling me, "You're such a bitch, so unreasonable." He'll call me a witch and a shrew, say I'm impossible to live with. When I start to get angry, he'll sneer, and tell me I'm a rotten mother because I am not considering the children. And there the children are, open-mouthed, watching him getting red in the face. Gary said to me, "Daddy's horrid to you, I don't like him now." That really made me feel terrible, as though it really was my fault.'

Those hidden stereotypes about women and men *can* lead some people to believe that all relationship problems in marriage are likely to be the woman's fault: he brings home the bacon and she sorts out all the rest.

8

The Anger Problem

Love and marriage may often be sabotaged by hidden beliefs about the inferiority of women, for these beliefs are more widespread than women would like to think. Therapist Adam Jukes in *Why Men Hate Women* suggests that *all* men acquire a 'natural contempt' for women, and he comes to the deeply pessimistic conclusion that misogyny and gender inequality may be an inescapable part of human psychology. I will examine these disturbing ideas a little further in the section on families, but for now I want to concentrate on the meaning of anger in intimate relationships, both in marriages where the husband believes that women are inferior beings and in marriages where the partners are able to acknowledge each other as equals.

Men who despise women see no need to listen, and believe that they have the right to punish a woman if they do not like what she says. Tanya, who finally plucked up courage to leave her violent husband after ten years of abuse, told me:

> 'Every time I did anything he didn't like, he'd shout at me. Or if the children were untidy, or I was late with his evening meal, or – just anything. And if I tried to argue with him, he would hit me. The violence and abuse just grew and grew. He'd tell me to cry. "If you'll only cry, I can stop hitting you." I wouldn't let him get that much control over me, so I wouldn't cry. It was so unjust. I wanted to be a good wife to him and a good mother. I couldn't take it any more in the end.'

To her husband, Tanya's refusal to cry meant she had not accepted her wrongdoing. Most abusive husbands agree with the man who said: 'If you'd behaved better I wouldn't have to punish you.'[27]

Abuse can take many forms, but the underlying factor is that the woman is not allowed individual autonomy and integrity. As we will see in Pauline's story, the wife of a man who secretly despises her because she is a woman will find that expressing her views and desires brings only contempt and condemnation. Believing that as a woman she must conciliate him, she finds her sacrifices bring no benefits, so she loses power as an individual and a sense of her own value, and ultimately she may lapse into silence. The deep anger she feels at this loss of self-esteem is repressed, and any expression of anger becomes a further proof of her lack of value as a human being. A husband's secret contempt of his wife can thus lead to an insidious form of psychological abuse in which the woman unwittingly colludes in her own loss of self-esteem.

Dangerous Convictions: Pauline's Story

'I feel it's not safe to say what I think more often than not. Part of me believes I'm dangerous.' (Pauline, 28)

Pauline is auburn-haired, blue-eyed, and has a lovely smile. From photographs it is clear that she can, if she chooses, be quite remarkably beautiful. But she does not choose – and why is this relevant? Because youth and beauty mean she feels, not powerful, but trapped.

'Fat *is* a feminist issue. When I don't have this protective layer of fat as a shield, all men see is a sexual object. Last year I did get my body the way I wanted it, I looked good, and then I found I couldn't go out. My friend Jill made me go out to the pub one evening, she just came round and dragged me out, and I was quite pleased really. But when I got there, I didn't dare take my coat off all evening. When I'm fat, I'm safe. I'm not a threat to anyone.'

Her sense of being a threat to others is bound up in her awareness of her own powerlessness. Others attribute to her powers she does not want – she does not want to be seen as a sexual object, does not want to alienate women friends because their husbands drool over her, does not want to be called 'sarky bitch' when she turns a man's open invitation with a sharp retort. The safest thing is not to provoke such responses in the first place. They blame her, and so does she.

Those powers she does want are denied her. She is married to Bill, an engineer, and they have four children. The son of a regular soldier, he is a big, powerful-looking man with the build of a rugger player, who freely admits to many of the assumptions of the macho world in which he grew up. Admiration of his wife by other men makes him preen, for she belongs to him and he has no fears she will stray. She is glad to be valued by him for her looks, for she enjoys sex. But she also wants him to listen.

'I only ever argue if I am sure about the subject because I don't want to get into deep water and be shamed. So I have to believe strongly my beliefs are the right beliefs. Because I spend such a lot of time in silence, I think long and hard and that makes it even more valid. And to have it not listened to is really hard. Particularly with my husband. I find it incredibly hard that when I say something he responds with anger, and I *know* that if someone else said it he'd listen. They could say exactly the same words. Even just putting forward a suggestion, I've been ignored on many occasions. And ridiculed which I ... you know, the end result is it makes me ... I feel I'm not able to express myself very well.'

Only women ever told me they feared getting involved in argument because they could not express themselves. There are men who are inarticulate, of course, and perhaps I just didn't meet them, or they did not want to confess such weakness to a woman. But many women said they feel inadequate when it comes to speaking out, and this included some highly educated women and even a few academics. Furthermore, I particularly noticed that those who feel inadequate are by no means always those who really do find it difficult to express their meaning clearly and coherently.

Pauline is a case in point. Our conversations about argument were interesting: she is intelligent, articulate and willing to reveal deeply personal experiences because she believes that learning you have the right to say what you think is absolutely vital for women like herself. Being silenced and devalued always takes its toll and, as with Pauline, may eventually lead to explosion.

'We were living in this terrible flat, and terribly stressed a few years ago. And one day I exploded and went berserk, I was hitting him, it was absolutely horrible. He walked out, it was dangerous. I didn't have a blind rage, but I really saw red. We daren't get there again.'

What exactly was dangerous she found hard to say. She was frightened of her own anger, and yet she does not think she was 'blind' with rage, that is, totally out of control. She probably feared that her anger might damage their marriage irreparably. Possibly, too, she was frightened that her husband might hit her back and, given their relative size and strength, that *would* have been dangerous. She talked of his 'abuse' but would not be more than allusive: evidence from several hours of recorded conversations suggests that he both treated her with contempt verbally and aggressed against her sexually.

'In my experience anyway, freedom of loving is not easily retained when you are married because it is so much harder to get out of sex . . . I don't know, to me it's something on the lines of not feeling I have the right to deny . . . . I kept this all to myself because it didn't seem real, as though it was a figment of my imagination – it was very easy to believe things were not happening. When he was very abusive to me, I did my usual trick of minimising it. I was alienating people all the time, had arguments with everyone, like the whole world was an enemy. I felt like a really horrible person. Everyone tells me he is a lovely person, so it must be me, everyone else has friends, it must be me. So I changed. I didn't say a word.'

Her self-esteem was so weak as to be in danger of total annihilation. And yet she can be lively, full of wit and humour, as well as being a warm, loving and remarkably sensible mother (her children are appealing even to strangers).

Pauline apparently silenced herself when her eldest child, now 10, was still a baby. But being silent is difficult, especially to a woman who has learned that modern marriage is about communication. For several years she struggled to find her voice, and the more she tried to sort out how to be true to her own feelings and beliefs, the more she found that her views were belittled. Eventually, she insisted her husband leave.

As always, this was devastating for the whole family. Nevertheless, the consequences were largely beneficial. She discovered a support group which encouraged her to speak her own truth, made new friends, restored her battered self-esteem. Her children were no longer bullied as their father tried to enforce his domination. He discovered what he had lost, and wanted to learn why. They agreed to go together to Relate.

'It all had to do with totally undervaluing myself and undervaluing being a mother .... All the stuff that I hear about being able to hold on to your identity and so on, don't for goodness' sake get married and have children – well, what about those of us who want to do that? who want to get married and who want to have children and who see it as a very worthwhile occupation? There doesn't seem to be anything to help people like me hold on to our sense of ... worth .... I'm *totally* undervalued by society because I don't earn money. And as such I'm totally dependent on Bill. And therefore for a very long time I felt I had no rights. Eventually one learns after a time to reassert oneself, but it's been a very painful process.'

Her discovery that she has the right to her own opinions, and to her own feelings, has been crucial. She is no longer frightened by anger, for she knows quite clearly that there is a difference between *feeling* angry and what you *do* with that feeling.

'I have felt that anger was so dangerous, so destructive because I have been aware of how murderous I can feel. It's taken me a little while but I feel now that anger is a really ... yeah, is a good thing and I've been telling my children that. Actually being angry is OK, it's just what you do with it. Mothers are seen as nurturing and caring, and as a result we're not seen as human beings. We have to learn that these things are all part of us all.'

That her husband has been able to recognise this too was liberating. She recounted a recent episode in which she forcefully expressed the anger she felt, and the release she experienced when he acknowledged her right to her own feelings. They had been talking about her difficult relationships with her husband's parents.

'Bill told me I was over-reacting. Oh I was so *furious* that he would *dare* to tell me how I should or should not react that I left the room because I thought, I'm going to *not* present myself well, so I walked out. Bill, because of all the stuff that we've done, was switched on and sensible enough to know that he was walking on dangerous ground. And so he came into the kitchen where I had gone and he said, How are you feeling? and I said, I am really angry with you.

'And instead of responding to that he said, OK, tell me about it.

'I, really, I let rip! I said, Don't you fucking ever *ever ever* tell me how to respond. I will *never* ever put up with that. Don't you *ever* do that again. And I really really went for it [*tears in voice*] and it felt so good [*quiet*]. But when I'd finished, it had all gone. Completely gone. And we had a hug. The incident was so powerful because he had simply accepted it. He accepted that was how I felt, he didn't take it on board, you know, he didn't say, how dare you get angry with me or anything. It was just, OK, that's how you feel. And I felt so good.'

Words are actions, and here she was using words to convey a vital message to her husband. The words she chose were emotionally charged, and might have had a deleterious effect; fortunately Bill was willing to hear the message behind the words. The important thing is *not* that everyone has the right to *express* their feelings – what if you feel violent or murderous, for instance? The crucial thing is that everyone does have the right to *feel* what they feel, however bad and antisocial those feelings are, and if you cannot say that you feel angry, or even murderous, without being made to feel a vile and totally valueless human being, then you do not have freedom of speech.

Anger and Hostility

Anger is a normal human response to being belittled and discounted. It is also a widespread phenomenon in Western society that women like Pauline feel so devalued as they competently carry out the socially valuable task of caring for small children that they can believe they have no right to refuse their husbands sex, no right to express an opinion. Their very understandable anger at this injustice frequently means that they feel deep down they must be horrible people.

Pauline is finding her way out of the tenderness trap, and one part of that is to acknowledge your own feelings, and to know you have the right to feel as you do. She is right. Feeling angry is OK, necessary sometimes if injustices are to be righted. What is important is what you *do* with that anger.

How did Bill feel about all this? Well, he tried. He really did. He told me:

'We're so different, it's like shouting across a canyon. She seems to think she can say whatever she likes, and I can take it. OK, she's not the weak little woman my mother was, but sometimes I wish she was a bit more like her. My Mum would never talk to my Dad like she talks to me. What about my feelings? Sometimes I think I'm on a rollercoaster, and I want to get off. We just see things differently. We always will. If she wants to be equal, let her go out to work and earn a living – then she'll discover what it's like to be a man.'

Pauline learned to acknowledge her anger, and it came out very strongly. Before she had discovered how to manage it so that she could direct its powers to putting things right, rather than attacking her husband, he left for good. He heard some of the messages behind her words, but his beliefs got in the way. He thought there was nothing wrong with his own aggressive anger, his bullying of his children and occasional violence: the children 'need to learn to do as they are told', his wife 'should not provoke' as he 'might not be responsible' for what he did. Six weeks at Relate is not enough to eliminate thirty-three years of training in machismo.

Some readers have commented that Pauline's anger seems so extreme, they feel she is not like 'most women'. I suggest that that is because women are not supposed to be angry, and most especially they are not supposed to express their anger. We all know that. In fact, Pauline seems to me very like the large numbers of women who repress their anger for so long it finally explodes in extreme violence of language, if not in active violence against themselves, their husbands or even their children. In my consulting rooms, I see many women who are depressed, and who discover that it is safe to say at last what they have never dared to say before – that they are angry with their husbands. We work together on how best they can let their husbands know how they feel without leading to a rupture: divorce may be the best solution in many cases, but it is not always, and many women discover that they can after all say what they feel and be heard, and the world does not disintegrate about their ears.

Anger is a serious problem because we do not teach people how to handle it productively. We always see anger as a bad feeling between people: anger is a powerful force, which when harnessed can be directed towards sorting out the problem that created it in the first place. Anger is like electricity: a good servant but a bad master. It exists. It is there. So it needs to be controlled and directed in the most productive way possible.

Men too can feel belittled and discounted. They are particularly vulnerable to feelings of inadequacy when made redundant. Psychologists John Archer and Valerie Rhodes found that a man may grieve over the loss of his job in much the same way as we grieve over the death of a loved one.[28] If his wife does not understand and sympathise with his deep sense of deprivation, he may react in one of two ways: he may become seriously depressed, as Pauline did, a sign of deep anger repressed, or he may become indiscriminately angry.

Hostility can become a way of life. Oliver lost his job as a creative artist in his forties, and eventually found work with an insurance company. From his diary, he seems to be in a permanent state of anger: everyone in his everyday life, at home and at work, is liable to trigger an explosion and all his arguments appear to reflect resentment at his lack of a sense of worth. He and his wife quarrelled about 'whether or not I was treading on seeds she had planted in the garden' and he explains:

'I genuinely felt I wasn't treading on the bloody seeds! Also I *hate* gardening.'

They went shopping and argued about where to park the car. He wrote:

'I cannot stand interference when I am doing something that only I am involved in. Just because someone else thinks the job should be done differently is no excuse for sticking his/her nose in.'

Note that he is holding her at arm's length: she is not a special companion, she is just one of the world of other people, referred to as 'someone else ... sticking his/her nose' into his affairs. Unfortunately, I was unable to get his wife's views as she refused to take part in the diary study, perhaps because the request came via her husband, nor was she willing to be interviewed. On the evidence of his diary alone, one might venture to say theirs seems to be a distressed marriage. The grief and anger he felt about the loss of his job were never fully acknowledged, and they operate like a volcano, sending up frequent sparks and periodic eruptions of hot, molten anger.

Anger As Normal

Not all aggression and anger can be put down to a sense of being fundamentally devalued, however. The anger most of us feel at some time or other when arguing with a spouse has very little to do with the kinds of abuse described above, psychological or other. Most of us know what it is to feel angry and most of us know that we would not want to harm the other person, that our verbal conflict does not escalate into verbal or physical violence. Anger is a normal human response to many situations.

Any kind of disagreement can lead to anger and, worse than that, deep-seated disagreement about how women and men should or should not behave need not even be expressed to generate anger between couples. American marriage counsellor David Mace said:

> Marriage and family living generate in normal people more anger than those people experience in any other social situation in which they habitually find themselves.[29]

People who live together have more opportunities for anger; their irritating habits may become cumulative and distressing to each other; they often have a stronger desire to get loved ones to change; and they have a greater sense of safety in expressing how they feel.[30] We saw earlier that women tend to talk of 'feeling safe' in relationships in which they can argue.

Of course, safety is a relative matter: expressing unbridled anger within any relationship may render it unsafe. At least part of the reason why marriage appears to be a failing institution is that people seem to believe more and more that anger felt should be anger expressed: 'Don't let it fester', 'Let off steam before you blow a gasket.' The view appears to be that it is 'more honest' to 'let it all out', whatever the consequences to the other person. As one man, a 31-year-old singer, told Carol Tavris:

> 'In Gestalt therapy they taught me to express my anger at once and not let it fester. I used to be a person who never expressed anger until I felt it was legitimate to do so – I'd only present my grievances if I felt I had a case for complaint. Now I don't worry about legitimacy; if I'm pissed off, I say so.'[31]

This approach can result in constant sniping, increasing bad temper and a great deal of misery that one of the partners, if not both, eventually decides is not worth staying with.

Married couples are advised – in books, magazines, by marriage counsellors – that angry feelings should be shared and negotiated, but calmly, quietly, not in the heat of the moment. John Gray, the counsellor whose book assumes men and women are 'from different planets' (metaphorically speaking), has a whole chapter on 'How to Avoid Arguments'. He suggests that we fail to communicate in a loving way because we do not appreciate how our different ways of talking can upset the other:

It is not *what* we say that hurts but *how* we say it.[32]

'*When I get into an argument with someone, I know how to calm things down quickly*' was among the top five strengths rated by Americans in a national survey in the 1970s.[33] Psychiatrist Carol Zisowitz Stearns and historian Peter N. Stearns suggest that Americans have developed a nationwide desire to control not only angry behaviour but the feeling of anger itself.[34]

On the other hand, other pundits advise that fear of anger can be more damaging than expressing it. Desmond Morris, author of *The Naked Ape*, is quoted as claiming that suppressing hard feelings can damage your health:

Long ago, my wife and I were always nice to each other. Then we discovered it was bad to bottle things up, and now if we get angry about something we shout at each other and blow our tops. We're uninhibited, and our relationship is the better for it. So is our health.[35]

A number of British newspapers and magazines have published articles claiming that 'rows are good for you' and 'quarrelling is just another way of releasing tension'.[36] Sally, who is in business with her husband and so with him all day, says:

'There's nothing worse than an atmosphere you could cut with a knife and that's exactly what you get if you don't bring your feelings out into the open. Arguing for the hell of it is pretty pointless, but if there's something you want to complain about – then do it. Otherwise you'll end up feeling resentful, and that's when the rot sets in.'

And as we saw earlier, Pauline's rediscovery of her self-worth was closely linked to her ability to acknowledge and express her feelings of anger.

What is one to do with such contradictory ideas?

The fact is that anger is an emotion that belongs to the person who feels it; it does not belong to the other person; the other person does not even 'cause' it. If you are angry, you are feeling the anger, the other person did not 'make you angry'. This is a very difficult concept to grasp, as most people are quite convinced that they are victims when anger floods in. It is as though they were innocently standing by the seashore, and suddenly a tidal wave of anger just swept over them. But this tidal wave of emotion comes from within: it is your response to whatever the other person is doing or saying. It is your own interpretation that makes you angry. Your anger is yours alone. This does not mean that you should not feel what you feel – there are no *shoulds* when it comes to feelings, they just are. You are entitled to feel angry, and to tell the other person you feel angry. This does not, however, entitle you to belittle and destroy the sense of self-worth of the other. Oh, yes, and the other person is entitled to feel angry too.

Now what to do with it? Letting it all out as the American singer says he does, without consideration for its effect on the other person, is to behave like a child with a tantrum. But expressing anger is not (necessarily) to throw a tantrum. The difference is that you take responsibility for your own anger and *explain* how you feel: 'I feel angry' allows the other person to hear, whereas 'you make me angry' puts the other on the defensive.

Two angry people who can say: 'When you do X, I feel angry (or unhappy, or whatever)' rather than 'You make me so angry when you do X' will find that this is like a magic formula for calming the stormy waters. There is no arguing with feelings. If you the reader were to tell me, 'When you say that this is a magic formula that works, I feel really angry', my only response *can* be, 'I'm sorry you feel that.' No one can argue about someone else's feelings – though some people will probably try to shift the ground by claiming that you should not have those feelings. This is to be resisted. Feelings *are*. Express how you feel without attacking the other person. Saying 'you are . . .', 'you do . . .' is the equivalent of aerial bombardment and sends the other scurrying to full-scale anti-aircraft defence.

Anger has different meanings for different people. Some people see anger as cleansing, some as frightening; some people experience anger as empowering, some as losing control. Two people arguing may have completely contradictory notions about what is happening when anger is expressed, and if husband and wife have opposing ideas, this adds to the difficulties they have in communicating.

Note that I have been talking about 'people' feeling angry, and I did not say that anger has 'different meanings for women and men'. Many readers may have expected gender differences to enter the picture here, for there are many myths around that women and men have different attitudes to anger and *this* explains why some quarrels just go on and on. Women are said to become depressed rather than angry; hide their feelings because to express anger would be unladylike; make snide remarks because they never dare come out with what they really mean; be afraid of revealing their feelings. Men are said to be allowed to feel angry; encouraged to be aggressive and express anger as part of their masculine role. Stearns and Stearns note that during the nineteenth century some purveyors of advice to parents assumed that little girls did not even feel anger: it was boys who needed to learn how to control their anger, while girls had to learn to be cheerful. And yet . . . this is one gender difference that surely does not stand up to scrutiny. Most of us, male and female alike, must have had personal experience of both women and men losing their cool, and psychologist Carol Tavris, in her book *Anger: the Misunderstood Emotion*, has pointed out that men may have the same kind of hang-ups about anger as women.

But these gendered attitudes to anger are yet another aspect of the Division of Labour we have already met. Woman's task is caring for relationships: it follows that she should not show anger, unless the relationship she is caring for is endangered – exactly what we find in diary accounts of argument. Men's task is to deal with relations in the external world, and to protect their loved ones: it follows that anger is acceptable in certain circumstances, for a man is expected to be ready to fight his enemies. Neither is expected to express anger within the confines of their own intimate relationship, but allowances may be made on both sides. Wives will say:

'I shouldn't have brought it [a practical household matter] up then because I knew he was tired.' (Sheila, 34)

'He's never at his best when he first gets home, so I brought it [his anger] on myself.' (Carla, 28)

'He's very worried about money at the moment. I think my bringing up the phone bill just then was too much. He's very good usually.' (Liz, 45)

Husbands will confess to strong anger, especially when the issue is something that relates to their supposed expertise in the outside world, and then say they backed off:

'I was extremely annoyed at her suggestion I had made a poor deal on the furniture. But I had no intention of changing anything, so I dropped it.' (Ivan, 33)

'I felt very angry, but it was only momentary. She has this infuriating habit of interrupting. The salesman wanted to talk to me, and I can understand her annoyance – she'll be driving the car after all. But it made me look a fool – just for a moment there I felt murderous. Of course, I wouldn't say anything in front of someone else.' (William, 58)

When Communication Breaks Down

My investigations show that many couples argue regularly and often about everyday facts or about practical matters like who should do the shopping, cooking, cleaning, driving, washing up, which television show to watch, where to go on holiday, but that such disagreements do not necessarily lead to unpleasantness or misery.

Women are inclined to conciliate both lovers and husbands unless the issue is very important, and most appear to hide what anger they feel. This was measured by asking diarists to indicate on a 5-point scale, first, how heated the argument was, and, second, how angry they felt even if they did not express it. Men rarely report hiding anger, though they may say the strong anger they felt was short-lived, but women do hide anger, especially with husbands: they claim the arguments were 'temperate', but that they were angry, with an average full point difference between. Husbands rated the arguments with their wives as hotter than their wives did, but not as hot as the wives *felt*. The blazing rows of popular imagination were rarely reported by either.

Many husbands do tend to back down when the issue is not significant to them; most wives do tend to conciliate, and to hide the anger they might temporarily feel; but both can still feel free to make their point of view known. Many couples also feel able to argue even about such dangerous topics as politics or religion or money or sex.

Deborah Tannen claims, in *You Just Don't Understand*, that women and men talk differently: that women are interested in 'rapport' talk and men are interested in 'report' talk. While this does apply to many people, my studies suggest that both women and men are capable of both kinds of talk. Problems arise when protagonists are out of sync, as in the numerous cases cited in Tannen's book: this happens to us all at some time.

One of the great pleasures many couples discover as they grow to know each other over time is that they can move from one kind of talk to another, they can talk to build and develop their intimacy, and they can talk to exchange information. 'Report talk' and 'rapport talk' depend on the context, and happy couples can enjoy communicating either way because they can read each other's signals.

Until, that is, their relationship is threatened in some way. Then the myths of feminine and masculine ways of thinking take over. No longer does the man listen carefully to what she says because his deep-seated, possibly unconscious belief that she is irrational and emotional interferes. The woman focuses on the 'metamessage' ('what is he really saying?'). She tends to believe he must understand what she is trying to say, and so his refusal to take her feelings into account 'really' means he no longer cares, or has some hidden motive. She feels betrayed, and angry – and the danger to their relationship *demands* she make her feelings clear. A woman may shout and scream in these circumstances in an attempt to be 'heard'. The man feels threatened when a woman tries to express violent feelings, and a blazing row may develop. Or he may clam up, because he 'knows' that women 'understand' mysterious things about feelings and he does not, and he refuses to try to communicate in 'her' terms. He is angry too. The appeal of writers who claim that we are arguing across a cultural canyon probably lies in the way such arguments can escalate and dismay. Once the relationship itself is in question, no argument is safe.

Love is widely held to be the prerogative of the young – especially by the young – and yet the evidence suggests that maturity and experience make it easier for a woman to say what she means in a way that will be heard. Young women in their twenties frequently complain to me that their husbands 'won't listen', or 'feel threatened' when they express their thoughts, and frequently confess that they themselves find it difficult to say what they feel. Older women seem to become both more demanding and less worried: those in their thirties and forties seem determined to escape the toils of the tenderness trap. They expect their husbands or lovers to take account of their feelings when feelings are at issue, and are quite prepared to take drastic action when things go wrong: at the same time, their lives do not revolve around love alone, and many are gladly and happily building comfortable reciprocal relationships with men who have learned to talk to them.

This happy picture does not apply to everyone, of course, and most especially it does not apply to large numbers of women in their fifties. This appears to be a potentially catastrophic decade for many married women today. These are the post-war girls and the 1950s brides, who were expected to 'snare' a man to keep him at home. Their husbands are the men who grew up with the myth that romance trapped them into marriage, who developed the myth of the male menopause, and who feel perfectly justified in restoring their own sense of youthful virility by seeking out willing younger women for their own sexual fulfilment. These women have been left stranded, for many of them believed they should be 'unselfish' and care for others before themselves, so have never learned how to stand up for themselves.

Margo, the mother of five adult children, is now 58 and a grandmother, and has never worked outside her home. A few months ago she discovered that not only was her husband carrying on an affair, he had also brought his mistress home while she was away visiting a married daughter, and they had slept in her bed. Not unnaturally, she was outraged.

'It wasn't so much the affair I minded, because I knew about it really, deep down – it was the insult. How dare he sleep with her in my bed? He promised never to see her again, but it was a lie, like all his lies. My sons want me to throw him out of the house now, but I just can't do it. How would he manage? And how could we throw away 38 years of marriage?'

A lifetime of caring and nurturing was not enough to protect her. Margo and her husband 'never argued'. For years, they had not talked properly, and did not know how. Perhaps they never did. Now that she is facing divorce, she is devastated, and desperately ashamed, and quite unable to talk to her husband even now. In her own terms, she has failed, and she does not know how to deal with her anger and anguish.

Some older couples, now in their seventies and eighties, told me of long-standing disputes which went on for years. Their problem was not that they 'never argued', for they argued year after year about the same issue, but that the conflict remained unresolved. Vera and Brian could not agree how to decorate the house they had bought together in the 1960s. Vera wanted to knock two rooms into one while Brian refused, and the issue rumbled on for years. Vera wouldn't invite visitors in until 'something was done'. Brian said: 'She gets these ideas in her head, I don't know where they come from, they're completely impractical.'

She thought he should be able to do for them what he had done professionally for other people. ('He's the expert.') But to Brian, this was nagging. Twenty years later, they agreed to drop the subject, the rooms were decorated the way Brian wanted, and Vera was prepared to let people into the house. She told me:

'He's so pig-headed, you can't imagine. I tried. But I've given it up now. And he's made it very nice, hasn't he? We spent hours choosing the wallpaper.'

Dennis would refer jokingly in company to the 'great central heating dispute', but it was not until he retired that he discovered that the house really was cold during the day, and he agreed to install the central heating Sarah had been asking for for years. Sadder still, Margie wanted to move to the country, but Fred refused, even when he retired. Their house was on a main road, which had become busier and noisier over the years, and Margie eventually had a permanent headache until she died – except for two weeks a year, when she visited Cornwall. But Fred had a big garden that was his pride and joy, and would not listen to her needs: he was partially deaf, so the traffic didn't bother him.

All these long-standing arguments created misery for the wives, because their husbands simply would not budge. The problem for the wives was that they wanted to change the status quo, and their husbands did not see why they should countenance a change that did not suit them and would cost money. The most serious aspect of these disputes, though, is that the husbands did not hear the unhappiness their wives felt in the face of their intransigence. I am not arguing that the husbands should have 'given in' to their wives. But I am arguing that if they had truly 'heard' the distress all these wives felt, they would have known that a creative solution to the impasse had to be found. Vera's refusal to have visitors was surely evidence of unhappiness, Sarah was constantly cold and Margie's physical distress was evident even to a stranger. But their husbands took refuge in the notion that 'women are always fussing about something, it doesn't do to take too much notice'.

My research suggests that young couples would be unlikely to allow a dispute to go on for years without resolution. Perhaps this is one reason why marriage is so likely to end in divorce: few women under 50 would accept a unilateral 'No' from a would-be dominant husband, and though divorce is hardly a creative solution, it is one which many people choose. Here are just a couple of examples of how a woman can approach the need for a creative way through.

Katherine was offered a major promotion, which meant moving from Manchester to Brussels. Her husband was a partner in a big firm of solicitors, and simply assumed she would turn the job down, no arguments. When Katherine realised how unhappy she would be, she went to great lengths to make sure he *heard* – she arranged a weekend away together, so that they could concentrate on each other, she emphasised how important he was to her, and how important it was to her that they think about this together. Because they loved each other, and tried to communicate rather than domineer, this couple did find a solution which allowed Katherine to take the job she wanted, and as it happened, benefited her husband too. Once he had begun to think about possibilities of change, he realised that expanding his business to Brussels could work for him too.

Creative approaches to disputes do not always bring such benefits, but do open doors to understanding that otherwise might have been missed. Tina, whose second marriage is to a farmer, found that her own businesslike approach to getting jobs done was making her very critical of her new husband. He would listen good-naturedly to her suggestions, but to her distress, their discussions apparently made not the slightest difference to how he behaved. She assumed he must have too much to do, and so decided to join him in the fields and the barns, to help with the lambing, the hedging, the haying, the mending of tractors and the mucking out of barns. She told me:

'Now I know why jobs don't get done. You can't work that way on a farm, everything's linked with everything else. I feel really good about it, we're working together now both literally and figuratively.'

The Division of Labour between the sexes can have different effects on different people, but it does seem that only those who discard stereotypical assumptions about the relations between women and men can find long-term happiness in love. No woman can be caring and nurturing at all times, no woman can always conciliate without denying her own needs, her own thoughts, even her own feelings. And no man can be conciliated and nurtured at every turn, with every whim catered to, without loss of his own ability to empathise and acknowledge his own emotional responsibility to others. Nor can he be always rational and logical and 'reasoned' out of his feelings. So it does seem to be true – as the relationship guidance experts tell us – that women and men need to be willing to talk about their true thoughts and feelings. They need to risk the pain of feeling the jabs of the reality of the other person, so that they can learn to adjust to the otherness of the other, and like porcupines in the wild, discover how to make love safely.

9

Of Families and Feuds: Simply Hating Mother

Behind so much of the anger is a simple HATRED OF MOTHER.[37]

These words introduced a review of a history of rock 'n' roll in the *Observer*, and the capitals are the editor's. The book's authors (Simon Reynolds and Joy Press) had taken the unusual step of examining the lyrics of popular rock songs, and found

> that rock is rooted in a virulent misogyny, that rock's 'rebellion' is all about flight from Woman, terror of domesticity, contempt for emotional commitment .... Always the theme is the same: that man is a free and heroic spirit, and that woman is an enslaving nag.[38]

So the popularity of rock seems to be yet another youthful manifestation of what Carol Tavris and Carole Wade call 'the longest war', that battle between the sexes.[39] As so often, resistance to women is equated with hatred of mother, though how *can* hatred of so important a person in one's life be 'simple'?

Misogyny is the most dangerous consequence of the Division of Labour: it leads not only to the danger of physical abuse, torture and murder, not only to the danger of sexual harassment and rape, it also leads (as we have seen in Pauline's story) to insidious forms of psychological abuse in which the woman may unwittingly collude in her own loss of a sense of value.

Men who hate women do not consider there is any need to listen to a woman. Men who hate women believe that they have the right to punish a woman if they do not like what she says. Men who hate women find it easy to believe that a woman does not mean it when she says 'No', or ignore it anyway because her desires don't count, or operate with the conviction that any woman who inspires lust in him does it deliberately to annoy and deserves anything she gets. They are in illustrious and long-established company: in the Middle Ages, St Bernard of Clairvaux believed that 'To be always in the company of a woman and not have intercourse with her is more difficult than to raise the dead.'[40] Eight hundred years later, Judge David Wild gave it as his opinion that

> Women who say no do not always mean no. It is not just a question of saying no . . . . If she doesn't want it, she only has to keep her legs shut and there would be marks of force being used.[41]

For their own safety alone, women need to find a way to stop misogyny at source. And that source is said to be ourselves as mothers.

I imagine that many readers will have a resistance to any suggestion that hatred of women is a key factor in the psychology of argument. When Germaine Greer wrote 'women have very little idea of how much men hate them',[42] she aroused a chorus of denial and mockery: it is neither pleasant nor safe as a woman to imagine that all men are our enemies, and seems as improbable as the complementary notion that all women hate men. I myself did not think of misogyny as something to which I needed to devote a whole section until a chance conversation with my daughter Akita. She said, 'I find it very difficult to be friends with women who are blatantly bringing their sons up to be misogynists.' I asked her to explain what she meant. She told me of Sheila, whom she met each day outside the primary school and who yells and screams at her two sons in front of everyone:

> 'I think it's because she lets them get away with things, and then when she needs to put her foot down she goes completely over the top. These boys have no respect for her because she has no control, and then she humiliates them in front of everyone, and

the other women call out "Hit him!", "Give him a good wallop!" These boys are growing up to be woman-haters.'

She may be right, because a boy's early experiences with his mother determine to a large extent how he will relate to women. Equally, a girl may learn to hate in the same way. But the same argument can be applied to fathers: if a young child of either sex is abused physically or psychologically by a parent of either sex, this becomes part of the child's expectations and understanding of what it is to *be* a woman or a man. So humiliation may be a source of misogyny – and of man-hating too. (Interesting to note that I can find no single word for the latter.)

Psychoanalysis and the Wicked Witch

Many writers, though, attribute misogyny to very much earlier experiences of the mother. Therapist Adam Jukes, author of *Why Men Hate Women*, suggests that all human beings have to deal with a desire to destroy their mother because of her absolute dominion and the inevitable frustrations she has caused in their earliest years. A similar point is made by psychologist Dorothy Dinnerstein.[43] Both go along with Melanie Klein's view that the babe in arms projects on to the mother all its frustrations in those early weeks and months of life, and the real mother becomes 'split' into the 'good mother' who provides nourishment at the breast and the 'bad mother' or witch who is dangerous and life-threatening.[44] Jukes writes:

> The male infant makes a decision never again to allow a woman to have the degree of power over him that he experienced his mother to have during his early life.[45]

He also goes along with Freud's theory that little boys acquire a 'natural contempt' for women when they discover they do not have a penis. These beliefs lead him to the deeply pessimistic conclusion that misogyny and gender inequality may be an inescapable part of human psychology.

Dinnerstein suggests that female domination of early child care has crippling consequences for both women and men. She believes that women actively collude in the present Division of Labour, which gives them power over emotions and men power over the world; this collusion works with men's desire for dominance and deprives men of the possibilities of deep feeling they might otherwise discover in heterosexual love. Jukes is unhappy at the notion that man is victim of this arrangement:

> While I am conscious of the costs I am far more aware of the benefits, for men, of accepting the Law of the Father and the entry into male freemasonry. It should be clear that I believe the notion of men as victims is profoundly undermining to attempts to help men to change. My experience is that we first need to see our role as oppressors and the power we, as men, have over women. Men are more victims of our expectations of women than we are of the male Law.[46]

Having watched three children and four grandchildren of my own develop, having studied what experimental science has learned about developmental psychology,[47] I find Melanie Klein's beliefs about the baby's terrors unconvincing. Early experiences are undoubtedly the key to later psychology, for it is on what we have learned that we build at every stage. But a baby can have no concept of good or bad, it can only have sensations of pleasure and pain; and if the mother is associated with both in the infant's developing mind, there is no evidence to support the theory that the infant splits the mother in two. In any case, a baby as young as five or six weeks may fuss when mother goes out of sight, and quieten, even smile, when she reappears: to the simple mind, this seems to indicate a pleasure associated with the mother's presence, and discomfort with her *absence*. Since language does not begin to develop before the end of the first year, and takes several years to be fully established, by the time the child is old enough to make decisions like, 'I'll never let a woman have this kind of power over me again', his decision is unlikely to have much to do with early hunger pangs or dirty nappies. It is much more likely to arise out of the frustrations associated with growing away from a protective or dominant parent. Seriously neglectful or cruel mothers will inevitably teach the growing child not to trust a woman, but they are fortunately rare, and cannot be invoked to explain normal development.

My view is similar to but not entirely the same as that put forward by sociologist Nancy Chodorow in her famous book *The Reproduction of Mothering*, though I do not share her positive attitude to psychoanalysis.[48] Psychoanalysts always seem to see the process of differentiating the self and the mother as a problem for the infant, which they then explain in terms of theories which perpetuate the gender differences we are attempting to understand. Furthermore, clinical practice relies on verbal recall, which cannot by its very nature tap pre-verbal stages of development, i.e. that first year which analysts claim is so fundamental to an infant's concept of mother. Psychodynamic theories are unprovable, which is why they contain such a powerful mix of magic and myth.

Chodorow argues that girls have no problem with their sense of femaleness, can remain identified with their mothers, and can grow up with a capacity for empathy and relationship built into their self-definition. Boys, however, do have problems: for them maleness is problematic because their early oneness with the mother provides them with

an underlying sense of femaleness that continually, usually unnoticeably, but sometimes insistently, challenges and undermines the sense of maleness.... Learning what it is to be masculine is defined as not-feminine, or not-womanly.[49]

Boys grow up with a tendency to devalue all things not-male and to define individualism and autonomy, which are culturally valuable, in terms of separateness and difference from women. Chodorow suggests that misogyny could be eliminated if men were to share equally in parenting.

But why does Chodorow need psychoanalysis for her view anyway? It is surely sufficient to recognise that girls learn that to be female is to be like their mother (and not like their father), and boys that to be male is to be like their father (and not like their mother); and that men have a vested interest in devaluing women in order to justify their privileged position.[50] She herself emphasises that 'gender differences and the experience of difference are socially and psychologically created and situated' and that they 'do not exist as things in themselves'; gender is a process which develops out of and reproduces inequalities of power.[51] Recourse to psychodynamic theory suggests that differences are so deeply embedded in our early development as to be immutable, however much one argues their socially constructed origins. And how does she expect the men who had such difficulty in differentiating themselves from their mothers now to be able to be transformed and show nurturing care to their small infants? The very solution she offers to the problem as she states it suggests that the psychodynamic element is unnecessary.

Men who hate women are unlikely to be very good at parenting, it's true. They are pretty awful husbands too. Adam Jukes claims – shockingly – that all men hate women, but that again derives from his belief in the psychodynamic origins of misogyny. The men he deals with as a therapist are, by definition, those who batter their wives, and we can all agree that a woman's ability to communicate with her husband in these circumstances has been effectively destroyed.

While we must be careful to avoid blaming the victim, women do need to take responsibility for their contributions to men's hatred of them. Mothers and teachers, in particular, have the opportunity to show the growing boy that women can be gentle and understanding (ah, yes, those tenderness trap qualities), and also firm and reasonable and strong (qualities more usually associated with men). Little boys learn about women from their mothers, aunts, grandmothers, older sisters, teachers – all the women in their lives. Little girls learn the same – they learn from their mothers and the other important women in their lives what it means to be a woman. A woman who screams and yells at her child uncontrollably, and humiliates him or her in front of friends, evokes the wicked witch of our fairy tales. Which mother has not gone over the top once in a while? But when it gets to be a habit, resentment and fear may turn into hate. Gentleness and tenderness *are* important qualities in the lives of infants and young children: it is not surprising that they loom large in people's concepts of what it means to be a woman when they are adult.

94

This is but one of many reasons why fathers have a crucial role in reassessing the Division of Labour. To the extent that they become involved in the care of babies and infants, they learn to show gentleness and tenderness too. Practice brings pleasure; the more they nurture and care for their growing children, the better they become at allowing others to be as they wish to be. But it is not easy, and men are not encouraged at any stage to renounce the male power they acquire by birth. Jukes believes that men will never renounce their power and control over women, and so will never be willing to take on 'feminine' tasks. Certainly the media's New Man has more to do than take a crying baby for a ride in a car (as in a recent TV advertisement). *Both* parents could teach their children that *both* sexes can be gentle and nurturing, and both can be firm and reasonable and strong.

As my daughter so cogently pointed out, it is every mother's responsibility to teach her son that when a woman says 'No', she means it.

Mothers and Their Adult Sons

'There's no point in arguing with her, she never listens. She's too stupid to understand what I mean anyway.' (Bob, 24, accountant)

'She's too dense to argue against me.' (Jim, 28, graduate research psychologist)

These are young men talking about their mothers. Where do they get this attitude from? British psychologist Halla Beloff has shown how all-pervasive is the belief that mothers are not as clever as fathers, despite the fact that psychologists established more than eighty years ago that there are no sex differences in general intelligence.[52] She asked university students to guess their own, their mothers' and their fathers' Intelligence Quotient, and as recently as 1990 she found that men estimate that their own and their fathers' intelligence as considerably higher than their mothers': given that the average IQ for the whole population is 100, Beloff's 265 male undergraduates guessed that their own IQ would be around 127, their fathers' around 125, and their mothers' around 118.[53] It should be noted that women share, and presumably help to reinforce, this erroneous belief in a sex-related difference in intelligence: 502 Scottish female undergraduates guessed their own and their mothers' IQ to be around 120, but attributed the higher score of around 128 to their fathers.

As Beloff points out, it is not sufficient to argue that these estimates of mothers' intelligence probably reflect the reality that men want to marry women who are less clever than they are (psychologist John Campion suggests this);[54] in any case, it is more usual for geneticists to talk of 'assortative mating' in which most people marry those similar to them. The crucial point is that the young women in her sample (and in numerous other similar studies) evidently share the view that women are less intelligent than men.[55] Not only did they guess their mothers' IQ was lower than their fathers', they also guessed their own IQ was both lower than their fathers' and lower than the self-assessments made by their male colleagues. Beloff assures the sceptics that this was not a reflection of reality in the University of Edinburgh. (In passing we might note that in Scotland, girls had been achieving significantly superior school-leaving examination results since 1984, while similar results began to show in Northern Ireland in 1989 and 1990, and emerged in England in 1994.[56]) By any objective standards, Beloff's female students were by no means less intelligent than the males. They just thought they were, and the men agreed.

Mothers' generally low standing in the IQ stakes may explain why so few of the men who sent me argument diaries reported arguing with their mother. Those who did said that, for various reasons, they were 'unable' to communicate, and the few accounts I did receive revealed great discomfort. Roger, a 39-year-old bookseller, found himself arguing with his mother about her 'projected purchase of a suite of furniture', but 'I failed to be honest about my reasons for having reservations'. Peter, a 27-year-old computer programmer, wrote:

'Difficult to communicate with her. She gets so emotionally involved I usually try to avoid clashing head on.'

Getting 'emotionally involved' is a standard criticism of women, and many men seem to assume that argument with their mother would involve her trying to talk about feelings. As several women said to me, 'Men don't seem to want to talk about feelings', and they don't. Graham, a 30-year-old engineer, had been explaining to me that arguing with his mother always made him uncomfortable, and I noticed that everything he said presupposed talk about emotions. So I asked, 'What about arguing about ideas?'

'Oh, anybody can talk about ideas. There is an important psychological distinction between feelings and ideas. She tries to take feelings apart and I don't really like that.'

Well, did he ever argue with his mother about ideas? He supposed so, somewhat dubiously. 'I'm always prepared to talk about ideas with anybody . . .' and his voice trailed off. Evidently mothers and ideas are not so easily associated as mothers and emotions.

Many men in their twenties and thirties confess to 'a difficult relationship' with their mothers, and in the words of one chartered surveyor, 'I can't talk to her.' Some men even go so far as to accuse their mothers of emotional blackmail. It frequently seems that any comment by a mother may be interpreted as a snide remark or as an attempt to manipulate and take control. Emotional blackmail is usually interpreted as meaning the mother is trying to reassert the powers she had over her son as a child. Leslie, a 30-year-old university lecturer, complained:

'She heard what I said, but it was ignored. My thinking was treated as irrelevant. She still thinks she can have power over me.'

Part of the difficulty seems to be that men have a problem with the fact that their mother has had intimate knowledge of them in a way no other person could. Why this should pose difficulties is not clear since that early intimacy with a carer applies to every human being: it is perhaps this mysterious sense of being known by a powerful Other that gives rise to widespread acceptance of psychoanalysis and its notions of separation from the mother. One man in his mid-thirties mused:

'With my mother I suppose I feel vulnerable. I feel vulnerable because she's my mother, she's got intimate knowledge of me. Yes, a long time ago, but I still feel it.'

Young men apparently get annoyed if their mothers 'try to boss them around'. Their need to assert their independence begins of course in their early teens, and may establish a habit of resistance difficult to break.

Perhaps lots of mothers are bossy, but the evidence suggests it is more probable that mothers remain concerned about their sons' well-being. If they do go beyond an expression of concern and try to offer well-meant suggestions and advice, this is *interpreted* as bossiness, mixed with manipulation of feelings of guilt and obligation. Another 30-year-old man admitted:

'Whenever she tries to tell me what to do I get irritable. It's as though she thinks I owe her.'

By the time a man has reached 30, it certainly seems reasonable to suppose he does not need his mother to tell him what to do. But simple comments may easily be construed as interference, and offers of help as intrusion. Simon, another computer programmer, commented:

'My mother was always trying to tell me how to run my life, made me really irritable. Seems to happen less now, though, now Emma's around to boss me instead.'

Does this man *like* having a woman to boss him around, or is he merely interpreting his companion's suggestions as bossiness? It is impossible to tell without being a sparrow at the window.

The mothers themselves tend to believe they are careful to acknowledge their children's right to think and act for themselves once they have become adults. Ellen was concerned that her 20-year-old son, 'a young and enthusiastic Christian', had become over-keen to evangelise.

'I suggested this can be a bit of an impertinence and should only be attempted within a real friendship . . . . He knew I wasn't "ticking him off", only making suggestions to which he was prepared to listen.'

Gillian's elder son was at university (she is a farmer):

'I really rather enjoy being able to discuss and argue about things when he's home. At least he listens, even if he does think I'm wrong, which is more than my husband ever does. We can even argue about politics and we'll never agree there. At least he lets me say what I *do* think, and that makes a change.'

But alas, communication may often be less effective than many mothers believe. Some evidence suggests that young men humour their mothers. Malcolm, an electrical contractor, explained:

'My mother gets really bored with her life, and I like to give her pleasure when I see her – it's not that often. If she wants to talk about politics or even about how I should run my business, I go along with it. It lets her let off a bit of steam, and doesn't do me any harm.'

And Patrick, a civil engineer, said:

'She only ever gets involved if she thinks we're not doing something right for the children, so I know she doesn't mean any harm. You know, she'll comment on how you're disciplining them or something, and it makes you mad. But I let her have her say; after all she's been there and I know she means well.'

Mothers and Their Daughters

Mothers and daughters have a less difficult time now that feminism has spread the word they can be friends not enemies. Every parent and child seems to need to go through a bad year: one saying I remember that sustained me through my own daughters' adolescence was, 'The two worst years of a woman's life are when she is 13 and when her daughter is.' It helped to know that others had been there too.

Daughters hate it, though, when their mothers argue with them, even when they have left home, started a career, got a family of their own. They seem to interpret any disagreement or well-meant comment in terms of what one called 'that power thing'. They fear being controlled by others, and are angry at any suggestion that even mother ('who is supposed to provide love, support, comfort and happiness') refuses them the right to independent thought.[57]

In diaries, daughters report feeling very high levels of anger, even when the argument is about trivial matters. Daughters in their early twenties record strong and heated arguments about 'what the time was', 'whether my mother had sent a birthday card to my cousin', 'my plans for the following day' or even 'why I thought she should lend me her Hoover'. There is an element of immaturity in all these diaries. A schoolteacher who still lives at home writes:

'My parents realised they should not nag me. I was cross that my mother had left specific food for me to eat when they are on holiday.'

And the student psychiatric nurse who wanted to borrow her mother's Hoover writes:

'I just kept repeating my views and ignored what she said. My stepfather joined in the argument when it was nothing to do with him. This irritated me because he did not know the facts. I reacted by arguing even more with my mother and ended up in tears and then left.'

Like the sons in the previous section, some daughters are convinced their mothers are stupid anyway:

'My mother's inability to listen to logic really annoyed me. She spends so much time moaning and talking that she never listens properly. What I was saying was important information, but she just focuses on trivial aspects. This is similar to her normal behaviour and I wanted to tell her this.' (Gemma, 20)

And Rita, a young management trainee, reports a 'blazing row' with her mother because 'she refused to listen, refused to accept my account of what had been said'.

Other daughters write that they rarely argue with their mothers, now they are growing up. Louisa, a 20-year-old student, writes:

'At home, I very rarely have arguments. I think that this is because most times it's easier to accept a point (domestic) and do a job rather than argue and feel selfish and lazy, however busy or tired I feel. Also I don't feel that it is actually my home any more and therefore do not have much say in what goes on there.

'For arguments of a wider nature, I tend to agree basically with my family views and being away from home most of the time, there is not much chance to discuss anything in more detail. Also, where this arises I tend to agree with my sister and she will argue more convincingly than me.'

Louisa's sister Nell (22) also kept a diary: she had just completed her first degree and was at home with her mother, working as a temporary researcher while awaiting a place to do postgraduate work in law. She records several arguments with her mother about politics and other social issues. Most are not heated, but are characterised as 'mild discussion':

'Have basically same politics, but get there via somewhat different beliefs/values/background, therefore have relatively minor disagreements in any discussion. Just part of a normal discussion, testing our political views mainly, but also just an academic exercise. Not really antagonistic.'

However, certain topics may become 'heated'.

'We totally disagree about this [heterosexuality] and don't really try to argue as we know we disagree. But the subject sometimes comes up, so we have a friendly row, not really trying to influence each other.'

This family has a tradition of argument, and a young woman hoping to go into law (as Nell does) must expect to be able to argue her case without distress. But in other families, when the disagreement is about important issues like politics or sexuality or women's rights or children, some mothers and daughters find it difficult to remain on warm and loving terms. Laura, a 22-year-old secretary, was very angry with her mother's attitude to her plans to live with her boyfriend.

'She refuses to accept that I am old enough to look after myself and make my own decisions. I felt I had to convince her that I would be all right. She was so determined that it wouldn't be the right thing, so I had to argue because it is what I want. I couldn't let it rest at her thinking she had won me over to her point of view.'

Marsha, a 23-year-old barmaid, was 'more upset than angry' with her mother's attitude to her pregnancy:

'To hear my mother talk, you'd think that men never do anything wrong. Every time I try to explain why I want to have this baby without getting married, she goes on and on about "poor Matt" and how he's being deprived of his rights. He's not. If he's prepared to stick around, he can be a proper father if he wants. I just don't want to get married. I never want to be some man's property, so he can never never say, "You're mine" like my stepfather said to my mother. Honestly, you'd think she'd know better with her experience. But no. It's all, "Think of poor Matt" until I could scream. I just can't take any more.'

And Diana (a boutique owner in her thirties) told me:

'Her ideas about Jews or black people or, in fact, about anyone who is not English make me feel so sick and angry, I can't believe she is my mother. I just avoid talking about these things if I can, because she never hears when you tell her that her facts are wrong. So she's lived longer than I have – that doesn't make her right.'

Once again we find women explaining these clashes with their mothers, or indeed with their parents as a couple, as differences in values:

'She's not really open to new arguments. A lot of her ideas are really sensible, but she can't really understand that people can have different values.' (Beryl)

'They have a different set of values.' (Patricia)

'A complete clash of values.' (Valerie)

These arguments can lead to long-term rifts that make both

profoundly unhappy. Women who lead lives which are different in some way from that expected or hoped for by their mothers still *want* to love their mothers, and be loved by them. All would like to have their right to make their own choices acknowledged.

Women, as we know, are not always tender and nurturing, and mothers can be as vicious and vindictive as anyone else. The problem is, their barbs go deeper as daughters are perhaps more vulnerable than anyone else, and the pain lasts. In a moving collection of letters between mothers and daughters, editor Karen Payne quotes a 30-year-old woman:

'I believe that the relationship between a mother and her daughter can be the most destructive of all conceivable relationships, even more so than between a husband and wife in a bad marriage. I've certainly found it was in my case.'[58]

Martha told me recently, 'I think this year I shall succeed in divorcing my mother. Then I'll be free.' She is in her forties.

My own mother, on the other hand, always made me feel that my point of view was valid. Even when I was a teenager, that most notorious of rebellious times, she would always ensure that I knew that she was not disapproving of me as a person even when she disapproved of what I wanted to do or disagreed with what I said. From a very early age, I learned to make a distinction between the person and what that person says.

This may well explain why I studied argument for my doctoral thesis, for I was astonished to discover as I grew older how few people are able to conceive of themselves as separate from their ideas. As American psychologist Bob Abelson says, 'Ideas are like possessions'.[59] Somehow if I argue with you, and want to suggest you change your ideas, you may feel I am taking something away from you. Whereas to me, ideas exist out there, in a kind of social cognitive arena where they can do battle independently of those who use these ideas or produced them in the first place. That is what books are about – they are ideas written down, which others can read and consider without needing to be concerned about the feelings of the author. Books assist in objectifying ideas, so that we can examine them coolly and in our own time.

An essentially unfeminine approach, one might say, and yet I believe that I owe this approach to the concern my mother felt that as a developing girl and woman I should not feel belittled when she criticised my words or my actions. I have always felt grateful to her for making me feel valued, but it was only when I came to write this book that I realised quite how unusual she probably was. Like writer Ann Scott,

> I have never understood how anyone could think women are inherently men's inferiors. The taken-for-grantedness of that is very deep in me . . . . I never learned conventional 'femininity' at her hands – and so never had to unlearn it either.[60]

Mothers also report arguing with daughters, and they see things somewhat differently. Those who have young children record some high levels of anger, especially when daughters – and sons as well – refuse to do their household chores. Watching TV, staying up late and running up telephone bills also rate strong arguments, while mothers say they are 'extremely angry':

> 'Daughter agreed she knew she's not supposed to watch TV during the week but went ahead anyway.' (Jenny)

> 'He hates washing up, thinks his sisters should do it. I felt he had to make some contribution to the household chores. He doesn't.' (Maria)

> 'If the bill goes up everyone will suffer in as much as we will have a lock put on the telephone to stop unnecessary use.' (Jill)

One mother of school-age children writes:

> 'I found myself shouting at the children on numerous occasions, but did not argue (e.g. to get dressed or to eat nicely). At times these were numerous and are the general main source of frustration. In the past I have completely lost my temper but not during this week.'

And Marion, whom we met in Part One, said:

> 'I never argue with my teenage daughter. I tell her. She knows what I say goes.'

As daughters become adult, mothers' accounts reflect their acknowledgement of their separateness, and the anger and need to control younger children diminish, but perhaps not as much as with their sons. There is a sense that mother knows best, especially when the issue relates to something she has more experience of. Eva (in her forties) wrote of a 'very important' argument with her daughter about 'practical approach to childbirth':

'We share the same values about the issue. We argued because I feel she is not realistic and practical enough. I felt my experience should be helpful in a situation she has never faced before.'

Though we cannot be sure, it is probable from the other diary accounts that Eva's daughter was not pleased to be 'helped' in this way and that she interpreted it as an attempt to 'control'. We have been told that as mothers we must let go, and these diaries reinforce that injunction.

Many women would like to think they are good friends with their daughters, and Michele (Nell's mother) confirmed the picture of a household in which political argument is the norm:

'We have many quite heated discussions – on politics and social issues mainly . . . . An element of verbal gymnastics, but mainly a genuine and mutual interest in exploring solutions to serious social questions. These discussions . . . usually ended in some form of agreement (as far as I know!) and at least on my part, with no anger at all.'

Many mothers say, though, that they dare not argue with their adult daughters for fear of a permanent rift. The anger so many daughters report suggests they are right to avoid argument, at least while their daughters are in their twenties and establishing themselves as adult in the adult world. That thirtieth birthday is like a watershed, after which it becomes possible to establish a warm and lasting friendship as one woman with another. My own experience with my two daughters confirms that they disliked very much being told what to do, but might occasionally, in their twenties, ask for advice if left alone. Now they are both in their thirties, we have begun to be able to discuss almost anything and enjoy the experience.

Women can encourage and inspire each other, and they can inhibit and destroy initiative. Not just mother to daughter, but daughter to mother: mothers have lives that continue after their daughters have grown, and communication *can*, when you are fortunate, develop into something mutually beneficial. Friendship across generations increases our strength and our ability to build on what has been achieved by others.

10

Iron John *and the Flight to Father*

The Greeks understood and praised a positive male energy that
has accepted authority. They called it Zeus energy, which
encompasses intelligence, robust health, compassionate decisive-
ness, good will, generous leadership. Zeus energy is male
authority accepted for the sake of the community.

(Robert Bly)[61]

Given that Robert Bly's concept of 'healthful male power' includes
not only those favourite male stereotypes of authority, intelligence
and leadership, but also takes over those widely admired 'female'
qualities of compassion, generosity and good will, it is hardly any
wonder that his book *Iron John* became a bestseller in the United
States. For he promised to show men who felt angry or frustrated
or lost in the middle of arguments about the relationships between
women and men how they might rediscover what he characterises
as 'male energy'.

Bly's thesis is that young men today are growing up with a
wounded image of the father. Those who have listened to women
have become more nurturing and more gentle, but have lost a vital
fierceness, have become 'soft'. He argues that the boy needs to
separate himself from the mother, needs a positive image of a father
who should lead him to find the Wild Man inside himself. He
mourns the disappearance of male initiation rites in our society,
and uses the Grimm fairy tale of 'Iron John' as a symbolic
enactment of the stages through which a young man needs to go to
achieve full growth.

The aim is not to *be* the Wild Man, but to be *in touch with* the

Wild Man. No sane man in Greece would say, 'I want to be Zeus'.[62]

There is a lot of good sense in Bly's book, considerably more than one might expect from some of the commentaries on it. It is true, for example, that it is helpful and illuminating to use the Jungian concept of the psyche as 'a community of beings', of which the Wild Man would be one; helpful, that is, so long as one does not hear voices or feel invaded. Bly's 'beings' are different from those described by Carl Jung, and are images taken from fairy tales which are meaningful to him: the Princess and the Wild Woman are aspects of what Jung would call the Anima, the feminine in the man's psyche; the King is an aspect of what the boy knows of authority, the Trickster what he knows about gaining power illegitimately and so on. All the 'beings' relate to what the person has learned about different aspects of life, they belong to the individual and may even operate unconsciously if not recognised, a factor of great importance in Jungian analysis but actually ignored by Bly.

What is harder to accept is Bly's thesis that men have been emasculated by learning about feelings from their mothers. He says that he first connected with feelings through his mother, which '*entailed* picking up a negative view of my father, who didn't talk very much about feelings'.[63] Why did it entail any such thing? Having learned empathy, as required of a woman, this mother is now blamed for her ability to empathise. Her question 'Are you feeling sad?' not only provides him with words for what he is feeling, but also with a weapon with which he later beats her. This is misogyny in a very subtle form.

Failure here lies, as Bly himself acknowledges, with fathers who are remote, who refuse empathy, are not tender. The conclusion is similar to that we came to earlier: fathers should be involved with their children too.

But Bly is far more radical, for he calls for separation between mother and son to protect the son's masculinity. The Wild Man is that natural primitive male who has been enchained by the mother: 'A mother's job is, after all, to civilize the boy, and so it is natural for her to keep the key.'[64] The boy's task is to steal the key for himself.

Few women are likely to believe that men need to go off into the woods to 'find' the Wild Man inside them. To most of us the problem is that that Wild Man is too easily discernible: how many women can walk alone at night, anywhere, without at some level fearing attack by some unknown mugger or rapist who thinks a lone woman is easy prey? How many women can honestly say they have never encountered the threat of violence in their own homes? No, the problem is not that men are 'soft' and need to toughen up. The real problem is that they need to *recognise* that Wild Man in their psyche, and by recognising get him under control.

To the extent that Bly's book, and the Back to the Wilds movement it led to, help men to recognise the primitive within them, these can be seen as a hopeful sign. But celebrating that 'three percent of DNA material'[65] that differentiates a man from a woman is damaging when it leads, as it appears so often to do, to a reaffirmation of misogyny.

Bly's concepts of masculinity, for all their poetic imagery, are those of a sophisticated teenager. He writes as though the Wild Man is really the Wise Old Man, but the myths and stories he recounts make it quite clear that the Wild Man lies in wait for the youth, he is the ancient primitive male power that the lover needs to win the daughter of the King. In other words, it is that testosterone-driven urge to mate, overlaid by the cultural and intellectual complications of the developed human mind. The Back to the Wilds movement is a retreat to adolescence, to that period in human lifetime when we reach the peak of our instinctive animality, and male and female both are swamped with the biological imperative to reproduce their kind.

The Battle with the King

Accounts by fathers of arguments with their sons put one in mind of those ancient myths in which the Old King must die in battle with the New – or evoke those splendid wildlife programmes we have all watched on TV, where the old lion must defend his territory every year against new pretenders, until at last he is defeated in bloody and fatal combat, and the victor takes over the pride – such is the level of aggression and anger.

We have already met Darren whose father threatened to throw him out of the house because of an argument. Darren also said 'I felt like hitting him', and it was probably the realisation that both were capable of violence that devastated him, and made him avoid arguments in future.

Other fathers and sons take a different path, and the streets of our cities are strewn with the cardboard beds of homeless youths slung out by angry fathers. Peter, who is now in his thirties, actually went white when recalling an incident when his stepfather grabbed him by the collar, saying he would throw him out of the house. He was 17.

'I don't even recall what the fight was about, it was something utterly trivial – I think I was expected to mend my sister's bike, I know she was involved and crying. He never listened. But he'd never tried violence on me before. I stood my ground, but if he hadn't let go, I really would have hit him. No, I'd never been involved in fights at school, I'm not an aggressive type.'

You may feel that *step*father is part of the explanation – an element of jealousy on both sides in their relations with the wife/mother. However, natural fathers throw their biological sons out of the house, and others get angry enough to threaten similar drastic action. In diary accounts, fathers report serious criticisms of their sons' behaviour.

Oliver wrote of a series of arguments with his 18-year-old son about 'his attitude to his work at college'.

'I thought he was wasting much of his time. He was flippant. I managed to catch him having done nothing but watch TV since he got up, and still in his pyjamas and dressing gown, talking about the amount of work he had to do. This really caught him red-handed.'

He was 'very angry' and the issue was 'extremely important'.

'I could see his future being jeopardised by his own laziness.

And my money (which is short just now) is being used to finance his "efforts".'

Kenneth's arguments with his adult son were about 'his general character and behaviour': he said he was not angry, but his son's 'deep-seated resistance' left him 'extremely depressed'.

Sons do indeed seem to be deeply resistant to being told by their fathers what to do. Few arguments were reported in diaries, but in interviews young men would characterise their fathers' attitude to them as 'interfering', 'domineering' and 'antagonistic'. Diary accounts were about trivia. For example, Allan (20) argued strongly about 'a train timetable' and was 'very angry', even though he conceded: 'I was wrong and there really was a train and I couldn't read the timetable properly.'

Serious rifts are recalled in interviews. Walter, now 50, remembers his implacable anger at his father's criticism of the woman he chose to marry at 23, and never spoke to his father again. Brian, 24, says he would never go home if it were not for his mother.

However, few men actually say they want a final break with their fathers, and just talking generally with young men left me with the impression of a powerful ambivalence. Like the young women quarrelling with their mothers, young men need both to insist on their autonomy and independence of parental dominance and to be able to rely on a father's love and understanding. Perhaps it is the cultural demand that girls learn to talk feelings and boys learn to talk tough that makes it so difficult for men to deal with these conflicts.

Writer Laurie Flynn, in his contribution to a collection of essays on *Fatherhood*, confesses that

> When I quarrelled with my father, I resented him as much as I loved him . . . . Those late teenage years included some major conflicts, some memorable rows. I would stop out. I would forget to say when or even if I would be home. For a while there seemed to be an almost limitless variety of causes for disputes – my first encounters with poverty and petty dishonesty as a transitory solution; my first bouts of drink; my first all-night parties; my first CND march.[66]

But eventually he discovered that, as he put it, his parents were 'open to messages from the other side' and he was able to convey to them that he needed time and space to try out the world. As he put it to his father:

'I mean, Vincent. Have you heard of the youth revolt or what?'

Looking back, he recalls his father's kindness, his love, and writes:

Even some of the conflicts and rows that I experienced make some sort of sense now I steel myself to re-enact them or some of them with those children I live among and directly influence for better or for worse.

Living with the Enemy is the title of a BBC TV programme on how to cope with a teenager in the family, and both parent and teenager may see each other as the enemy as the new generation seeks to assert its autonomy. Mothers and daughters quarrel, and fathers and sons may come to blows. Yet given time and avoidance of a permanent rift, fathers and sons too may at last rediscover pleasure in each other's company.

Fathers and Their Adult Daughters

There are no examples in my research of fathers reporting arguments with their daughters. This cannot be because they never occur – daughters do report such arguments, though they too are rare. But it is the one relationship for which I have absolutely no evidence whatsoever.

Very few women diarists reported arguing with their father. One who did was 20-year-old Gemma, who still lives at home. She recorded a number of arguments with her mother, all of which left her angry or annoyed, and half a dozen with her father: almost all of them were joking and good-humoured and 'having fun'. The only one that was not joking was about 'who should cook the dinner', and she reports that 'I gave in'. Rosemary, the administrator we met in Chapter 5, told me that she never argued seriously with her father:

'We joke around, but I never really argue with him. When I was living at home, I'd only ever fight with my mother. She was the one who tried to tell me what to do, what time to get home, you know. He didn't get involved.'

And Anna recalls:

'My Mum would decide where I was allowed to go and what time I had to be back. My Dad would be the one who came to fetch me. I needed a lift most times unfortunately, because of where we lived, but he didn't seem to mind. We had some good times, laughing about me being tight and singing songs – the time I was disgustingly drunk, he was really kind. It was my Mum who told me off.'

There is a sense that neither fathers nor daughters want to engage in arguments that would emphasise their separateness. As Rebecca told me,

'We argue a lot at home, but I'd never argue with my parents about important things. It would upset them.'

This is quite a typical response from women in interview – when asked about arguments with their father, they respond by talking about their parents in the plural. Just as when women are asked about arguments with close women friends, many say they can't think of any, or that they 'would never argue' with a close female friend, so similar responses arose when they were asked about fathers. It seems to be easier to talk about parents in the plural, for that includes mother – and no one seems to be concerned about arguments with her.

When women do talk about arguing with parents, their memories are usually painful, and they invoke the same concern about values as we saw in the section on arguments with their mothers. As Judy says, arguments with parents can be never-ending and always about the same things: 'Non-stop arguments to do with expectations and different value systems.' A few women do recall their fathers as getting personally involved in their arrangements with boyfriends. However, though this occasionally led to some anger, it did not always result in argument. Pat said,

'He'd storm outside, and find me and my boyfriend having a cuddle, and send him packing, and I'd feel so mad at him. But for some reason, I could never say. He'd be shouting at me, and I'd feel, well at least he cares about what happens to me.'

Of course, some daughters do argue with fathers, about going out with boyfriends and about the suitability of their dress and whether they should wear makeup and what time they should be home. We all know this. The odd thing is, though, that no one in my research actually recalls such arguments themselves.

Unless, that is, they also recall that their fathers were violent and that they were afraid. Irene told me in interview of a long series of violent arguments with her father, starting in her teens and continuing in an unpleasant exchange of letters when she left home.

'When I was 30, I did try for a better relationship with him, because I thought my children should know their grandfather. It was always edgy though. It was only when he died, I felt really sad and wished I'd tried harder. He always seemed to blame me when my mother left home. He seemed to feel he could take it out on me and it wasn't fair.'

Other women have talked of being afraid of their fathers, and wanting to leave home at the first opportunity. They rarely talked of arguing.

The only diarist who had a 'blazing row' with a father was 24-year-old Gina, and this was with her *father-in-law*:

'He's an arrogant bastard who doesn't listen to other people even when it concerns their property. I felt like murdering him, so just arguing let him off lightly.'

The 'extreme anger' Gina felt may perhaps have been because this intimate relationship was imposed by her recent marriage and so was much more like a non-intimate relationship – women do sometimes report high levels of anger in arguments with men with whom they do not have a close friendship.

One public argument between a father and daughter took the UK press by storm: in May 1994, 28-year-old Victoria Scott, whose father just happened to be Nicholas Scott, Minister for Social Security and Disabled People, denounced government policy on disability, and in a round of interviews with journalists and TV reporters, demanded her father's resignation. Shocking disloyalty? Or admirable idealism? Readers and commentators alike were divided.

Perhaps even more striking, both father and daughter seem to have maintained an amicable relationship even while disagreeing fundamentally, and vehemently, and in public. And two years later, when Nicholas Scott was deselected by his constituency, daughter Victoria rallied to his defence, in print.

Commenting on the public disagreement between father and daughter in *The Times*, Janet Daley wrote:

> Almost all ideological conflicts between parent and child are based on sincere conviction.... Disagreements over principles or politics can lead to complete breakdown between the generations in a family.[67]

Perhaps it is fear of such a breakdown that inhibits women from arguing with their fathers. Or if they do, they were not telling me.

11

Of Families and Feuds:
Some Conclusions

They fuck you up, your mum and dad,
They may not mean to, but they do.[68]

Philip Larkin's gloomy view would be shared by many of the diarists I have quoted. Parents are indeed a primary factor in how you feel about one's right to a point of view, and what happens when you dare express it.

Journalist Stephanie Calman confessed, in an article in *The Times*, that even in her thirties, a few hours with her parents are enough to reduce her to childish resentment:

> Where, I want to know, is that mature detachment, that inner security which renders the parental criticism a mere statement, as neutral and harmless as a news report? Why do they continue to issue their assessments as if we were still five years old? ... If we are so young and helpless, how do we travel, pay taxes, buy homes? By the same token, if they're such bossy, blithering old idiots, why do we care what they think at all?[69]

YOU'RE STILL A CHILD TO THEM was the headline to Calman's entertaining article. The problem really is that they are still a parent to you (to us). No one can make an adult *feel* like a child – we do it to ourselves. The escape is to see mother as a person, a woman in her own right, and father as a man, a separate man, in his own right. But as my daughter Akita commented, when reading a draft of this section:

> 'Precious few people see their mothers as a "separate person". I

believe most can never see their mother as anything more than a *mother* who is supposed to have provided them with love, support, comfort and happiness. Most people have tunnel vision about mothers.'

Mothers, as we know, are expected to be caring and nurturing, so their adult children acquire the belief that any argument from their mother is a failing on her part. It is fine for her to tell small children what to do, for that is her job, but when she tries to tell her older offspring how to run their lives, she is being interfering, bossy and failing in her duty as a loving, accepting parent. Since we all need to understand *why* people do whatever they do, adult children explain their mothers' attempts to put an opposing point of view as evidence of their lack of intelligence, their stubbornness, their inability to understand new ideas; as their desire to exert power, to boss, to dominate; or worst of all, as their lack of love.

Women know that these are risks they run, but many are inclined to insist they too have a right to say what they think. If their children demand the right to be treated as adults, why should their mother not have the same right and be treated as an intellectual equal? But there is a very widespread assumption among people in their teens and twenties that mothers are in fact *not* their intellectual equals at all.

Fathers, of course, are expected to give opinions, for argument is a male occupation. The hostility which develops between fathers and sons may be partly a result of surging testosterone in the adolescent male, but this is also overlaid and enhanced by consequence of the Division of Labour. Relationships with those outside the in-group, politics, religion and all ideology are the legitimate domain of the dominant male, and the newly adult male demands the right to make his own decisions. Can there be two dominant males in one household? For many men, their sons' aggressive arguments for a different viewpoint are seen as attempts to undermine the father's authority, and must be crushed.

Sons insist on defending their right to their own views, their own values, their own life. This can lead to blows, even rupture. Daughters seem to feel less need to defend themselves, often because their fathers do not appear to pressure them as much; this does not, of course, apply to daughters who suffer abuse or violence, and their main aim is just to escape. The Victoria Scott story does suggest that young women may be feeling freer to express their intellectual convictions than in the past, even if this brings them into conflict with their fathers, but such disputes figured very rarely in my research.

Families are more than parents and children, and arguments between brothers and sisters loom large in many people's lives. Many diaries reported feelings of warmth and pleasure at being able to exchange differing views with a sibling. David, for example, who says he tries to avoid argument with friends, told me of his brother: 'He's always open to new ideas. I always feel I can talk to him.'

A large proportion of the reported arguments between brothers turned out to be about religion: this was not only between young men who were seeking and questioning, as young men so often do, but also between men in their sixties. Apart from one case where the diarist was trying to persuade his brother that he was wrong to get involved with a religious sect, and felt 'sad and angry', these arguments are pleasant and laid back, even though the topic is rated 'extremely important'. As Alfred (60) wrote:

'Quite obviously – conflicting egos! Try converting any one of 1,500 different religions!'

Sisters, like Louisa and Nell, find they enjoy talking about differences because they 'share the same basic values', and Kathleen says she can argue with her brother because 'deep down we understand each other'.

Where this pleasant sense of sharing does not exist, feelings can be painful, and siblings are strongly criticised. The historical relationship seems to lead to an assumption that the speaker 'knows' that any fault lies with the other person, most especially if the other is a sister:

'She has this rigid approach, a fixed view of right and wrong that nothing will budge.' (Beryl)

'She'd never admit any weakness to me, so if we differ, my values must be wrong.' (Irene)

'She's just stubborn, and will never listen to reason.' (Paul)

Some young women, though, contrast the more 'sensitive approach' of their sisters with the aggressiveness of their brothers. As Anna said:

'I find I argue with men, and especially my brother, much more than I do with women, and that is because they assume they always know best. This infuriates me. I know my brother means well, but I wish he would not always try to tell me what to do.'

And her brother told me:

'I don't understand why she gets so upset. I'm only trying to help.'

Words which can madden: mothers, fathers and siblings all 'try to help' and the recipient of advice feels belittled and fights back. Families are our training ground for relationships in the outside world, so it is no wonder that sometimes we make mistakes and relationships get strained.

Families also differ in their attitude to argument. Some parents try to prevent any arguing and bickering, emphasising that 'nice people get along with others and don't argue', so that resentments are pushed underground. Others encourage a free-for-all, in which the older and stronger are likely to dominate and tempers flare. Sean French writes in the *Observer* of his experience growing up as one of three brothers:

When anybody starts proclaiming brotherhood as a civic virtue and a basis for policy, it can safely be assumed that internecine slaughter and civil war will shortly commence .... Anybody who has grown up in a family in which all the children are boys will have learnt that the everyday reality of brotherhood is to be found, not in some utopian vision of communal bliss, but in those conflicts in Bosnia in which neighbour fights neighbour.[70]

French assumes that fighting for dominance is a male trait, and it certainly is part of the Division of Labour which requires men to be prepared to fight the outsider if necessary. Yet not all brothers relive the tale of Cain and Abel. Other families develop their own tradition of arguing, and Charles told me:

'My brother and I have the same style of arguing as my parents. So we can communicate. Though he is more stubborn than I am over practical things.'

Practical issues predominate in family arguments, and brothers and sisters are frequently seen as stubborn when they won't give way.

Families are usually regarded as places where people are expected to stand up for themselves. This is the case even in families where everyone is also expected to 'get along', an impossible dilemma which can lead to simmering resentment and sudden explosions of anger, and may well contribute in great measure to the ambivalence so many of us feel about family gatherings.

This is yet another version of the porcupine's dilemma. All our intimates can jab us painfully with their demands to be acknowledged as separate, different individuals. When mothers and fathers and daughters and sons refuse to play the roles we assign them and insist on being what they want to be, we are being asked to recognise them as who they are, and to love them still.

Part Three

Janus-faced in a 'Post-Feminist' World

'I don't think it's a problem for us. We don't attack men, you see, and they know we want to co-operate. We can be friends these days. It's different from the way it was for you.'

(Suzy, 24)

Young women today mostly believe this book is not about them. They believe the problems their mothers faced as second-class citizens are fast disappearing, and as the media tell them, this is the 'post-feminist era'. Young men they meet admire their confidence, their ability to be independent and support themselves, their willingness to be frank and open about sexual relations.

Young women think they have got it made, and men are inclined to agree. That best of all possible worlds is on the horizon, in which women are independent and men have all the sexual partners they could desire. For make no mistake about it, men still see young women as sex objects, and those same young women are not entirely sure they are unhappy about that. Rampant hormones and a natural urge to seek a mate add spice to the dull workaday world, and today's young women feel more confident in their ability to deal with sexual advances when they become excessive or are unwanted. Many young women believe that sexual harassment became a serious issue in the 1970s and 1980s because women were becoming threatening to men at work and may have appeared aggressive and hostile in their behaviour. Today's young women do not feel hostile, they feel friendly towards the men they meet, whether at work or at play, and are convinced that their refusal to engage in hostilities and their unambiguous friendliness allow men to see them as equals.

It is, of course, part of a woman's 'task' to be friendly and nurture friendly relationships. Young women believe that many of their mothers rejected friendliness in the struggle for liberation, but now the truly liberated woman can feel free to be friendly again.

For this is the 'post-feminist' world, Suzy and her friend Maureen both agree. They know that some things remain to be changed if they are to achieve full equality with men, but they are confident that their future will be different from that of their mothers – and that of the older woman psychologist they are chatting with. Maureen told me:

> 'We don't want to fight men. We want to get on with them, and they know we want to be friends. Everyone knows fighting is destructive, and you have to work together. We just don't have a problem with that.'

As an afterthought, Suzy added, 'We do realise it is thanks to women like you, struggling for equality in those early days. We do appreciate it, you know.'

So why Janus-faced? Janus was a Roman god, with the enviable ability to look both ways at once: his two faces gave him eyes in the back of his head. He was the god of doorways and new beginnings; the first month of the year, January, commemorates him, for at this time we look back to the old year and forward to the new.[1] Janus looks forward to the future and the brave new world of which some of us dream and which some of us fear, and he looks back to the past, to the old ways that to some of us were intolerable and to others may appear more desirable than the uncomfortable present and disruptive future.

Western society is hovering in the passageway between the old Division of Labour between women and men and the new as yet untried relations of equality. It is natural for people to resist when old certainties seem to be under threat. The struggles by feminists to be heard have been largely successful, in that their demands for equality of treatment have led to enormous changes – in attitudes to women at work, in legislation, in response to victims of abuse, violence and rape, even in our general willingness to accept certain kinds of language. But such changes have alerted many to the kinds of transformation in social mores that will be needed if we are to create a truly equal partnership between women and men, and not everyone is sure they want to carry on down that path. For some, we have gone far enough. Janus symbolises this conflict within society, and the problems of communication it creates.

Many people (especially advertisers, politicians, journalists and media gurus) have discovered the power of language to create images in the mind, and they know that there is no need for external reality to reflect these images for them to affect people's beliefs and behaviour. This is George Orwell's Newspeak, and we are, indeed, post-1984.[2] For some people in powerful places, the changes in relations between women and men are experienced as a threat, and considerable effort is being put into imposing on people a picture of a transformed society in which women now have all the freedom to achieve what they want and men offer full support. If you are aware I wish to create an image in your mind, you have complete freedom to examine this image, and if you disapprove of it, to discard it. But when the listener is *not* aware that the speaker is attempting to create an image, then it can creep into the mind with an insidious appearance of truth, and unexamined will remain as 'something you feel you know'. This is what has happened to people, and especially young women, who believe we are in a 'post-feminist' era. They have heard the words, and are unaware of the power ploy behind them, so accept the image of enlightened gender equality without critical examination.

Analysis of what people say about real-life arguments demonstrates quite clearly that gender equality has not yet been achieved. Such analysis also shows that expectations of difference between women and men and your response to what they say depends to an enormous extent on what your relationship with that other person is.

In Part Two we examined argument with that great variety of people formally known as 'intimates', whose good opinion is important to us – close friends, lovers, wives and husbands, mothers and fathers, children, sisters and brothers. Here in Part

Three we will examine the psychology of argument with casual friends and acquaintances, strangers, and then in those more formal situations where your relationship with the other person depends on interpretation – traffic wardens, for example, or plumbers or doctors. You may be wondering when we are going to look at work, that extremely important part of one's life where argument can be a serious problem. Part Four will brave the complications of the workplace after we have established a few key ideas about people arguing with someone they don't have to learn to live with. The psychology of argument is more complicated than we would like to think.

Janus was also a god of communication, which makes him a suitable symbol for this section on the psychology of argument with people who – well, to be blunt, don't really matter that much to us.

12

Arguing at Leisure

It is the nature of idea to be communicated: written, spoken,
done. The idea is like grass. It craves light, likes crowds, thrives
on cross-breeding, grows better for being stepped on.

(Ursula Le Guin)[3]

Many of our acquaintances come from places where we work. To
understand what is going on when people argue, it is important to
be clear whether the relationship is a formal work one, or a friendly
informal one. Here we will meet some people who got to know
each other through work, but whose arguments bear all the
hallmarks of informal friendly relationships. Their arguments are
not *at* work, and they are not *about* work. Surprisingly, this makes
a lot of difference.

'I Love to Hear You Talk': A Cautionary Tale

When 20-year-old Lucy was told by James, a 24-year-old solicitor,
'I love to hear you talk', she did not feel as though she were being
patronised. Far from it. She felt good. There she was, a secretary in
a law firm in Manchester, having drinks in the pub with three
good-looking men from the office, and they were taking her
seriously.

David, the oldest man there (he must have been at least 30),
nodded. 'You have a lovely way of arguing. I do enjoy talking to
an intelligent young woman.' Andrew, the third man, laughed and
added, 'You should study law.'

Why should she be suspicious? She looked good, she felt
confident, and these three attractive men at the office had asked her

to join them for a lunchtime drink. She knew the dangers of being treated like a dolly bird, but it hadn't been like that. There had been a discussion of the meaning of prejudice. Just in case they had expected her to be a decoration and just sit there, she made sure she took part by giving her opinion, and arguing for it when someone disagreed. She was an independent person, and these men seemed to like it.

Anyone who sees something degrading to women in this exchange must be paranoid.

Analysis of what men say after such conversations, however, does lead one to conclude that most are not as admiring of young women's minds as those young women would like to think. Men say things like:

'I just couldn't resist leading her on.' (Ian)

'It was quite amusing to hear what she had to say.' (Don)

Of if the argument is less friendly:

'I argued because I didn't like her ideas. But I didn't really try to convince her. Not worth the effort.' (Keith)

'She was just making an emotional point, really.' (Charles)

All these are extracts from diaries by young men recording arguments with young women who are not close friends in situations like the pub or other informal gatherings. The overall picture is of men who do not take women seriously, reporting, with a detached superiority, arguments which were 'not important'.

Most of these supposedly trivial arguments are about political or social or moral issues, matters that become 'very important' when the interlocutor is another man. Other topics include more personal questions to do with what a person is wearing, 'whether Dr Marten's boots are associated with the National Front', or practical student affairs. All these arguments are reported to be 'not at all important' and the male diarist usually claims that he was 'not angry at all'. The highest level of anger any diarist reports is 'mildly angry' (2 on a 5-point scale), always about a political issue: in many cases, the anger *expressed* was much higher. University student Tim, for example, recorded a 'heated' argument (4 on the 5-point scale) about the Shah of Iran though he was only 'mildly angry' (level 2): in other words, he was subjecting the young woman to a high level of anger he did not even feel. He explained:

'She was stubbornly right-wing in her views.'

In the argument about Dr Marten's boots, the same student wrote:

'I didn't like the implication that I looked like a Nazi.'

One might have expected genuine anger here, given the apparent personal offence involved, but no, Tim claims he was 'not angry at all'. He didn't get his point across, but this was simply because 'I didn't really try.'

These accounts are quite different from their reports of arguments with other men in similar circumstances. Remember, none of these are close friends – as we saw in Part Two, men enjoy arguing with their close male friends, but these are arguments with 'friendly acquaintances'. Men rarely talk of enjoying argument with other men who are not close; they talk of being challenged and of needing to win.

Young men – or indeed, men in general – may argue with each other about almost anything: half of all arguments reported in diaries are about how society should be run, but they also record arguments about sport, sex, the paranormal, morality, how others should be treated, practical issues and matters of fact. Most arguments are recorded as 'important', even 'very important', and very often are seen to arise because of 'misunderstanding': many men seem to find it worrying when another 'rational' man disagrees with them. If they fail to convince the other man it is because he is seriously at fault ('bigoted', 'entrenched in his own opinion', 'uninterested in any other point of view') or because the diarist 'didn't have time'.

Thus we see that young men take argument with another man seriously, whereas they assume it is perfectly in order to dismiss arguments with a woman as unimportant. BBC Radio broadcaster Gordon Astley insists that the point of a 'good row' is to win, and devoted a programme to finding the best strategy for doing so.[4] But men do not try to win with a woman unless she matters to them: they can't be bothered.

So what was happening to Lucy?

Lucy was young, attractive and a secretary: all three factors make her a pleasing companion for a lunchtime drink, and it may be that one or two or all of the men were exploring the possibilities of an affair. Being a secretary is a come-on for many men, for it is still a quintessentially female occupation, designed to make men's working lives as easy as possible (what some have called the 'office wife'). Men gather round attractive young women like wasps round a plum tree.

Of course they were work colleagues, and therefore people who see each other on a regular, even a daily, basis, but it is unlikely that the men were looking at Lucy in that light. A secretary is usually a subordinate (certainly one who is 20 years old), and argument from a subordinate leads to anger. It is improbable that they could have looked on her as an equal-status colleague, as they are reported as saying that she had a 'lovely way of arguing', and that she could even 'study law' and so become more like them. If they *had* seen her as a colleague, they would have dismissed her arguments as unimportant, but they would also have felt critical, characterised her as 'aggressive' or 'hostile', or thought she was 'taking things personally' (see Part Four).

These men were egging Lucy on, enjoying her arguments without feeling any need to get involved or angry. They indulged and petted her when she expressed a different view. But unless they are quite unlike all the hundreds of men whose accounts of argument I have studied, they were not taking her seriously. Yes, they did 'enjoy hearing her talk' because they were treating her like a pretty child performing for their entertainment. Remember Dr Johnson who compared a woman's preaching to 'a dog's walking on its hinder legs'. Substitute 'arguing' for 'preaching': perhaps they thought, as he did, 'It is not done well; but you are surprised to find it done at all'.[5] Lucy is not the first woman to find that expressing her opinion as a young and attractive female can be classed as a social accomplishment, keeping flocks of young men entertained. But she should not expect any of them to remember what she said.

Conflicts Between Rational Men

> He always had a chip on his shoulder that he was ready to use to kindle an argument.
>
> (Fred Allen)[6]

Some men can be found engaging in argument in almost any social situation. We know that university students are notoriously argumentative, for they are confronting new ideas and discovering the delights of discussing important views of society, the world, the universe, the meaning of life itself. But a relatively small proportion of older men seems to enjoy argument so much they seek it out, engage in debate at the drop of a comment, even deliberately provoke argument with friends and strangers.

Les (51), for example, will always make politically loaded comments in any company, and when asked why, says:

> 'If you believe something, you should be prepared to defend it. Politics is important, it's about how things should be done. I always want to know how other people stand.'

I suggested that some people might feel uncomfortable arguing politics at a pleasant dinner party, and that he could not be sure that people he did not know well would share his views. But he replied: 'What's the point of arguing if they agree with you? I want to stir people up.'

Which he does very effectively, to the dismay of any dinner hostess or host who looks for a harmonious discussion over the food so carefully prepared. William, who experienced Les's 'stirring' for the first time, said afterwards:

> 'I felt irritated, not so much by his aggression, as his assumption he knew best. Let's say, his confidence was not matched by his breadth of knowledge.'

When men disagree with each other at any age, and continue to disagree after argument, they do tend to be highly critical of each other. Just some of the comments made by diarists:

'He doesn't know what he's talking about.' (Jack, 38)

'Invincible bigotry.' (Sydney, 63)

'Bigotry – this wasn't a reasonable argument. Pertinent points were answered with dogma. I just couldn't believe that anyone could be so naive.' (Mark, forties)

This may look reminiscent of how men talk of arguments with wives and mothers. Women, though, are called irrational and frequently accused of stupidity and emotionality, because they are supposedly *unable* to follow rational arguments. By contrast, men are *expected* to be reasonable: bigotry and ignorance are frequent explanations for other men's refusal to agree, for what other reason could there be for the supposedly rational male to be unable to follow the superior reasoning of the diarist?

Like many other men who were annoyed by arguments with a male acquaintance, Mark deliberately scored out the term 'friendly' on his diary record. However, he was only 'mildly angry', and diary accounts suggest that that notoriously emotive topic of politics does lead to 'strong' and 'heated' disputes, yet the combatants are not really as angry as they appear.

The 'stirrer', who spreads irritation and annoyance around him, may himself feel cool and collected. Alfred (60), who reports many arguments about politics and similar issues, writes:

'As always, on this subject [politics], arguments can go on interminably, the whys and wherefores being inexhaustible. Always I am willing to argue on this subject, it being the right of any individual in this so-called Democracy.'

On many occasions Alfred also wrote that his argument was 'justified', and in his account of an argument with an acquaintance about 'sex without love' added:

'Riposte justified, as any thinking person will understand. Sex without love is just a matter of relieving body impulses. And however much people may argue, it very often reduces those who indulge [to] lower than animal level.'

His reiteration of the argument might suggest he was angry, but though the argument was 'strong' and the issue 'extremely important', he was 'not angry at all'.

Men do tend to get angry with each other when they feel under personal attack in some way. Edward, a former schoolteacher, wrote:

'I felt indignant at being accused of an attitude entirely opposed to what I had practised as a teacher.'

Henry (34) was angry 'Because I felt (as it turned out justifiably) that I was about to get bulldozed into doing something that I did not want to do. Hence anger and intractability.'

Issues of fundamental morality can also lead to extreme anger. Tony, for example, was 'very angry' in an argument about 'breaking the law'. And Jim told me: 'I was so incensed by his pernicious ideas that I threw him out of the house.'

Indeed, in my analyses of levels of anger *felt* in non-intimate relationships, men report they feel overall significantly more angry with another man than they do when arguing with a woman in similar circumstances. Since this is the *only* relationship in which men are the object of higher anger than women, it is worth exploring this point further. Everyone seems to get more angry overall with a man who insists on winning in a social or informal situation. Yet there are many occasions when an outsider might think that disputants are about to come to blows, and the men themselves say, 'I was not angry at all.' Not only is this an interesting puzzle, it also means that when men *do* get angry with each other, their level of anger is high: statistically speaking, their low 'not angry at all' has to be outweighed by some pretty high levels of rage to produce the significant difference I found.

Ashley (late fifties) wrote a long and detailed letter, discussing his attitudes and explaining why he frequently engages in argument: he distinguishes between discussing a practical issue, and becoming entrenched in an emotional position; he analyses usefully the differences between discussion, argument and quarrel; and he even justifies those escalations into violence that so dismay most observers.

'I could argue the pros and cons of who is going to win the Tour de France all day and feel no strain. You see it is my sport and whilst it is important, I have no vested interest in who will win and who will lose. Such an argument is based upon a comparison of excellence. However, let's give the Tour a slight twist. Let us imagine the argument turning aside slightly to a holidaymaker, a dyed in the wool motorist, joining the argument by saying, "I was a day late getting to the Med, because those bloody fools blocked the main road – the whole damn bunch of them should be banned!" In the next minutes, or as long as it took me, I'd set about demolishing his complaint, and if possible demolishing him, his family, his car, and anything else I could introduce to cause him distress and annoyance. In simple terms, I would go all out to see my point of view prevail.'

Road rage explained? Certainly this kind of irascibility is no new phenomenon, and the eighteenth-century writer Oliver Goldsmith is reported to have said of his contemporary Samuel Johnson:

'There is no arguing with Johnson, for if his pistol misses fire, he knocks you down with the butt end of it.'[7]

Since there is no evidence that Dr Johnson actually engaged in physical violence – and why would so eminent a wit need to descend to the level of a street brawl? – this sense of threatened physical violence is presumably a vivid metaphor for the rage some men feel in some arguments.

There seem to me to be two factors involved here. First, men see argument with another man as 'important', and part of its importance becomes persuading the other person to see your point of view. As Gordon Astley said (quoted earlier), the point of having a good argument is to *win*. But the fact that argument is important means that if the other man is not convinced, then the arguer has a problem he needs to deal with. If he sees argument as a battle he must win, and he does not win, he has lost, and this is experienced as failure. Writer Marc Nicholls suggests that 'failure is what a man fears most'.

To a man, all other men are rivals. Whether it's boardroom, gym or bedroom, we can never (ever) face the notion of being judged second-best.[8]

Second-best is what a man feels when he is 'defeated' in open argument. Sometimes he will explain this defeat by claiming that he did not actually have time to put the necessary effort into the fight, with the implication that in other circumstances he would, of course, have prevailed. On other occasions, the other person was so 'bigoted' and 'entrenched in his ideas' that budging him from his absurd position was impossible.

Which brings us to the second factor involved: men's primary social task of dealing with enemies of the in-group. This, as you will remember, is men's share of the Division of Labour which we examined in Part One. Clearly, any man who is so bigoted and entrenched as not to be able to accept the arguments put forward so rationally must belong to the out-group. Or in the case vividly depicted by Ashley, the motorist has asserted his difference from the Tour de France enthusiasts by, as they see it, aggressive verbal attacks on their in-group. It follows that he is an enemy. Depending on your views on the place of aggression and outright war in relations between groups, it may follow that physical violence or even attempts at total destruction of the enemy are in order.

It would be quite wrong for the reader to infer that Ashley has actually perpetrated any illegal violence, however provoked he may have felt. I have absolutely no evidence that he has done, or would ever do such a thing. However, he does express in his letter (from which I quote above) the kind of *feelings* of rage that many men do experience when confronted with another man who seems to threaten their well-being. It is the sense of threat that evokes a desire to wreak violence, and the threat reflects this sense of the other as out-group member, as enemy.

Other men have said in conversation that on occasion they have felt so angry with another man's views they wanted to kill him.

'I wanted to smash his head in.' (Tom, 58)

'I wish I could have killed him. People like that are the scum of the earth, and it would be good for society if they were destroyed.' (Noel, fifties)

'He's lucky I'm too much of a coward. I wanted to murder him. He should have been strangled at birth.' (John, 48)

For all the failures of our global society and the wars that persist between people, we can at least be grateful for the level of civilisation we have achieved. Without it, violence would be worse, and especially between man and man, for what is it that prevents these men from carrying out their destructive murderous impulses but civilisation?

Bringing Women into the Equation

> I never make the mistake of arguing with people for whose opinions I have no respect.
>
> (Edward Gibbon)[9]

Arguments do not, of course, always lead to such extremes of rage, and indeed, men's anger in argument with male acquaintances is usually reported to be low where men can see themselves as debating those issues which are rightfully theirs – how society should be run. This is widely known as 'putting the world to rights', and is a male sport, like football. Ashley too draws a parallel between arguing and sport:

> 'Both try to arrive at a win or lose conclusion, and both are a wonderful safety valve to emotions. If you have an argument bottled up inside your mind, it can do a great deal more harm than if it is allowed to go free.'

Arguing as a game is so central a concept to understanding what is going on when men argue on some occasions that I have devoted a whole section to 'Games Businessmen Play' in Part Four.

Women, however, do not usually see argument as a game. If they enjoy the flexing of verbal muscles and sparring with ideas – and many do when the other people are not very close – they still fail to understand why there should be any need for one person to win and the other to lose. For women, discussions with friends and

made what I considered to be rather a bigoted and arrogant
ment during a conversation. I felt my hackles rise and felt he
t to explain himself.'

'very angry', though in the end the outcome was positive:

ealised I thought he was a bigot, so we both did some
ning of the concepts involved, and we then found that we
robably "on the same side".'

does not matter to most women whether they end up
nd 'on the same side' so much as that the man *listen* and
e he knows best. As Doreen wrote:

d because I thought he was very dogmatic about the
[Francis Bacon] and dismissed his importance. I put
a considerable number of points and eventually he
ith some of them. At least he heard what I said.'

old me:

ly was interested in what he could tell me [about
archaeology], but because I actually asked questions,
nade comments of my own, he seemed to feel under
etimes these men make me mad. Am I not supposed
mind of my own?'

hanie Calman also wonders why men have such a
arguing with a woman. Writing in *The Times* under
THINK, HE KNOWS, SO WHO WINS?, she describes
of dinner-table chat in people's homes:

atter under discussion is almost always open to
one view should be as good as another. Yet
ntly find themselves marginalised. A thesis pref-
...' just doesn't have the same resonance of
It is ...' This gives the impression of objectivity,
irrational the notion. How much more impres-
le, to be the bearer of 'well known fact', rather
experience of people you know.[12]

acquaintances over the food and wine can genuinely be an
interesting exploration of different ideas. They do not feel any need
to demolish the other, and cannot see why dinner-table debate,
which can be fun, need degenerate into a verbal war.

Put these two attitudes together, and you have a recipe for
misunderstanding. Mix well with our assumptions about the
differences between women and men, and you have a broth of
dismay, resentment, simmering anger, even contempt. The contempt, I regret to report, is what I discovered in some men's diary
accounts of arguments with women in social settings.

This attitude is fairly widespread, as Victor Seidler, Senior
Lecturer in Social Theory and Philosophy at London University's
Goldsmiths' College, confirms. In a book analysing men's
response to feminism and their need to rediscover the meaning of
masculinity, he writes:

> We have inherited a historical identification of masculinity with
> reason and morality .... It is always others – usually women –
> who are emotional, if not hysterical. It is always us who have to
> wait patiently for them to calm down, before we can add the
> weight of our arguments to the situation.[10]

The American writer and philosopher Henry David Thoreau was
emphasising the need for the truth to be *heard* when he wrote:

> It takes two to speak the truth – one to speak, and another to
> hear.[11]

For many women, Thoreau might have been speaking about all
men in their attitude to women in argument. The man speaks and
the woman is supposed to hear.

Alfred wrote of an argument about 'food prices':

> 'The other party was afraid to get into "Bad books" or whatever
> was meant by that. My argument was quite justified. She would
> never, at any time, consider ... challenging increases in food
> prices. Like many others of similar type, they just pay.'

Sydney wrote of an argument about 'teachers' pay':

'Diehard Tory with little or no experience of the teaching profession. I felt I had to pass on the facts.'

And Ivan, in another argument about pay for teachers, wrote:

'Could not resist getting involved with a bunch of teachers complaining about their lot.'

Now, none of these comments is very different from those of men reporting unsuccessful arguments with some other 'outsider' man: the other person's failure to hear reason is obviously due to some fault inherent in them. The difference that does arise is when the argument is successful, and the woman ends by 'hearing' or even by agreeing. Comments then are still tinged with a detached superiority:

'I was just setting right a person who had an over-simple idea.' (Sydney, 63)

'Other party had little grasp of the complexities involved, so I was able to put her straight. She's always talking about things she knows nothing about and makes a fool of herself.' (Bill, forties)

'Common sense tells us that there are two types of argument, and that both should be included in any definition of argument.' (Jack, 23)

Unlike close women friends, other women are not attributed with good qualities and reasonableness when they agree with the man. They have just been 'set right', 'put straight' or it was 'common sense' anyway.

As it happens, I was the 'opposite sex friendly acquaintance' in that last argument with 'Jack' and my recall is rather different. Indeed, his account even leaves me feeling rather irritated! This was another of those debates with people at parties I used to get involved in before I learned just to listen and gather material. Jack, like Marion in Part One, had expressed interest in my research, and then agreed to keep a diary. On this particular evening, he had asked me whether my definition of argument included quarrels,

and I explained that the definition was inte of disagreement and dispute, and we ta definitions which must delimit when comprehensive as possible. My memory argument at all. To me, he was seeking meant by 'argument', and conveying my definition still left doubt in some however, records that he got me to ag which I did not. I did hear what he s with any better definition. To Jack that his 'common sense' prevailed.

You may wonder why I am attr superiority to Jack's account, and typical of other accounts by men 'heard' what was said. Jack's di even though all diaries were kep a personal note: he must surel argument that he records with r evidence he includes. Was he, that all arguments were includ that he got his point across th and that 'any definition sho with him because this is 'cor the apparent evidence that labour the point. This is actually was in a positio research, and in fact I thin just two. I obviously di definition of what I was numerous occasions I female, how it might be about what was intend wrote,

'Men tend to thin infuriates me.'

It infuriates many v the man get away

Men accuse women of 'using anecdotal evidence' rather than hard scientific facts; of 'reacting emotionally'; of 'personalising' the argument. For women, these accusations are absurd. How can you argue without using what you know of human experience? And if pointing out that the other person – the man – is not being consistent in what he says and what he does is 'personalising' the argument, then they cannot see what is wrong with that.

Interestingly, this may be a major philosophical difference between women and men, and I have never yet managed to persuade a man that the following argument is valid, though it seems to me – and to any woman I have discussed it with – perfectly sound, not to say obvious.

Philosopher Trudy Govier points out that whereas academic philosophers examine the propositions of an argument for their logical relationships, in real life, arguments are between people who 'argue back and forth because they have different beliefs'. This has certain consequences. Since arguing is a social practice, it is governed by rules, norms and assumptions:

> People . . . presume that [other] people are communicating their real beliefs, which they are trying to back up with what they themselves see as good reasons. That is, they presume a kind of argumentative sincerity. If this is lacking, the statements are best understood not as argument, but as an attempt to persuade or manipulate by means other than good reason.[13]

In other words, if you argue that protecting the environment demands that everyone co-operate by using unleaded petrol and recycling plastic bags, it is a valid attack on your stance to point out that you use four-star petrol and have never approached a recycling bin in your life. It is *not* a refutation of this attack on you if you respond, 'Oh, you're just personalising it.' Nor does it help if you have studied philosophy and retort: 'That's just an *ad hominem* argument, and won't wash.'

Govier thinks that *ad hominem* and *tu quoque* arguments are perfectly valid in real life, and so do most women. She writes:

> *Tu quoque* allegations disturb an arguer's credibility because

they suggest ... that he is not properly participating in the practice of arguing, but only appears to do so.[14]

However, I have never managed to persuade any man of this. Even my own husband, with whom I have many enjoyable debates and who is a source of inspiration for many of my ideas about how women and men can learn to argue without pain, even this paragon among men claims that personal sincerity has nothing to do with argument:

> 'I agree that a personal attack might be persuasive to a third party, but it is not a logical attack on the argument. It does nothing to undermine the principles of the argument, which have nothing to do with what I personally may do. Taken to its logical conclusion, your approach would mean nobody could criticise anybody else unless the critic himself were perfect, which is absurd.' (John Tyerman Williams)

Of course the internal logic of any argument remains undisturbed by what a person may do, or wish others to do. So we agree on the philosophy of argument in principle. But the whole point of this dispute is that when it comes to a real-life situation, most women tend to believe that the credibility of a person's argument *is* undermined by proof that he says one thing and does another. What a woman requires is for the other person to *justify* this difference between words and action.

This is not the same thing as having a corrupt hidden agenda. To take my husband's favourite example, let us imagine a county councillor promoting the merits of routeing a new road in a particular direction which, unknown to his listeners, will bring him in a fortune. My husband argues:

> 'Even if his motives for arguing the merits of a case are corrupt, that does not undermine the logic of the argument itself. The route he proposes may in fact be the best one for the community as a whole. A person's sincerity has nothing whatsoever to do with the logical value of an argument.'

Difficult to disagree with the principle, but is that the real issue?

Surely most people (men and women) would agree that bringing the councillor's hidden agenda to light *would*, in fact, destroy his credibility and thereby undermine his argument in the minds of most of his listeners. Because it is a real-life situation, logic is only one part of the equation, and people's motives and sincerity are important elements in persuasion. Where we disagree is over whether any argument where a person does one thing and says another requires justification, whether or not the motives might be said to be corrupt.

The reason men and women are in conflict here is again a reflection of that ubiquitous Division of Labour. Men know that logic and argument are theirs, and they have, in Seidler's words, 'inherited a deep and unspoken investment in seeing (them)selves as "rational beings"';[15] they cannot therefore be seen to acknowledge any interference from extraneous non-logical factors; the motives of arguing a case have nothing to do with its internal logic, and they are not about to give up their hold on the principles of argumentation itself. Women are perfectly able to understand the principles of argumentation and of logic, but they usually can't be bothered to 'play' at argument: they are more aware of the need to include the human factor in arguments about practical or social issues than they are of any need to keep logic and feelings separate. This makes arguing about social issues extremely irritating for both. It is no wonder women often prefer to argue with other women.

Conflicts Between 'Emotional' Women

It was a woman, Ursula Le Guin, who wrote:

> They argued because they liked argument, liked the swift run of the unfettered mind along the paths of possibility, liked to question what was not questioned.[16]

We saw in Part Two that, as women grow older, they rediscover the joys of arguing and exploring ideas with their close women friends. Many women also find they enjoy arguing with less intimate friends and acquaintances, and this is true of much younger women as well. They report arguing about an enormous variety of topics, and most may be summed up by the comments:

> 'We were debating and quite willing to listen to each other.' (Gemma, 20)

> 'Enjoyable argument – not bad-tempered. Friend is reasonable and can see both sides of argument.' (Maria, 29)

> 'Mild discussion – interesting!' (Theresa, 31)

Sometimes the argument *is* important to the diarist, especially when she wishes to dissociate herself from a particular position. The response of the other person can determine whether the woman feels angry or not. For Irene, her friend's willingness to discuss their differences was positive:

> 'I felt it was important to make my views clear on this issue – I did not want her to think I thought otherwise. Also – my position seemed so clearly sensible, I felt she should agree if I got her to see my reasoning! As it turned out, the principal problem was one of definition and once this was clarified, our positions were not very different.'

Vera, who is a retired schoolteacher, found a very different response and was angry.

> 'The other party started a long tale about what a fool the Archbishop had made of himself by saying we don't need to go to Ethiopia to find real need. Everybody else seemed to be agreeing and I thought if I don't say anything it will seem as though I am agreeing as well, so I wired in. The other party is one of these blind Conservatives who really believe that there is no real poverty in this country.'

Women do feel angry when the other person appears to take no account of information, facts and knowledge they bring to the dispute. That the other person disagrees is not the problem, and as we have seen above, women are inclined to enjoy exchanging different views. As Lynda put it, recording a potentially explosive argument about 'Role of women's and blacks' sections in the Labour Party':

'I was listening to her and learnt something about the other side of the argument.'

So differing ideas about running society do not necessarily divide, nor do arguments about other equally sensitive topics, like a person's plans for the future or their personal relationships. Indeed, several diarists write of arguments with a friendly acquaintance whom they have unsuccessfully tried to persuade to do one thing and who has remained determined to do another. Jenny, for example, tried to persuade a friend that her plans to sell her house and move to a cottage by the sea were impractical:

'She accepted all my statements of fact, but did not want to accept the logical conclusion. I argued because I really felt concerned for her well-being.'

This was a 'mild discussion' with no anger. Lynda records a similar argument with a 'friendly acquaintance', though on this occasion she did get her views across:

'She was clearly in need of talking about recent events in her family. She had already begun to feel her behaviour had been inappropriate.'

So women appear to be willing to argue about almost anything, from politics through practical issues to personal relationships, and these only seem to lead to anger if a woman's expertise is not recognised. Margaret, a psychologist, told me she felt 'angry' recently when a friend had not accepted she had relevant expert knowledge.

'She was telling us about a TV programme on twins, and seemed to think that it had shown that twins growing up on different sides of the world found they had similar accents and used language in the same way. I tried to explain to her that this was impossible, as language was not genetically determined. She said, That's not what Chomsky said, so I felt I had to try to explain what Chomsky actually had said, and what could and could not be said about the genetic inheritance of language. It is something I have studied after all. She must have understood because then she shifted ground, and "wondered why I was arguing about language". I was angry because by shifting ground, she seemed to try to make it look as though I was being aggressive. It left me feeling very bad, as though I should never open my mouth.'

This is a common feeling among women who find that acquaintances and friends rarely turn to them for information in their special field and even treat them as aggressive when they try to explain that actually the other person has their facts wrong. Freda, for example, had made a special study of the law relating to small shop owners and restaurateurs – not as an expert, but as a person who did not want to make mistakes when opening her fish restaurant. When an acquaintance blithely recounted her plans to open a small shop selling home-baked goods, Freda felt she should warn her she might be infringing certain regulations. This led to a very angry argument. Freda told me:

'I felt really upset because I was only trying to help. I thought she would be glad to know before she got into real trouble. But she just got really nasty, and when I went off to the Ladies, she said to my husband, Who does she think she is? You tell her, I'm not putting up with her interfering like that. And he actually apologised for me. As I came back, I heard him saying, I'll have a word with her. I've never been able to forget that. He says, people don't want to know. But why don't they?'

I have had similar experiences, and even more infuriatingly, have had women ask me to ask John (my husband) if he would help them in areas that I know as much or sometimes more about. He is a social historian, and well read in philosophy and theatre and English literature, and has recently published two witty books, *Pooh and the Philosophers* and *Pooh and the Ancient Mysteries*: anyone wanting information in those areas is well advised to turn to him. But he is not better informed than I in areas like psychology, or aspects of language (I first trained as a linguist), or even journalism and publishing (I was a journalist before taking up psychology, and have been an editor for ten years). But if I say, 'Can I help?', most women say: 'Oh, I think John will know.' What do they think I do all day?

(John asks me to add that he has become aware of this happening since I first pointed it out, and now makes a point of referring people to me in areas of my greater knowledge.)

Deborah Tannen writes in her well-known book *You Just Don't Understand*:

> I do not enjoy 'grappling' when I feel personally challenged, though I certainly enjoy intellectual discussion if I feel my authority is respected.[17]

Tannen's authority as linguist is well established in academic circles (and issues relating to authority at work will be dealt with in Part Four), but even she may find it difficult to establish her authority in casual relationships where people wish to see themselves as equals. Authority and expertise are considered irrelevant when people are at leisure (except of course when someone actually wants to discover some fact from a useful expert who just happens to be present). Women do not want to be told that another woman 'knows more' than they do when arguing at a party or in a pub.

This is, of course, a similar situation to the one where 'men think they know best'. Women do dislike it when a man insists he knows best. But they dislike it even more when a woman does the same thing. A woman argues happily with another woman just as long as both can continue to experience each other as equals.

Looking Both Ways

> The truth is rarely pure and never simple.
>
> (Oscar Wilde)[18]

So women and men are divided in several ways when arguing in their leisure hours.

First, men appear to assume they know better about anything that might be subsumed in their special domain of the outside world, and that means just about anything except feelings – and babies. Of course, individually they are perfectly well aware they don't always know better. But the male attitude to argument which requires them 'to approach an argument with almost military defensiveness' (Stephanie Calman's words) because they must win and the other lose means they feel they need to *appear* to believe they know best. Many arguments between women and men in this non-intimate casual relationship occur in mixed company, which means it is even more imperative for the man to appear confident. Even if it does not matter whether he wins or loses with a woman, it matters a great deal with another man.

Second, men do tend actually to believe they know better than women about most things (except feelings and babies). We have met this before, as it arises from the Division of Labour and our cultural myths about differences in ability and aptitude between the sexes. This is why they dismiss arguments with a woman as unimportant, make little effort to persuade her of the validity of their views, and accuse her of getting emotional.

Third, women do not think it is necessary to fight when arguing. Indeed, they rarely see a discussion or debate as a contest. They like to explore ideas, and as they grow older, many women will say they prefer to exchange ideas with other women rather than men.

Fourth, women believe that each person should be able to prove their argumentative sincerity and that accusations that 'you say X but you do Y' need to be answered. Men appear to believe that what they do has absolutely nothing to do with what they say they *should* do, or other people should do. So men can build a grand edifice based on ideas and concepts that to women appear to have no relation to reality. To a woman this is irrational, or deliberately deceptive.

Fifth, it is an advantage to a man to be a real expert in mixed company, and a disadvantage to a woman. The man will be deferred to in his special area; the woman will be resented.

Anger is also a distinguishing factor but is not so easy to add to the list. Except when issues of 'expertise' arise, women do not usually feel angry with another woman, but they frequently feel angry with a man. Men rarely feel angry with a woman either. So women in normal friendly social situations should rarely find themselves on the receiving end of another person's anger.

Men too may find themselves engaging in friendly arguments without rancour. They tend to see arguments with other men as 'very important', and they are often reported to be 'strong' or even 'heated', and yet they say they were not really feeling angry. On the other hand, sometimes arguments between men can become very unpleasant indeed. Men report feeling 'very angry' or even 'extremely angry' (levels 4 and 5 on the 5-point scale) with another man, and some even talk of 'wanting to murder him'. These high levels of anger are so extreme that statistically they more than counterbalance the very low anger felt when debating with casual friends and acquaintances. As the rest of this book will show, this relationship is the only one in which men arouse more anger than women.

13

Arguing with a Stranger

'It was a slanging match, not a reasoned argument in which anyone tried to see the other point of view or compromise at all.'

Nell was canvassing in the local elections, and got involved in a heated exchange with 'a random person in the street' (a man).

'I was there to argue, and I was very angry at the stupid political statements he came out with. I knew I wasn't going to affect his views – it was more for enjoyment than anything else.'

So she reports feeling 'very angry' (level 4 on the 5-point scale), yet she says she enjoyed the argument. Indeed, there is every evidence that arguing with a stranger is far less distressing for a woman than arguing with someone close. Even an argument about a car accident, that quintessentially anger-provoking situation, does not necessarily leave the woman feeling upset after views have been properly aired. Ellen was 'very angry' because the collision

'Obviously was not my fault. The other driver had taken a bend, at speed, on the wrong side of the road. He *did* apologise. Annoyance prompted my self-defence, but we were grateful no one had been injured. This tempered anger. I was also concerned that I should not have to face a bill for repairs to my car.'

It was a car, too, that led Karyn to get involved in a heated argument, this time with 'a woman from whom I bought a second-hand car'.

'The car is dangerous and I have to spend a lot of money on it. I

148

wanted her to give me some money back. When I made an unanswerable point, she burst into tears and put the phone down, thus ending the argument.'

Clearly the argument did not have a satisfactory outcome, and Karyn was left feeling angry, with no sense of pleasure. Was this because of the topic, or might it have something to do with the fact that the other person was a woman and the previous two arguments reported were with men? Absurd though this question may appear at first sight, there is some evidence that women do find a dispute with another woman who is not a friend much more upsetting overall than with a man, and such arguments can lead to some very high levels of anger, both felt and expressed. As we will see later, arguments with a woman neighbour or the doctor's receptionist or a shop assistant can be very anger-provoking: these are what I will call 'formal' relationships because society has certain rules and assumptions about how they should be carried out.

On the other hand, why should a woman not see a female stranger in much the same light as a casual acquaintance? If she did, her response to a dispute would be more low key and even enjoyable. Does it depend on how the dispute arises, and what it is about, and whether she gets her point across?

Diary reports of arguments with strangers were rare, and men report very few. Tim does record a number of arguments with fellow students because he was canvassing in student elections, and all of these are very low key and his comments casual. One argument with a woman he interprets as follows:

'She was going after me, and therefore being obsequious and attentive.'

Younger women in interviews say they would never get involved in an argument with a young male stranger unless they like the look of him, as it is usually interpreted as a come-on.

Men have talked in interview about getting involved in heated arguments with other car drivers, but as Henry said: 'It's the element of danger that makes you so angry. Who cares what a stranger thinks anyway?' Is it this indifference to the views of the stranger that explains why men recorded so few arguments in their diaries? Or is it that, except in special circumstances (like a car accident or electioneering), people are not seen as strangers once you have got involved in an argument, for example at a party or in the pub?

American psychologists Gerald Miller and Frank Boster believe that people are much more likely to argue with strangers than they are to engage in conflicts with people who matter to them. This is rather different from what we have found so far, though it is true that women say they avoid arguing with close women friends and men say they back off from arguments with their wives. However, Miller and Boster write that:

> We believe that most people are reluctant persuaders, and that they are especially reluctant to persuade those with whom they have personal relationships .... By contrast, persuasive communicators in casual acquaintanceships and transient encounters with strangers are more likely to perceive they have little to lose relationally.[19]

They talk of 'incurring costs' which may mean the other person 'may capitalise on the norm of reciprocity to enlist our compliance at some later date'; or the argument may produce 'considerable hostility towards the parent' from a child persuaded to clean up the garage, or create 'frustration and tension' between waitress and kitchen after attempts to speed orders.[20] All these examples come from the same paragraph in their chapter on 'Persuasion in personal relationships', but in fact they are talking of three very different kinds of relationship.

To understand the psychology of argument, we need to think very clearly about the precise nature of the relationship involved. The distinction Miller and Boster make is whether or not the outcome has an effect on the relationship's future. But we have already found that other factors are involved: intimacy is one, gender is another, age is yet another. In the sections to follow, we will find that status and formal expectations are enormously important, as are the complexities of relations at work, and all of these are mixed up with the recurring theme of gender.

The psychology of argument is immensely complex, and we need to try to understand just how differences in relationships come into the equation. One way of disentangling some of the extraneous elements is to get strangers to argue together. Why? Well, if you remove from the equation all the elements you can, what is left should represent essential elements that can be found in all arguments. Strangers may be characterised as those people about whom you know nothing except their gender, their skin colour, and their approximate age. If two people are matched by the experimenter for age, education and/or occupation, and racial origin, then they should bring to their encounter few expectations that are not related to gender.

Race is of major importance in most Western countries, and I did include race as a factor in some studies – but I have to put cross-racial argument information to one side for the time being. Interviews and diary reports from people of varied racial origin are included in this book, and where I happen to know who is who, I see almost nothing in their accounts to distinguish a black man or woman from a white man or woman – and where such differences occur, I make it clear. However, in experiments where strangers argued together, the colour of the other person was such a complicating factor in how the argument was conducted, let alone in the outcome, that I will not even begin to address it in this book. Class is another factor, especially in the UK, but was not included in my investigations.

So I want to get strangers to argue, and I need to match them for age, education and/or occupation, and racial origin. Any differences in their accounts will then be most likely to relate to gender – a factor which cannot be eliminated – and to the argument itself. I do not want them to bring extraneous ideas to the argument itself, but I do want to be sure they will actually argue. I need to find a topic on which they will have different opinions, but it must not be something emotive or value laden – like politics or social issues – or I might find they simply interpret what the other says as 'what can you expect of someone with such pernicious political ideas?' I want to be able to establish whether differences do have something to do with gender and people's assumptions about women and men.

Whodunnit?

I invented an experiment in which pairs of strangers were brought together and asked to solve a murder mystery, but a mystery with a difference: it has five plausible solutions built in, and is based on an ingenious whodunnit, *A Case for Three Detectives* by Leo Bruce.[21] I therefore anticipated – as it turned out correctly – that if each person is asked to decide who murdered the unfortunate victim first, then when two people are asked to discuss the mystery and come to an agreement as to which solution is best, they would start out with different ideas. To fulfil their part of the implicit contract, that is to carry out the experimenter's instructions, they would have to argue. And I hoped that the exercise itself would be enjoyable.

Furthermore, because I control all the information people use in their argument, I can also determine who influenced whom, and whether the two people really agree with one another after the discussion or whether one is just complying publicly while actually thinking something else.

Participants in the experiment were 36 women and 36 men, all strangers to each other, and all from the Oxford University Department of Experimental Psychology Subject Panel – which means they are called on by various research psychologists to take part in experiments. For this reason, in the questionnaires completed by participants, two questions checked that they had not met before and were really strangers. All were.

It worked as follows. Each was given an outline of the murder, complete with clues for the five different solutions, and had twenty minutes to work out who was the murderer and how it was done. Each then completed Questionnaire 1 (Q1), which asked for an account of the murder and evaluation of all clues.[22] Then they were asked to work together in pairs: 12 pairs were all women, 12 pairs were all men and 12 pairs were mixed. They were told this was an investigation into 'whether two heads are better than one' and asked to discuss their solutions, and to come up with one which suited them both. The experimenter repeated that there were five possible solutions, and that therefore no single solution was 'the correct one'. After a further thirty to forty minutes, each then separately completed Questionnaire 2 (Q2 – essentially a repeat of the first), as well as a third questionnaire, asking about the argument itself and their reactions to their partner.

Asked to find an agreed solution to the mystery, participants eventually belong to one of the following groups:

1. Influencer: Keeps own (Q1) theory
                     Partner agrees after discussion (Q2)
2. Influenced: Change from own Q1 theory
                     Accepts partner's Q1 theory in Q2
3. Mutual Influence: Both change from Q1 to new theory
                     Both agree Q2
4. No Influence: Partners disagree in Q1 and Q2
5. No Change: Partners agree in Q1 and Q2

An Interlude: Who Influenced Whom?

Who do you think persuaded whom? Given the makeup of the pairs (all women, all men, and mixed), would you expect there to be any differences depending on gender? Would men influence women, or vice versa? Or would you expect no difference? Which pairs do you think would be more likely to come to new joint solutions? And which pairs do you expect to disagree at the end? And do you expect to find more public compliance in any group (i.e. one person publicly agrees while privately disagreeing with their partner)?

This section provides a brief interlude in which we look at how people – 'experts' and non-experts – *expect* arguments to turn out. We will then return to the main topic of the book, how people report they actually *do* turn out.

SENIOR PSYCHOLOGISTS (1987)

Before running the first Whodunnit experiment, I canvassed ten senior researchers in the Department of Experimental Psychology, Oxford University, for their views. In line with the then gender (im)balance, eight were men, two were women.

Each senior researcher was approached in the course of

conversation, given an outline of the new experiment and asked what differences, if any, they would predict in outcomes for the three different sets of stranger dyads, matched for age and education level. I explained that I had developed measures that would distinguish public compliance from real agreement.

These were their predictions:

FOR MIXED PAIRS, eight men and one woman predicted that the women would show greater influenceability and would be unlikely to defend their views strongly with a man, while one woman predicted strong argument, followed by public compliance with a male partner's views in order to fulfil the experimenter's request for an agreed solution.

(Prediction: high Influencer = male)

ALL-WOMEN PAIRS were expected by six of the eight men to have difficulty in arriving at an agreed solution, as women would be unwilling to defend their views.

(Prediction: high No Influence)

By contrast, both the women and two of the men expected that women's 'willingness to listen' would lead them to an agreed solution, quite possibly to one new to them both.

(Prediction: high Mutual Influence)

ALL-MALE PAIRS were universally expected to be competitive and the potentiality of several solutions was expected to lead to failure to agree since rational choice was not possible.

(Prediction: high No Influence)

It appears that the ideas of equality we are told had taken over society in the 1980s had not yet ventured into the hallowed halls of Oxford University. One might expect that psychologists would be the first to acknowledge the power of stereotypes, but those hoary old assumptions that 'man is assertive and rational' while 'woman is conciliatory and easily influenced' still lurked in the minds of these senior academic researchers. One very distinguished male researcher told me firmly: 'That is because stereotypes have their origins in reality.'

PSYCHOLOGISTS IN A 'POST-FEMINIST' AGE

Before I tell you what actually happened in the experiment, let us complete this interlude by looking at what experts and non-experts expected in the mid-1990s. To provide an up-to-date 'post-feminist' perspective, I approached a different set of psychologists, all researchers and delegates to a British Psychological Society conference, chosen at random.

Six women and six men were given an outline of the experimental situation as above, and asked for their predictions (individuals are identified by F for female and M for male and a number). All except one woman expected some effect of gender, though their reasons differed widely, and there was strong and widespread resistance to the investigator's desire for clear-cut predictions.

Five of the six men predicted quicker agreement between man and woman:

'Women are more accommodating' (M1) or 'more flexible' (M3).

'The woman might move towards the man's solution because of the technical or mechanical component in the mystery.' (M4)

'One of the pair would submit. Not necessarily the woman; the man might be chivalrous, or the woman would submit in a gender role way.' (M2)

Thus men expected agreement in mixed pairs, and more influence from man to woman (though the chivalrous male might lead to an opposite outcome). One man also suggested that it would depend how attractive the female partner was:

'Men are more gullible with an attractive woman, but would be more directive if there was no magnetism between them.' (M5)

One man who began by suggesting that men 'tend to dominate and be assertive' added that 'some women are keen to be assertive', and that it would depend how involved the woman got, because 'some women enjoy games more so she might try harder' (M6).

Of the women, one insisted that all results would depend on personality, and one expressed an essentially separatist view:

'Women make decisions intuitively, and would find it more difficult to fight their ground in a mixed pair; the man would have a more concrete argument.' (F2)

The other four women agreed that women tend to defer to men in groups, but in pairs where neither had power or status over the other:

'Women might be more dominant if anything.' (F6)

'Women are more confident today. Twenty years ago, they would have given in to men. But now she would feel she has as much expertise in a murder mystery as any man.' (F4)

Generally, more influence was expected from woman to man, even if the man did choose to explain it to himself as 'chivalry'. One woman proceeded to turn sexism on its head:

'Would depend which was the stronger. If the woman won, it would be public compliance because I certainly don't think he would agree just because he was convinced by pure judgement. He would feel a very cold wind round his ego because he had been worsted in argument. So you'd see the outer duvet of acceptance because he has been chivalrous, and underneath his ego wrapped in a thin and holey sheet.' (F3)

Same-sex pairs led to conflicting predictions. One man suggested:

'Men might discuss the relevant evidence more fully, whereas women would agree more quickly.' (M2)

By contrast, another man thought:

'Two males would be satisfied with the first solution they could find. Women would be more likely to explore, so you'd get a wider variety of solutions.' (M3)

Looking at public compliance versus private conviction, one woman expressed sharp views:

'Men merely maintain standpoints, and can be easily changed through respect for the other person. He has to feel he has been convinced. With women you can be absolutely certain their agreement is genuine, because it will be more to do with discussion of the issues than with cherishing a perception linked with self.' (F3)

Female psychologists tend to expect public compliance from men, and male psychologists expect it from women, because all agree that influence in argument will depend on 'which is the stronger', and all tend to think that applies to their own sex.

There was considerable resistance to making any predictions, but when urged to say something, most men's predictions tended to reflect standard gender stereotypes. These include the effect of a woman's physical attractiveness making a man 'gullible', and the notion that if a woman did influence her male partner it would be because she 'tried harder'. One distinguished male researcher who predicted 'small differences' along stereotypic lines added: 'I do hope I'm wrong.'

Women psychologists tended to adopt a firmer stand, expecting men to experience problems but to be less anxious to accommodate them than in the past. Most repudiate any notion of intellectual difference. Or if there *is* a difference, they are quite certain the advantage is to them.

NON-PSYCHOLOGISTS

To provide an up-to-date view from 'ordinary' non-experts, I also sought the opinions of five young men and five young women whom I approached by telephone. They are all known to me personally, but knew only that I was 'investigating argument'. They are all British, white, from a variety of occupations, and ranged in age from 26 to 35. Given a brief outline of the experiment, they were asked 'Would you expect any differences?' if partners were both male, both female, or mixed.

Unused to such questions, non-psychologists unanimously began by insisting it depended more on the individual character of the participants than on gender. Pressed to think in general terms, most went on to see some differences, but one man maintained:

'It's totally down to individual character. I can't see any reason for gender to make a difference. If there's a logical solution, both would come to it. The man might be convinced he's right, that his logic is right, but women tend to be stubborn. It would just depend which had the stronger character.' (Gordon)

The assessment of each sex is different, but the outcome is the same. Another man also insisted on strength of character being the deciding factor, though he thought that women might be more willing to seek agreement than men:

'Both are on a par, so on the whole both are likely to argue their case. So it would depend on how well the person delivers her or his opinion, how convincing it is. Of course, the woman might not argue if she finds she's got a bolshie guy on her hands, and they've got to agree in the end.' (Gareth)

There was general agreement that men tend to try to dominate and are competitive, but even here a lone man had a different view:

'Women are more competitive, more inclined to want their personal opinion accepted. With men there would be a greater level of teamwork.' (Peter)

Three of the men and all of the women agreed that women would work harder to find agreement, and that this would lead to greater flexibility in all-female pairs, who might be more likely to come up with a new solution:

'They would discuss their solutions, neither would be immovable.' (Molly)

'It might be easier to express uncertainties with another woman, and redefine the problem.' (Ella)

'Depends on character of course, some women avoid argument. But they'd be more likely to work together and find a new solution.' (Cathy)

'They'd be more likely to have a reasoned argument and see each other's point of view.' (James)

'You'd find better agreement with women.' (Sam)

Though one man expected 'teamwork' in all-male pairs, everyone else expected them to have greater difficulty in agreeing on a solution:

'Depends on character, they might not agree.' (Sam, Gareth)

'Both would believe they are right.' (Molly)

'Could be difficult if both want to be top dog.' (Susan)

These differing expectations did lead to contrasting predictions for the mixed pair. All the women expected the men to try to dominate the discussion:

'Men believe they are right and are reluctant to believe a woman could know better.' (Molly)

'Men like to dominate, so if the woman wants to solve the mystery, she would have to defend her opinion.' (Susan)

'The woman is likely to give in before the man. She would give it a good shot, but they would end up with the man's solution in the end.' (Cathy)

The women saw it as essentially a battle between the sexes, and this view was shared by three of the men, though they did not appear to think they themselves would treat it like that:

'There is a tendency for men to be overbearing and force women to agree with them. Less so when people are better educated.' (James)

'The woman might not argue if she finds she's got a bolshie guy on her hands.' (Gareth)

'The woman would be more competitive, want her personal opinion accepted.' (Peter)

However, this last man thought that the differing points of view of man and woman could be creative, and lead to production of new solutions. And another man thought that women's influence on an argument would include an effect of their personal interaction.

'It does depend on who they are. I guess with mixed pairs you'd get extremes, either very good interaction and so they'd agree, or very bad, so they'd be farther apart at the end.' (Sam)

To summarise, all-female pairs are expected to have a high level of agreement, and high Mutual Influence; all-male pairs are expected to have a low level of agreement (high No Influence); mixed pairs are expected to have a high level of agreement, with male as Influencer (and some public compliance from women), and some Mutual Influence.

Summary of predictions of direction of influence

	Mixed	All-female	All-male
Psychologists 1987	Influence = M F Compliance	No influence or Mutual influence	No influence
Psychologists 1994			
Male	Influence = M F Compliance	Mutual influence	Mutual influence
Female	Influence = F M Compliance		
Non-experts	Influence = M F Compliance some Mutual	Mutual influence	No influence

And What Actually Happened?

No one got it all right

Gender did not appear to affect who influenced whom and, *pace* our distinguished Oxford psychologists, there is no evidence whatsoever to suggest that women are more easily influenced than men. All outcomes were found nearly equally in all groups. Though there is some suggestion that mutual influence might be more likely with a woman partner, this is countered by its being equally likely that they would not agree at all.

Summary of Whodunnit outcomes

(a) Number of pairs in each group compared by dyad

	All-female	All-male	Mixed
Influence one way	4	6	5
Mutual	4	2	3
No influence	4	2	4
No change	–	2	–
Compliance (individs)	3	4	8 (6 = M, 2 = F)

(b) Number of women and men in each group

	Women	Men
Influencers	7	8
Influencees	6	9
Mutual	11	7
No influence	12	8
No change	–	4
Compliance	5	10

(c) Numbers in each group compared by gender of partner

	Female partner	Male partner
Influencers	6	9
Influencees	6	8
Mutual	12	7
No influence	12	8
No change	–	4
Compliance	9	6

Contrary to everyone's expectations, there is some evidence that men are more inclined to express public compliance with views that contradict their private convictions than are women, particularly if their partner is a woman. Twice as many men (10) as women (5) were found to have publicly complied with their partner, and this includes half of those men with a woman as partner. It is interesting to note that public compliance by men could be predicted from diary accounts in which they report arguments with women as 'not important' and that they 'did not really try': this suggests that men find it less worth 'making the effort' if their partner is a woman. The criteria for inclusion in the compliance group were very strict. Public compliance means that they expressed *in words* the solution agreed with their partner, but all other measures requiring participants to evaluate the importance of clues show quite clearly that they thought some other solution (usually their original one) was much more likely.

Presented with this information, many of the original Oxford psychologists spent some time trying to dissect the experiment: the measures were not effective, participants complied with the female experimenter's bias, the people were not properly matched, etc. When all objections were overcome, the conviction remained with some researchers that 'the men must have been inadequate, and not properly representative of the population as a whole': a damaging notion, since so much of Oxford's experimental output depends on its Subject Panel population. Eminent academics, even in the best of all possible universities, are only human and need a little time to change their minds about things that we all 'know' because we learned them in our cradle.

So where does this leave us in our exploration of the disadvantage women face in argument? One might imagine that these objective measures are clear evidence that women's demands to be treated equally have effectively changed men's attitudes towards them. But alas, these changes are not as deep as we might hope. Just as the words some participants use to express public agreement hide their true convictions, so we can show that the words these strangers use to describe their debate also hide deep-seated beliefs about the relations between men and women.

Furthermore, no one realized at first what I worked out later, that the high rate of compliance by men concealed an even more significant finding. We know that 6 of the 12 men arguing with a woman pretended publicly to go along with her ideas while privately thinking differently, but what of the other 6 with a female partner? Two were Influencers and persuaded their partner to accept their solution, and the other 4 ended with no agreement. This means that women only appeared to influence men: *none* of the men actually had his ideas changed as a result of a woman's influence after all.

14

Whodunnit? Making Sense of the Argument

Arguing with a stranger about a fictional murder mystery is about the purest situation we can find to enable us to tease out the meaning of gender in argument. We have seen what people in general ('expert' and non-expert) *expect* to happen, and we have already learned that, though gender did not have quite the predictable effect on who influenced whom, it may be the case that men 'did not think it worth while' arguing with a woman. Let us now examine what those who took part in the experiment actually told us about the argument.

On this occasion, names will not be invented. Identification is by letters and names in brackets, as follows: F1A and F1B, M1A and M1B and so on were partners in same-sex pairs; X1F and X1M and so on were partners in mixed pairs.

Woman to Woman

'Neither of us assumed any superiority over the other.' (F4B)

'She wasn't over-pushy or under-assertive.' (F1B)

'It was just a friendly discussion.' (F4A)

'She was willing to listen to my points, didn't interrupt or make any stupid suggestions and worked with the evidence.' (F9A)

Though these comments reveal that the women may have felt

apprehensive about working with a female stranger at the beginning, most found these discussions pleasant and friendly. Emphasis by most women in all-female pairs is on the usefulness of rational discussion, and on the clarification that 'talking out loud' seemed to afford. Where the women came to a mutually satisfactory new solution, they thought that 'different perspective and perceptions' (F7B) helped solve the mystery.

A quarter of the women (6 out of 24) did feel annoyed with their female partners:

'She kept finding reasons in people's characters for them having done it without giving very compelling arguments.' (F6B)

'She interrupted me.' (F10B)

'When I thought we'd just agreed on a solution, and then she started us on another irrelevant track.' (F10A)

'She interfered with my train of thought. Two minds go off in different directions – confusing.' (F6A)

This annoyance appears to be linked with a sense of personal challenge, with the other seen as a potentially hostile stranger. One woman wrote:

'I think I probably concentrated too much on the task and doing it myself. I would have got further by questioning my partner to draw out what I saw as weaknesses in her solution.' (F10B)

Others who developed greater liking for their partner enjoyed the discussion. Changes of mind were explained by using such phrases as 'we agreed', 'we decided', 'we both thought'. Even where they failed to come to agreement, most thought the discussion helpful, and the difficulty of solving the mystery did not upset them. Typical comments at the end were:

'I enjoyed the experiment and liked my partner.' (F3B)

'I enjoyed it very much. I found it totally absorbing, mainly because it was too difficult for me. It was interesting that I changed completely my solution to the crime after discussion.' (F5A)

Man to Man

'A variety of approaches helps lateral thinking.' (M9A)

'The great amount of evidence presented was better sifted through by two people ... in the limited time allowed.' (M9B)

'Found completely new approach. Things fitted more rationally, loose ends tied up.' (M5A)

Men arguing together in all-male pairs mainly found the debate a rational, objective, friendly affair, and most agreed that 'two heads are better than one'. Those who accepted their male partner's solution explained this as due to 'partner's reasoning' and said that the other's solution was 'more likely' (M9B):

'I had not been satisfied with my original solution, which was a stopgap: [his] solution was entirely plausible.' (M10B)

This objective, detached air is maintained by their partners:

'We both agreed that the facts were consistent with my interpretation.' (M10A)

'My working hypothesis was possibly strengthened by the discussion. We came up with no better solution.' (M9A)

Communication between men was not always as good as these comments suggest. Asked if his partner had changed his mind after discussion, one man wrote:

'I think he didn't actually tell me his first impressions as to who or how.' (M4B)

His partner was one of the small number of men (4 out of 24 in the all-male group) who report feeling annoyance, and another wrote:

'I wanted to put across a point and didn't feel I was succeeding.' (M8A)

Though most claim that joint discussion was helpful, in some cases they do not appear to have been listening very hard to each other. One man attributes his solution to influence from his partner:

'I hadn't a clue (pardon the pun) at the outset but with J. I was able to continue what was basically his thought.' (M12B)

His partner however gave a different solution. These men were essentially operating independently, using the other as a sounding board.

By an unlucky chance, two of the all-male pairs started out with the same ideas, so that they did not have the same pressure to argue, even though they needed to discuss the evidence to provide a more detailed solution. One of each pair confessed to not trying very hard, a situation that had been predicted by one of the male psychologists in 1994. As one man put it: 'I let my partner do the work' (M2B).

Across the Gender Divide

'He was reasonable and friendly, so we had an interesting and good spirited discussion. Twice as many ideas with two people.' (X12F)

'Discussion presented a more plausible murder sequence.' (X2F)

'More of the evidence accounted for. We were both in much the same position . . . . It is useful to try out ideas on someone else to see if they think they are good/bad/indifferent.' (X2M)

These are comments from people in mixed pairs who came to a new joint solution. Most participants thought the discussion helpful, though the partner of one of the women quoted above was negative. He clearly found the mystery difficult, and explains that he changed his mind because he 'became less sure as evidence sunk in'.

'Neither of us had much confidence about the solution, two heads didn't help.' (X12M)

One woman apparently anticipated possible male dominance, and was pleased to find she was mistaken:

'He was not trying to push his ideas as the right ones, but was willing to discuss possibilities fairly. I was surprised at the ability to discuss with a stranger without competing for one's ideas to be the accepted ones.' (X8F)

Her partner, however, did not think the discussion useful:

'Because there was no right or wrong answer there was no necessity that even the most logical thinking on the part of one person would help the other.' (X8M)

He also reported that 'because there was no firm idea in my mind at first I was quite flexible'. Not flexible enough to adopt his partner's solution though: they ended with no agreement.

Men who 'accepted' their female partners' solutions said:

'I had only very vague theory at start of joint discussion, so hadn't formulated solid theory that I would try to assert.' (X9M)

'That there were at least four plausible explanations was a bit frustrating.' (X11M)

A third showed his detachment, subtly implying the outcome was unimportant:

'The other opinion seemed plausible. She seemed satisfied. Her argument seemed quite sound.' (X5M)

Their 'influential' partners all explained the others' change of mind by referring to the evidence and to their joint discussion:

'He decided my solution had more evidence.' (X5F)

'His mind was not made up to start with.' (X9F)

'He thought it was Miles, but since Miles isn't mentioned at all in the last part after the murder, we thought that it couldn't be him.' (X11F)

This last woman added that she enjoyed the debate because 'we could work logically together'.

Only two women and one man of the 24 people in mixed pairs reported that they felt angry or annoyed: all were partners of people whose solution finally prevailed.

'Tendency to assume he had the right idea and wouldn't allow interruption.' (X1F)

'Slightly foggy rambling approach.' (X9M)

'He was uncertain, did not have any new bright ideas, looked down most of the time. I get annoyed at men anyway generally and may have been aggressive.' (X10F)

The first two comments reflect standard stereotypes; the third is a somewhat truculent approach to the stereotypical 'battle of the sexes'. However, this woman further reports her own public compliance, both to her partner's solution and to gender role expectations:

'I did change my mind – officially – in order to reach a consensus in limited time. Because I'm naturally self-doubting anyway.' (X10F)

Her partner apparently did not notice her self-reported aggression:

'Discussion followed logical reasoning and neither of us were intransigent or assertive.' (X10M)

He explained that he did not change his mind, but his partner did, because 'alternatives did not include evidence that I considered important'. He also thought that 'different ways of approaching the problem lead to confusion'. Perhaps his partner had some justification for her truculence.

A second man apparently saw the exchange as a contest and explained that his partner changed 'because I convinced her!' He does however acknowledge she had some part in the discussion:

'I still had to justify my argument to her and she questioned the various points well.' (X1M)

So there is some evidence of men trying to dominate, as well as evidence that they did not always take the discussion very seriously, but women comment favourably on being able to discuss the evidence logically and rationally with their male partners.

The Hidden Assumptions

So far, the picture may be encouraging, but becomes less so when we analyse the more objective measures of attitudes to partner and to the argument itself. The third questionnaire included both open-ended questions, from which I have quoted above, and rating scales. When people answer open-ended questions, they use their own words, and so provide evidence of what they believe to be socially acceptable replies. Overtly stereotypical attitudes are considerably fewer than our experts anticipated. On the other hand, when people are asked to circle a number on a rating scale (e.g. How assertive were you, on a scale of 1 to 7?), they find it hard to tell what the overall pattern of responses will reveal.

It should be noted at this point that most of the significant differences found in this experiment were between *influence groups*, and that who influenced whom and whether or not agreement was reached was the major differentiating factor on most scales. Nevertheless, gender was important, and since this is the topic of our book, it is on gender that I will focus here.

The graphs on p. 172 illustrate in a fairly dramatic way how gender was implicated in persuasion strategies. Don't worry if graphs make your heart sink: I will go through all the relevant details. But just a glance will show lines zigzagging and crossing over, demonstrating quite clearly that it did matter very much whether one was a man or woman, and which one's partner was.

Participants were asked to 'indicate to what extent you used the following persuasive strategies' during the discussion:

	A great deal						Never
Logical reasoning	7	6	5	4	3	2	1
Suggest compromise/use of bargaining	7	6	5	4	3	2	1
Make other feel her/his ideas are good	7	6	5	4	3	2	1
Were especially charming	7	6	5	4	3	2	1
Were assertive	7	6	5	4	3	2	1
Were intransigent	7	6	5	4	3	2	1

This wording was based on the work of American psychologist David Kipnis and his colleagues which shows that people's accounts of their persuasive strategies depend on relative power.

They asked people in a variety of relationships 'How do you get your own way?' and eventually classified the replies into three main types of strategy: the *hard*, the *soft*, and the *rational*.[23] People in positions of power tend to use the *hard* technique (summarised by Kipnis and his colleague Stuart Schmidt as 'being assertive' and 'being intransigent'); people in positions of weakness tend to use *soft* approaches (summarised as 'being especially charming' and 'trying to make the other feel good'); equality leads to use of a *rational* approach (summarised as 'using logical reasoning' and 'suggesting compromise' or 'use of bargaining').

The experimental situation offers a rational problem to be solved by weighing the evidence, and carries with it no emotional connotations for strangers of equal status. Thus we would expect participants to emphasise *rational* strategies. On the other hand, the stereotype is that women are relatively powerless in relation to men, and so women might be expected to focus more on *soft* strategies in mixed dyads. It is interesting to note in passing that 'soft' strategies are closely related to those recommended by Dale Carnegie in his hugely successful book *How to Win Friends and Influence People*. According to the same stereotype, men are seen to be relatively powerful in relation to women, and might be expected to use *hard* tactics – though some of our 1990s female psychologists suggested that *women* might use them when dealing with men.

Let us see what the participants in this experiment actually told us.

Given the kind of problem participants were asked to solve, it is not surprising that both women and men emphasise that they were rational and logical. All gave 'logical reasoning' the highest rating. Furthermore, no single item on this questionnaire differentiated groups, and it is only when patterns of relationships among items are analysed that differences are found: data for each experimental group were correlated, and the relationship of each item with all others plotted separately in the graphs over the page.

Some of the major differences will be noted, concentrating on correlations greater than +/− 0.2. You will see that same-gender pairs have solid lines on each graph, and mixed-gender pairs are

Correlations of self-reported persuasion styles, by gender

"Rational" styles

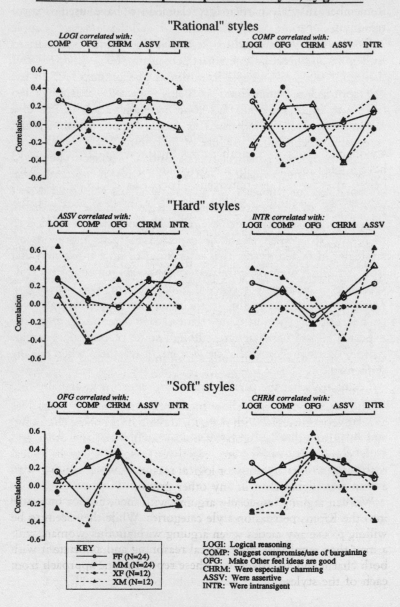

LOGI correlated with:
COMP OFG CHRM ASSV INTR

COMP correlated with:
LOGI OFG CHRM ASSV INTR

"Hard" styles

ASSV correlated with:
LOGI COMP OFG CHRM INTR

INTR correlated with:
LOGI COMP OFG CHRM ASSV

"Soft" styles

OFG correlated with:
LOGI COMP CHRM ASSV INTR

CHRM correlated with:
LOGI COMP OFG ASSV INTR

KEY
FF (N=24)
MM (N=24)
XF (N=12)
XM (N=12)

LOGI: Logical reasoning
COMP: Suggest compromise/use of bargaining
OFG: Make Other feel ideas are good
CHRM: Were especially charming
ASSV: Were assertive
INTR: Were intransigent

shown by dotted lines: females are circles and males are triangles. Remember that all participants claimed to have used 'logical reasoning' most.

Let us look at the graphs for 'Rational' styles first.

Women arguing with women show a positive correlation of logical reasoning with all strategies, which suggests they may have made use of all techniques at various stages in the discussion. When arguing with men, however, only 'being assertive' is positively associated with being rational.

For men, compromise is a rational technique when arguing with a woman, but not with another man. Furthermore, men's claims to have argued logically with a woman are strongly associated with being assertive and intransigent. These 'hard' tactics are not associated with arguing with a man. Thus the implication is that men tried to dominate a woman partner.

The 'Hard' style graphs confirm this.

Both hard tactics are strongly associated with logical reasoning when a man argues with a woman (LOG, ASSV = 0.648; LOG, INTR = 0.416), but not with a man (LOG, ASSV = 0.093; LOG, INTR = −0.048). We can see that men appear to construe women as relatively powerless and report that they did try to dominate with hard tactics.

By contrast, women show some use of hard tactics when arguing with another woman, but with a man intransigence is out (LOG, INTR = −0.565), and if they are assertive then they may try to be 'charming' too.

The 'Soft' style graphs show that women do not see themselves as relatively powerless with men, for though both 'being charming' and 'making other feel good' are associated with each other and with compromise, they are negatively associated with logical reasoning: women's rating for logical reasoning when arguing with a man was higher than in any other group.

Women arguing, especially arguing with men, do not fit neatly into the Kipnis persuasion style categories. While they seem to be willing to use any tactics when arguing with another woman, with a man they emphasise their logical reasoning and associate it with both charm and assertiveness – these represent one approach from each of the styles.

Women's association of assertiveness with 'being charming' may suggest an attempt to sugar the pill. They want to defend their own ideas, but their awareness of the social expectation that women are 'nice' may lead to attempts to propitiate to a minor extent.

Men, on the other hand, fit the Kipnis categories better, especially when arguing with a woman. They associate both 'rational' styles as well as both 'hard' styles with arguing with a female partner, with very high correlations between 'logic', 'being assertive' and 'being intransigent'. Men arguing with another man seem to have selected a style, using either 'soft' or 'hard' on occasion, but rarely both.

In other parts of the questionnaire, women report feeling less able to 'develop own ideas' with a man, and did not enjoy the discussion as much as with another woman. They find men less friendly than other women, and less analytical too.

Men, on the other hand, did enjoy the debate more with a woman than a man, and they evaluate their feelings of friendship for their woman partner considerably higher than for other men, and higher than their partners did for them. They also rate women high on analytical skills – an interesting and unexpected reversal of roles.

Arguing with a Stranger: Some Conclusions

These are the main points which emerge when matched strangers are asked to argue about a non-emotive fictional topic.

Men reveal a sense of dominance in relation to a woman. The verbal accounts of the discussion give only minor evidence of men adopting a superior attitude, and some women comment favourably that their partners did not seek dominance. Nevertheless, the ratings on the persuasion style items show that men describe themselves as using hard tactics with women partners, tactics which Kipnis and his colleagues have found used almost exclusively when a person feels in a position of relative power.

At the same time, men report feeling more challenged by a woman partner than by a man, and rate their women partners as more analytical, logical and reasonable than another man. These objective measures are not reflected in the verbal accounts, but appear to contradict the above suggestion that men feel superior. Furthermore, many men report friendly feelings towards their woman partner, and rate the exchange as more enjoyable than with another man.

These paradoxical results reflect our earlier discovery that men have internalised the gender role of man as dominant and assertive, and assume that a dominant role is expected of them in relation to a woman. They feel more challenged by a woman partner when her assumption is that she is equal and she is therefore resistant to dominance. If he appears to accept any of her ideas (as some did), then obviously she must have exceptionally good analytical and reasoning powers: since the argument with her was unimportant, he could feel content with letting her do much of the work – and half the men did go along with their female partners' ideas without really being convinced. Indeed, we have seen that none of the men was *genuinely* influenced by a woman. Nevertheless, men enjoy women's company and expect the woman to be warm and friendly, whereas another man may see himself as a rival who must win.

Arguments between male strangers were detached, and accounts emphasise how rational they were. Those who liked each other do report some use of 'soft' tactics – 'being charming', 'making the other think your ideas are his' – tactics more usually associated with women and others who find themselves in an inferior social position. Rivalry was not overt, but its effects can be seen in the very poor communication between some men, and an air of disengagement with partners who did not like each other. Even the confession 'I let my partner do the work' reflects a refusal to get involved in an argument he would then need to win.

Women do not describe themselves as ready to conciliate their male partner. If they report using 'soft' tactics, this is only with another woman, and is rare, though many of those who claim to be assertive with a man also add a touch of charm. Most women write about the discussion in terms of the evidence (i.e. rationality), and they are willing to defend their views with a man. They found having a male partner was inhibiting, as they were less able to develop their own ideas and the discussion was less enjoyable than with another woman. This reflects their expectation that a man will try to dominate (an expectation that is justified, as we have seen). But they rarely describe behaving in a gender-stereotypical way, and stress their own logical and rational skills. Many comment favourably when a man does appear to acknowledge them as equals.

Women arguing with another woman appear to have started out with some apprehension that the other would behave like a stereotypical female: being 'pushy' or 'under-assertive', making 'stupid suggestions', being unable to 'work with the evidence'. Women are as affected by society's negative stereotypes as by their positive ones, and even when they themselves know they are firm, strong, intelligent and rational beings, they tend to expect *other* (stranger) women to be as society says women are. Stereotypical behaviour from another woman can infuriate, whereas an ability to work together rationally and logically leads to warm feelings.

Strangers arguing about a topic that is of no emotional or practical consequence show that they expect *other people* to behave in culturally standard ways. Because argument and logic are thought to be quintessentially male, men are cautious with each other but construct a view of themselves as dominant with a woman. Women expect men to try to dominate, but the majority now see themselves as men's intellectual equals, and so are ready to resist overt macho behaviour. They are also resistant to other women who appear 'pushy', or who fulfil their expectations by being irrational and illogical.

Out-moded conventions die hard. On the surface, we appeared to find a greater willingness to go along with social conventions of equality, with many men prepared publicly to adopt a solution proposed by a female stranger, or to work with her to find a new one. But we must remember that half of all the men with a woman partner did not really go along with the solution agreed, and only appeared to agree. Evidence from diaries and interviews already cited – and more especially from accounts of arguments at work to be reported in Part Four – suggests that men are willing to go along with a woman because they don't actually think it matters. Compliance stops the argument on a pleasant note without disturbing their own ideas. None of the non-complying men even pretended to be influenced by his female partner. Yes, most of the men enjoyed the experiment when they had a female partner more than when arguing with a man because, as the Division of Labour requires, female companionship is for pleasure. They argued with their partners because the experiment required this, and a few felt challenged by the situation and needed to win. But most, finding women uninfluenceable, simply chose to abdicate. By contrast, argument with a male stranger puts a man more on the spot; with another man, he has an atavistic need to win.

There is a tension between old expectations and understandings of gender relations and new, more socially acceptable notions of gender equality. This tension comes into focus when we look at relations between strangers. Imagine a seesaw, with warm intimate relationships at one end and cool formal ones at the other. Strangers form a central pivotal point, where the pressures of other assumptions are held in tension. Most people are aware of the old Division of Labour, and some resist and some (women) try to turn it upside down, but they still anticipate stereotypical behaviour from others even if they reject it for themselves. The results of this experiment reveal in their very unexpectedness that things *are* changing, but not at quite as deep a level as many would wish.

15

'You Are, Sir, My Obedient Servant'

Civil servants are servants and should be civil.

(Letter from irate male citizen)

We have seen that gender role expectations are involved even in arguments with strangers with whom we might say we are on an equal footing. We tend to expect other people to behave in gender-specific ways, even if we do not do so ourselves; and men tend to adopt a dominant attitude towards women, even if it is no longer socially acceptable to express this openly. What happens then when we argue with strangers who are also expected to provide us with a service?

Most of this section will provide a transition to that all-important Part Four, which is about work. For many of the strangers with whom we battle are themselves at work – tradespeople, receptionists, nurses, doctors, government officials. But there is an important difference between these arguments and those at work, with colleagues, subordinates, boss: arguments at work have long-term consequences, just as they do with the more intimate relationships we examined in Part Two. Most arguments with strangers in this more formal relationship are transitory, and though we would *like* to keep the same plumber, say, or doctor, we do not *have* to learn to live with them. It is easier to change one's plumber or doctor than it is to find a new job.

'No argument about God, or Mrs Thatcher, is as likely to arouse passion as one with a plumber who has done a botched-up job and insists that he knows what is best or that he is far too busy to come back.'

A distinguished academic, whom I will call Dr Cromwell, had just retired after many years working in a major university, and was commenting on one of my questionnaires. His life as researcher and university lecturer had of course been punctuated by numerous arguments in committees, seminars, at mealtimes and so on: and as an internationally respected historian, his status would usually have been high. For status now becomes an issue, and in my questions I had specifically made the point. He wrote:

'The disgraceful truth is that I get into far more arguments with people of "lower status", in your sense, such as shopkeepers, waitresses, garage mechanics. Or rather they are people who have temporarily, in this situation, acquired a higher status – and this touches off unwarranted anger.'

The anger may not always be unwarranted. For those from whom we expect a service also know that they are the 'expert' and that gives them power; or they may be able to prevent us from doing something we wish to do – speaking to the doctor, say – and that gives them power; or they may be able to make our lives more difficult, by insisting on arrangements at inconvenient times, or by being 'unable' to help in ways we might reasonably expect, and that gives them power. People with power like to use it.

Though I will examine the concept of power further in Part Five, here it is worth bearing in mind that power can usefully be divided into several kinds:

COERCIVE POWER

This is what most people think of when they think of power. It means you can force people to go along with your demands: a parent is bigger and stronger than small children, has sanctions available; an employer can refuse pay rises, promotion, take your job away altogether; a dictator uses military force to gain and keep power. Coercive power can include verbal aggression, threats and use of violence.

CONSENSUAL POWER

This means you are allowed to exercise power by general consent, but that consent can be withdrawn. This is the original source of the power of democratic government, in theory – we vote them in and we can vote them out. We vote to give certain people power so that our society can be run efficiently and defended effectively without our having to worry about details. By extension this consensus includes all government officials and civil servants: that is why they are 'servants' – they are there to 'serve' us, the people. We have agreed to the powers they have, but feel strongly inclined to revoke them when these civil servants are not civil or appear to think the consensual powers we freely handed over are their own to use coercively.

EXPERT POWER

This means that your knowledge gives you power in circumstances where others lack this knowledge and it is needed. Most people have expert power on occasions, but car mechanics, plumbers, electricians and other tradespeople wield this power most of their working lives. It is not surprising that many also abuse this power by being deliberately unhelpful, especially when dealing with people who socially are of higher status. Because, of course, status gives power.

STATUS POWER

This is tenuously linked to all three kinds of power mentioned, but comes with the job, so to speak. Status refers to a person's place in a given hierarchy, so that Dr Cromwell was high status within his university as a senior member of faculty (but not as high status as the Vice-Chancellor), and high status within the academic world for his work as a historian. On most social occasions, this high academic status would be reflected in the respect others feel for his learning and achievements. Similarly, doctors have high social status (in addition to their expert power), as do successful company directors and so on. Status is not necessarily linked to financial success, however, as any academic will tell you, and wealth is another kind of power.

MONEY POWER

Wealth gives the power to buy service of all kinds. For many people it is a powerful argument in itself. It is not relevant to this section, because in its presence the kinds of argument we are going to examine tend to evaporate. However, since most of us do not have that kind of power, let us just remember its existence and move on to the arguments that many of us encounter in our daily lives.

Arguments arise when legitimate consensual or expert power is abused, and especially when one feels that the person providing a service is refusing to acknowledge one's own legitimate powers – as civilian, employer, client and so on. Exercise of coercive power is always resented.

Man Disputing with Man

'I told him, I could see he thought he was going to take me for a ride and that I was extremely angry. The building work he had done for us was unsatisfactory in many ways, and I pointed out that his guarantee promised that he would come back and put it right.'

Ken was recalling a heated argument with a builder whose concreting had started to crack weeks after the job had been completed.

'On the whole I tend to be easy-going, but I was really very angry indeed, and expressed myself forcefully. My wife said she was surprised to hear I could sound so angry on the phone. It ended as usual with profuse apologies from him, and no action. We had to take him to court in the end.'

This is an extreme case of the 'expert' failing to deliver the expertise for which we pay. Similar anger is induced by the plumber whose botched job leaves the householder as badly off as ever. Peter recalls:

'A central-heating pipe under the floor suddenly started leaking, and was damaging our parquet floor. This complete idiot did stop the leaking, but managed to completely bugger the whole system. He tried to tell me we need to replace the whole lot. I kicked him out of the house, and called the one I'd wanted in the first place to come and rescue us. No wonder that fool was available immediately. No one would have him in the house twice.'

Arguments with experts are rarely this heated or this direct. The anger here is because the work has been done extremely badly, whereas many arguments are designed to prevent that happening. Malcolm, for example, recalls that a builder tried to insist he knew better how to prevent damp entering the ceiling of an old cottage.

'When he returned for the third time, I made him listen to my own theory. It seemed pretty obvious to me that the water was entering where the electric line came in and was travelling along behind the plaster, and I explained the logic very carefully. I was right. These damned experts make you so mad when they are so sure you know nothing and they have to be right. But the argument was pretty cool, as I didn't want to upset him so much he'd walk off.'

Oh yes, important words. Surprising though it may seem, given the extreme levels of anger men reported when arguing with male acquaintances (Chapter 12), the majority of the arguments with experts are fairly restrained, with male diarists sounding pretty easygoing. They don't want to upset the expert too much because they need his help. William remembers what can happen if you do upset a local tradesman:

'I had been warned that the plumber was very good but very lazy, and inclined to botch a job if he hadn't got the right tools or materials. So I decided to keep a special eye on him, and he obviously realised he was being watched. Some weeks later I heard that he was going round telling everyone we had not paid his bill – which we had not had. I was distinctly displeased, and got very terse with him. It wasn't really an argument in your terms, he just backed off, with a mixture of lying and apology. I told him to send his bill in immediately and we'd pay it.'

Builders, plumbers, electricians, garage mechanics – these are all experts whom we have to trust to a greater or lesser degree, and they know it. The expert himself does not like being questioned. As one electrician told me:

'If he thinks this is a botched job, let him do it himself. I don't need this kind of aggro. Who's got the qualifications? Him or me?'

Keeping disputes to cool rational logic works best. Sydney reports an argument with two Gas Board employees called in to repair his central heating, in which his 'reasoning' prevented the experts from making a mistake:

> 'One of the men thought that the upstairs radiator should have had 2 valves or something (the correct term escapes me) and that this was the reason for the malfunctioning of a *downstairs* radiator. I explained that this had always been the case and that until the present time all radiators had functioned normally.'

Of course, not all the men one disputes with are experts in this specialist sense. Many are simply there to serve: police officers, postmen and waiters for example. Sydney's argument with a Post Office employee was successful in this case because of

> 'Insistence and repetition. A letter from Paris having taken 15 days I requested an enquiry. It was extremely important, and I set down the matter in writing and addressed it to the Postmaster.'

Alan had a fairly strong argument about delivery of goods:

> 'I was persistent, and I had a reasonable case going. To have given in would have meant involving myself in unnecessary work, which could be avoided if I won the point. Which I did, partly.'

He did not explain the 'partly'! But we see that persistence is the theme when service is being demanded. And when the service is not forthcoming, the man may feel very angry, even if the issue is something as simple as delay in supplying a telephone directory. As Ian reports,

> 'I was very angry and frustrated at Telecom's inefficiency. The operator was not really interested. I keep asking but not getting the directories.'

University student Tim wanted to get a message to a friend in a theology college, but was frustrated and somewhat angry at being prevented from doing so by the gatekeeper priest:

'He didn't give a damn and wanted to get rid of me because of my haircut.'

Obviously in this case relative status operated against the person looking for a service. Relative status between client and waiter works the other way, and firmness is often sufficient to win the day. James had taken a young lady out to dinner, and the waiter tried to tell him they could not have their coffee in the lounge, as it was for residents only:

'I didn't like his manner, so I just said firmly, Please serve the coffee. And he said, Oh yes, sir, and went away and did it.'

Ian reports that he 'sorted out a stroppy waiter':

'I don't mind someone making a mistake, but I objected to his insinuation I had changed my mind. I made it quite clear that he should take the dish away and bring me what I had ordered.'

And Edward recalls with some amusement an occasion when he had taken his parents out to dinner:

'We had enjoyed the food, but we all agreed that the service had been appalling. And I had found the way the waiter treated my mother was quite objectionable – she had asked for water, and he didn't bring it until I repeated the request, and then plonked it on the table in a most offensive manner. So I paid the bill, but refused to give a tip. The waiter was so incensed he actually called the manager. My parents supported me and it was quite amusing really. The manager was placated by our assuring him the food was excellent, and the waiter slunk off, very woebegone.'

Being in a position of power oneself can mean arguments are low key and quickly over. Sydney again reports his successful routing of a would-be double-glazing salesman:

'To convince the hawker that he was wasting his time and mine, I told him I was an OAP. He asked me how much I thought it would cost. When I replied, "approx. £200" he smiled in a wan manner and backed rapidly and hopped it.'

Sydney was obviously having fun. But Alex was not – he was 'extremely angry' at the intrusion of a Jehovah's Witness on his doorstep: 'I was vigorous, not to say rude. Our conversation did not continue.'

Perhaps these variations in anger are a matter of temperament, for other men do not get angry when approached by a Jehovah's Witness. Indeed, Peter says he invites them in: 'I enjoy arguing with them, and trying to get them to defend their ideas. Mind you, I'll argue with anyone.'

Peter is like broadcaster Mike Dickin Shaw whom we met earlier – some men do enjoy arguing with anyone so long as there is no personal threat or involvement. However, the majority of the arguments in this section entail some kind of personal involvement, whether it is to do with repairs to one's house, one's car, or one's standing with dinner guests. As we have seen, anger is usually low (no more than 2 on the 5-point scale), and only escalates rapidly to 4 or even 5 when the other person fails to deliver or makes matters worse.

Anger can be used as a weapon – by both sides. The philosopher Bertrand Russell is described by a biographer as having a meeting with the builder and architect transforminmg his house, and immediately, without preamble, 'boiling over into a furious denunciation of everything' they had or had not done. He then returned to the car, perfectly cool and collected, and said, 'That's taught them a lesson I think.'[24] His explosion was designed to produce results – and apparently it did.

Andrew, a stage director, recalls a 'long and heated argument with a minor civil servant in a police station' who was deliberately trying to make him angry so that his request could be refused:

'I had just taken over the job, and found the chap I replaced had not got a licence to fire a gun – with blank cartridges of course – on stage, and the performance was that night. The situation was urgent, I had to get that licence, so I was very careful not to get heated. He was a pompous little man, and gave me a long lecture on the incompetence of stage people, he was doing his best to rile me. I knew he was trying to needle me into losing my temper, but I was extremely cool and extremely persistent. If I'd taken his No, not the first time, but half a dozen times, we would not have got the licence. But I kept cool and came out with the licence in my pocket, and literally shaking with suppressed fury.'

Police officers can certainly be aggressive towards members of the public, if our favourite television police soaps are anything to go by – and we are told that even police officers themselves like ITV's *The Bill* because it is true to life. In a recent episode, a middle-aged shopkeeper was demanding that police do something to find those who had broken into and smashed up his shop, and Sergeant Cryer told him rudely: 'Don't be bloody paranoid.' Later Cryer said to his colleagues: 'I just took control or he'd have walked all over us.'

An interesting attitude towards a victim of crime, but one that develops all too easily in people whose power to affect people's lives is reinforced by their own sense of righteousness.

Council officials and other representatives of petty officialdom operate in that uncomfortable zone between being powerful and righteous (as with the police) and offering an expert service. They have rules and regulations they can invoke, but we simply expect them to provide us with a service we have already paid for. They are our servants.

Arnold, a college porter, reports a series of arguments with council officials about 'why there was no refuse collection'. At first, the exchanges were mild and Arnold was 'not angry at all'. He explains that he listened to what the other said, and then insisted the other listen to him:

'By accepting his explanation as to why there was no service, in this way he could see my point of view.'

However, as the day went on, Arnold became increasingly angry, particularly as he found that the earlier explanation of lack of service was untrue:

'I discovered reason for no refuse collection was that the road was obstructed. I wanted to know if council would make sure this did not happen again.'

He got nowhere:

'They just quoted legal argument. I got fairly angry in the end.'

Arnold's job involves him in many a dispute with members of the public, whom he has to inform of college regulations and persuade to conform to college requirements or escort outside. His diary includes many arguments with 'visitors to the college' who are variously willing and unwilling to abide by the rules, but he never reports anger, even with the most recalcitrant. Only a council official who fails to provide the kind of service we all expect inspires any level of anger in him. It is quite likely, of course, that the *visitors* feel anger – other people's rules and regulations are always infuriating when they stop us getting what we want, and in their case Arnold would be in the position of the council official. It all depends on your point of view.

This section is entirely about men arguing with other men either to get something done or to explain – or perhaps merely assert – that it can't be done. Various techniques are used, depending on who the other person is: another person's expert power precludes use of aggression or assertiveness until that expertise has been found wanting, but cool persistence pays off in most other cases.

It is interesting to note that no man recorded any argument with a professional like a doctor or solicitor – though women did – and men did argue with nurses (but that's for the next section). All of these arguments might be said to be with other men of 'equal' or 'lower' status, some of whom have expert power, but from all of whom we expect help because we pay for it.

Men Dealing with Women

'I had told her exactly what I wanted. The incompetence of that woman has to be seen to be believed!'

Jem is talking about a librarian who has not yet located a book he has requested. Brian had a similar problem and wrote:

'The book was a long time (two months) and there were records showing ordering and date. Responses to my questions were inadequate, just repeating how the system worked was not enough. I wanted to know what she was going to do about it.'

He was 'very angry', as are many men who get into arguments with women in this more formal kind of relationship, where the woman is expected to provide a service. Women in jobs where they have to meet the public – receptionists, shop assistants, waitresses, telephonists and so on – talk of being on the receiving end of some pretty vile verbal abuse. As one waitress told me:

> 'Some men seem to think nothing of calling you a slut or a stupid bitch. Just rolls off the tongue. They're just disgusting beasts, and I ignore it.'

Psychologist Arlie Hochschild found that female flight attendants were targets of verbal abuse from men passengers, and that male attendants often had to be called on to deal with high levels of unwarranted aggression against their female colleagues.[25] Hochschild suggests that women's generally subordinate position leaves them with a weaker 'status shield'.

Not that any man reported using vile language. Far from it, for even when he reported being very or even extremely angry, the account was in temperate terms. One argument over the repair of an electrical gadget, with a woman receptionist, was heated and the customer did not get his way because '*she* was not reasonable, though I was'. And an argument from the other side, by an electrician with a customer complaining at the delay, was reported as completely unsuccessful because 'we were both bad-tempered'. One does infer that the confession of bad temper on his own side reflects acknowledgement that he was in the wrong. For when a man feels completely in the right, all blame is on the woman's side.

One morning Pamela found a police car outside her house, and the officer clutching the steering wheel, breathing heavily. Fearing he was ill, she offered help. 'Do you know Mrs X?' he asked. 'Is she a friend?' When she cautiously admitted to being acquainted with said person, he exploded:

> 'That bloody female, I'll have her up for wasting police time. Always calling us in to sort out her problems. Why her husband doesn't murder her, I don't know. Be a blessed relief to us all.'

Now naturally he was angry and not thinking what he was saying, so Pamela assures me she has completely forgotten *who* the policeman in question was, and has no idea what the dispute was about. However, policemen called in to domestic disputes are not always as sympathetic as their role as public servant and defender of the weak would lead us to expect. One male officer was quoted at a Scottish conference on domestic violence as blaming the wife for being beaten by her husband:

'She let her alligator mouth outrun her humming-bird brain.'[26]

Clever, but not what we hope to hear from a public servant paid to protect us. Of course, this is a report from the other side, so to speak. The police officers are the ones from whom we expect a service, and they are angry with or contemptuous of women who have asked for their help. When men are expecting a service from women, the women report high levels of conflict, but there are far fewer arguments with women in this relationship reported in men's diaries. William reflected:

'Most of the arguments I have are with men. Women seem to be so much politer with a man somehow. I have noticed that my wife will have arguments with a receptionist who is all charm with me.'

He did recall getting involved in a dispute with a woman, a dog breeder, who accused his wife of breaking some contract by arranging to have a bitch they had bought from her mated. His wife was apparently so upset by this accusation, and by the terms in which it was put, that he decided to deal with the dog breeder himself, in writing. He told me, with some pride and amusement, that he had finished his letter in the following terms:

'You betrayed so gross a disregard of the normal courtesies of civilised intercourse that I am unable to subscribe myself, Madam, your obedient servant.'

He did not tell me what his wife thought of his intervention, nor why she should want him to help her out. But he was obviously pleased with the wit and elegance of his valediction. As was Andrew, who told me of a stay in hospital where the ward sister was a stickler for tidiness.

'I had been feeling angry while I observed her and saw she was not interested in the comfort of the patients. I felt it was about time someone brought proper priorities to her notice, and when I spoke

I felt like getting an amusing jab in. So when she twitched my covers yet again, I said, I suppose your ideal ward would have wax models of patients lying under neat covers, with the patients lying on the floor hidden under the beds. She was not very pleased.'

On the whole, men appear to remember arguments with women in this relationship only when they have a story to tell. The everyday conflicts which women themselves recall are missing. As one diarist wrote:

'Arguments when unimportant are easily forgotten.'

Women Dealing with Men

'I'm feeling pretty smug, in fact, to have the matter turn out *my* way. I had researched the subject thoroughly, knew exactly what I wanted, have learned to say "no" readily, and took time to listen (during which time he "hung himself" with unprovable statements).'

Sylvia had gone shopping for a new car, and as everyone knows, dealing with a car salesman can be a worrying business. But Sylvia feels she came out on top:

'If I had not argued, I would probably not have bought the car – *or* I would have had to pay a lot more for it. I *had* to convince him of what I *wanted* (and what I didn't want)! He was convinced I should have a bunch of "frills" that were expensive and impractical and mostly for show. No deal!'

Other women too report successful arguments with salesmen, shop assistants and others expected to provide goods as ordered. Joan has been promised a piano, which 'through an administrative mess-up' was no longer available. But she sorted out the shop assistant over the telephone, and got what she wanted because, as she cryptically notes: 'Threats to have further discussion which – he probably hypothesised – might lead to loss of order.'

Fiona told me a similar story, this time about buying a music centre:

'I had the salesman's card, and phoned the next morning to confirm my tentative order. The older man I had dealt with was not there, and the head of department said the model I had ordered the previous day not only was not in stock, with my name on as promised, it was no longer being made. As this was precisely the model I wanted, I persisted, and eventually got the demonstration model which I had tested for several hundred pounds off. I feel it was a good deal, and I only got it because I was very polite and very persistent.'

Far from being tentative and anxious and fearful about putting themselves forward, as some myths have it, the women in my investigations are nearly all confident and willing to argue with any man. Indeed, the argument with the person of highest status in diary reports was from Elsie, who argued with a bishop:

'It was a discussion in committee about expenditure on decorations and refurnishings in a Retreat House. I think I got the point across because I felt it strongly and expressed it so. I felt like arguing because the money might otherwise go to more pressing social needs, which I thought imperative.'

Firmness, politeness and persistence are all elements that women emphasise in their arguments with men. Anger arises when they are not treated with courtesy in return. Professionals like solicitors and doctors seem to be frequent offenders here. Kathy reports an argument with her solicitor about

'Invasion of privacy – him invading mine! He didn't listen to me properly, probably because he felt strongly about what he was asking, and I *was* angry. I felt my solicitor had gone too far, and should be stopped! So I stopped him.'

Fiona recalls an argument she had with her divorce solicitor over his final bill.

'We ended up writing these long letters, to ensure – on my side anyway – that the other person really understood. In the end, he wrote to say he was glad I had explained so clearly as he had felt very fond of me and did not want our relationship to end on such a sour note, and he said he probably would not have understood my point of view if I had not written. I felt really good after that, and we remained good friends until he died. He even sent me tickets for Queen Elizabeth Hall, and as he said, he didn't do that for all his clients.'

This account does bring up a further issue when it comes to arguments between women and men, and that is 'fondness'. Women are generally expected to inspire affection in men with whom they have a long-term relationship, however formal. When she does, she is a *marvellous* woman' as one elderly Peer said of Baroness Young,[27] or a 'wonderful woman', as an academic in the Conservative Think Tank said of Margaret Thatcher.[28] Jenny recalls that she had an excellent friendly relationship with doctors all her life until she reached her forties:

'I was being prescribed drugs for high blood pressure, and I did not want to find myself taking pills for the rest of my life, so wanted to know exactly what was involved. My doctor said he hadn't got time to explain it all to me. I said that in that case we were wasting time, both his and mine, as I would not be taking drugs unless I knew what they would do. He said, "The trouble with you is you're too intelligent." What sort of a comment is that?'

What indeed? Doctors' attitudes to women patients are a frequent source of irritation, as many a magazine article will attest. Meg told me:

'When I walked into the surgery, he was already writing a prescription for tranquillisers. I said to him, How can you know what I need before I've even spoken to you? His reply was: "Are you questioning my professionalism?" I wanted to say yes, and walk out. What I actually said was that I did not want or need tranquillisers, I'd come because I had a lump. He was very nice and gentle then, but I decided not to go back to him. Fortunately, there are two other doctors in the practice.'

Firmness, persistence and insistence on their rights are themes in all the arguments reported by women with men. These may be with builders who don't turn up when promised, or whose job is substandard. Angela wrote:

'I just kept telephoning every day, until at last he had to come back and fix the bells. It was tiresome for him, but even more tiresome for me to spend so much money and still not have them work.'

And Rose said:

'I think the boss was really upset when I told him I was not happy with the way the builders had left the place. He promised to get them to come back and sort out everything. And the man who was in charge was really anxious to make sure everything was all right before he left. I felt pleased I had made the effort to complain properly, and to the top man.'

Few of these arguments seem to turn out badly, and these are usually men who enjoy abusing their power anyway. Sheila recalls an electrician leaving a real mess everywhere:

'He was one of those men who enjoys the power he has to disrupt your life. We'd had him in the house for three days because it was a major alteration, and when he came to leave, I asked if he had put the insulation back in the loft, because he had lifted it to lay cable and left it all over the place. "Not my job," he said, and walked off. But the carpenter who was with him raised his eyes to heaven, and went up to the loft himself to sort it out. As you can imagine, we'll have the carpenter back to do work, but the electrician never.'

Contrary to a wide variety of myths, many craftsmen and other tradesmen seem to go out of their way to help a woman who argues with them – so long as she argues firmly but gently. If she raises her voice or loses her temper, her charm as a woman has disappeared to be replaced by the image of witch and harridan. Natalie saw the other side when she hired a tree surgeon to cut down an enormous tree which was threatening her house. The delicacy of the job was such that the surgeon asked a neighbour for permission to run a steadying rope from a winch on their property as well. The neighbour, a woman, refused, to his astonishment and fury. Natalie told me:

'Steam was really coming out of his ears as he came back, he was raging with fury, and threatened to murder her. She really did upset him because the job was terribly dangerous, and by not allowing the winch, she was putting his life at risk. She's a really difficult person, and I had already tried to get her co-operation without success, so I did warn him. But he was so sure he'd persuade her because no reasonable person would refuse. Of course, she's not reasonable at all.'

Reasonable women do appear to get what they want most of the time when arguing with a man. Perhaps it is that they are more polite with men, as William suggests, than they are with other women. For 'other women' are usually seen as not reasonable at all.

Women Disputing with Women

Take Vivienne's argument with a female service receptionist: her TV needed repair, and she did not want to spend half a day off work waiting for the repairman to call. She got her way in the end:

'I insisted unrelentingly that I was *not* going to agree with the time she said the engineer was to call. I consider that having paid in advance for a service, it should be completed at *my* convenience and not the engineer's.'

She was angry; and so was Janet, when the dentist's receptionist refused – at first – to arrange emergency treatment for her husband who had severe toothache.

'I did not accept her reasons for preliminary unhelpfulness and made very reasonable and limited demands (for temporary dressing to kill pain). It was a practical issue with a simple solution: I felt that if she considered the issue rather than her own convenience, something could be done. It was.'

Both women found themselves dealing with a female stranger who was, in their view, being deliberately unhelpful and illegitimately exercising power. Both were angry even though in the end they got what they wanted: they were angry because they had to argue for a helpful attitude which they expected as a right. Receptionists are there to provide a service. So are shopkeepers. When Val found the prints of her photos were badly out of focus, she refused to pay for the printing, and a strong angry argument ensued. She too won her point.

'My comments were fair and reasonable and the girl eventually agreed with them. I felt my request not to pay for the printing of negatives was justified. I was willing to pay for developing of film and did so.'

When a woman does not get her point across, then she reports extreme anger. Susan, who rarely argues with anyone, sent me a note:

'At last an argument for your research, and I *still* feel cross.'

She was trying to arrange for a society to use a room in the Community Centre for their meeting:

'She didn't want to hear my side and was only interested in the small print of the lease. I felt my request was justified.'

Susan was 'extremely angry' and added the splendid *non sequitur*:

'The woman I argued with is married to a retired fire officer which I think explains everything.'

Kathleen reports a series of arguments with a librarian, and firmly circles the word 'subordinate' on her diary report. In this case, Kathleen gave a great deal of information, and it is quite clear that she does not enjoy getting into conflict with anyone. Nevertheless, she had a series of 'blazing rows' with this librarian. On the first occasion, she writes:

'She would not listen to me, and launched into me without warning. I could not reply as [other people] were there and I was afraid of inflaming her further. I did not argue back after a first statement of the facts. However I have not spoken to her since, which I hope makes her feel uneasy.'

Vain hope, as it turned out. Eventually Kathleen decided to fight back:

'She yelled at me for renewing books. I said there was no rule against it and I am working from them at the minute. She said it fouled up her system. She wanted to pick a fight with me. I felt I couldn't let her attack me as she was attacking me, and I was very cool about it. She is probably a bit jumpy because people have been complaining about her, but I don't feel that is my business. I am too preoccupied at the minute to do more than defend my position. I used to give in to her and apologise, but recently she has accused me wrongly, and now I think she has gone too far.'

Kathleen was extremely angry and extremely upset, though she kept 'very cool' in her behaviour. She wrote: 'It is becoming important though it shouldn't be.' Disputes with someone you see as a subordinate or provider of a service are liable to inspire rage if that other person does not provide the service and appears to expect *you* to fit in with them.

It is just as bad when communications break down, and the woman you are disputing with does not have the information you expect her to have. Julia, for example, was informed by a hospital receptionist that she was too late for her appointment, which made her very angry. She got her point across by 'Being assertive and insisting on my rights. The fault was not mine but incompetence on the part of hospital admin.'

Her troubles were not over, and a few days later she had a 'blazing row' with a nurse who wanted to send her husband away:

'It was extremely important as I was having an operation and it had already been explained to the surgeon my morbid fear of an anaesthetic and he had agreed to let spouse stay.'

No doubt her anxieties added fuel to the flames, but a high level of anger is extremely common in all reports of women arguing with other women whose jobs make them in some sense 'gatekeepers': the nurse who can allow the husband to stay, or not; the receptionist who can make you an appointment, or not; the librarian who can renew your books, or not.

When the other woman behaves in a warm, friendly and 'womanly' way, however, the argument can be low key, and even a traffic warden may not inspire high levels of anger if she responds in the right way. Beattie is a university messenger, and travels around the city on a motor scooter, delivering parcels from one college to another. She reports a mild dispute with a woman traffic warden who asked why she was parking her scooter in a 'no parking' zone. Beattie explains:

'When I am on university work I have reasonable access to such areas. This was discussed at local police station, who in turn allowed my parking scooter while on business.'

Most of us who have tangled with traffic wardens might be surprised to learn that this was accepted, and Beattie was only mildly angry. A kind of camaraderie of two women working within a complicated system developed.

Nevertheless, the majority of disputes between women do infuriate both parties, and diarists report that they only got their point across by 'being assertive and insisting on my rights'. This phrase is a constant refrain, repeated by many women who in other circumstances would never talk of 'being assertive'. Many more women have said in interview that they have *felt* extremely angry with shop assistants, telephonists, waitresses and others who are expected to fulfil requests willingly and without argument, and who don't, but much of this anger remains unexpressed. Fiona recalls getting so mad with a telephonist she demanded to speak to her supervisor, but this reaction is rare.

16

Living with a Stranger

A few mentions of neighbours have occurred *en passant*, and it is worth taking a quick look at this potentially difficult relationship. While most of us probably dream of a friendly neighbourhood, where 'neighbours become good friends' as the soap theme tune has it, many people find themselves living next door to people who make their lives hell. Indeed, television has spawned several series on 'Neighbours from Hell', and it seems producers have not been gravelled for matter.

Luck comes into this, and so I will not spend a great deal of time on it. But even here there do seem to be some gender differences worth noting.

Men arguing with men usually start out quietly, and if the dispute can be sorted in quiet 'gentlemanly' fashion, both feel satisfied. I myself have found that it is a good idea to get my husband to sort out any mild dispute with a neighbour (we did have a long dispute about some dying trees threatening our garden and greenhouse, and eventually persuaded our neighbour to have them felled): a man will more easily listen to another man when being asked to *do* something or to spend money. As we all know from reading the newspapers, a dispute over trees can lead to a great deal of anger, and to court cases. But my husband is old-fashioned and gentlemanly, and usually he gets his way through quiet persistent reasoning, helped by maintaining friendliness on both sides.

Men arguing with women tend to get very irritated very quickly. Len tried to laugh it off when his neighbour pointed out damage his builders had done to her garage, then got angry. In the end, he agreed to a quick repair:

'She was quite reasonable really, though a bit short-tempered at first. I was afraid I was going to get landed with a big bill, but she said it was an old building, and she just didn't want it to fall down. Seemed fairly reasonable so I told the builder to shove a bit of concrete in the cracks next time he mixed some.'

His neighbour told me:

'I knew it would turn into an argument, and he tried to tell me it had nothing to do with the heavy machinery five inches away. I just didn't have the energy to insist on a proper repair – so long as it didn't fall down, I felt that would do. The builder was there, and he knew what had happened, so he said he could do a quick repair without a major problem.'

So this argument was resolved by a compromise. Ruby was not so lucky. When her new neighbours moved in next door, she was appalled to see the man wandering around the garden in the nude. Realising that he might not take kindly to her comments, she caught his wife on her way home from work, and asked if she could persuade her husband not to spend all day in the nude in full view of her windows. The wife said she could not, and the dispute escalated until the husband attempted to climb the fence, still starkers, threatening to strangle Ruby, calling on his dog to attack, and the police were called. Whatever you think of nudity, and of Ruby's request that a man not wander around naked in his own garden, most people will agree that violence is not the way to deal with the issue. Nevertheless, anger from man to woman can be very high, and a woman can find herself frightened. Carla recalls that a neighbour's dog barked constantly and was driving her mad:

'When it had got to the point that I only had to walk into my kitchen to set the dog off, I decided that was it, and went round to talk to them. The woman was perfectly pleasant at first, though she said she couldn't stop a dog barking. What's she doing with a dog, if she doesn't know how to train it? But the man came storming out, and threatened to turn the dog on me. I was really scared then, but I told him I would call the police if he threatened me again. And I expected him to train his dog properly. It did get better after that, actually.'

Women arguing with women neighbours can also infuriate, though any threats they make are legal rather than physical. Beattie reports:

'Neighbour questioning the right for my daughter to park her car at the rear of my flat, i.e. she claims if car is parked there she is unable to get her car in & out of her garage – this is not so, the space is plenty large enough.'

Beattie was 'extremely angry', though she believes she got her point across. Even when the women are not obviously fighting, anger may intervene. Ellen reports in her diary what appeared to be a 'mild discussion' about a Russian vine on the boundary between her garden and her neighbour's:

'She liked it. I didn't and it was on my side. I had removed it, which gave me a view into her garden. She just mentioned it when I was weeding, and I felt much angrier than I expected, because I felt somewhat in the wrong. I had removed her screen without asking her and not quite realising that it would affect her.'

Neighbours are people with whom one has to learn to live, though one may really wish to have nothing to do with them. Disputes are almost invariably about a sense of having been invaded in one's home, which, as we know, is every English person's castle. When invaded, we understandably feel a need to defend ourselves. It is noticeable, though, that women seem to get the brunt of much of the anger from both women and men.

17

Playing Power Games

So this brief survey of arguments between people in what I am calling 'formal non-work' relationships reveals almost the reverse of what happens in 'informal' casual relationships. Women usually engage in mild exchanges of opinion and discussion of differences with other women acquaintances; with people expected to provide a service, it is mainly men who report low-key arguments with other men, though women report arguments with men that succeeded through persistence and assertiveness. Anger, aggression, even threats of violence and murder among casual acquaintances were all directed at men. In formal non-work relationships, however, high levels of anger, aggression and threats of violence are mainly directed at women – by both men and women. This difference extends even to neighbours, who might be expected to be more like casual acquaintances: anger is very near the surface and ready to explode in any dispute with a neighbour, especially if the other person is a woman.

Why should women be the targets of so much anger and aggression? Psychologist Arlie Hochschild, whose study of airline attendants we mentioned earlier, suggests that women are supposed to master anger and aggression in the service of 'being nice', while men's job is to take action against those who break the rules, wield anger and make threats. This is the Division of Labour again: women are expected to bring their special understanding of feelings, their ability to 'do relational work', into the marketplace. 'Nice people don't argue'; any woman who does argue is failing in the job she is there for: to carry out subordinate tasks smoothly and make everyone around feel good.

The other side of the Division of Labour is that a woman who acknowledges a man's expertise is likely to get good service, for she is making him feel good about his special male power. We saw that women were pleased when the results of their 'persistence and assertiveness' with tradesmen produced what they wanted without unpleasantness. I too have found that I can get better results from talking to a plumber or carpenter or electrician than my husband can, not because I have any special knowledge or lack thereof, but because these experts are always pleased to be able to show off their knowledge to a woman, and the more detail we get into the better. My numerous arguments with the experts transforming our house have led to excellent working relationships because they get me what I want and the man has found the process a great boost to his ego. Arguments between men in such situations can be construed as interference.

But of course I am the one requiring the service. Arguments with a man to whom I am supposed to provide a service are a very different thing. We have seen that men did not report any arguments with 'high-status' professionals, and as a chartered psychologist providing psychological services to individuals, I cannot recall any man arguing with me. (I have certainly had arguments as an employee, but that is different – see Part Four.) If we look at the diaries and interviews, it is women who report arguing with high-status people, not men. (Of course, such arguments occur, but we are taking the reports of the hundreds of people who voluntarily contributed to this research as reflecting important *attitudes* to argument.) This contrast may arise because men are more conscious of and willing to subscribe to hierarchies, and I will examine this idea more carefully in Part Four. But men *do* make a difference in how they construe their behaviour towards men with expertise, whom they treat with caution, and women whom they see as there to serve. For women are frequently found in jobs that require them to serve the public: more women than men are receptionists, shop assistants, telephonists, nurses, secretaries and so on.

If women providing a service to members of the public face aggression every time they dare to argue or to justify their actions, it is no wonder they develop ploys of sullen resistance which allow them to use what power they have. We have all come across the sulky shop assistant, who makes it quite clear that you as the customer are a tiresome nuisance, but who just manages to stay this side of being rude enough for you to make a complaint; the receptionist who carries on with her conversation because she 'just didn't see you'; the telephone operator with the bored voice, who doesn't know who could deal with your query, or where the person you want to speak to has gone, and can't find out or take a message. These young women are all expressing their anger and frustration in one of the few ways available to them when direct expression of their views is out. Playing power games is a way of getting one's own back without retribution.

Take the receptionist/nurse at your doctor's surgery, for example.

You: I have an appointment with Dr Snarf at 11.45.
Receptionist: Oh, Doctor's running late. Please have a seat.

This exchange is taken from Robin Lakoff's book *Talking Power: The Politics of Language*, in which she analyses the political meaning hidden behind the façade of politeness.[29] We have probably all been subjected to this attitude. No doubt few of us expect to be able to walk straight in to see a doctor, the very nature of whose work makes time-keeping problematic, though we'd like evidence of some attempt at making appointment times meaningful. But whether or not the doctor's poor time-keeping is a power ploy, the language used shows the receptionist is playing a power game. Lakoff translates the subliminal message as follows:

'Doctor is more important than you. You'd better be subservient because you need us more than we need you.'

This is infuriating enough, and Lakoff reports tales of people invoicing their doctors for time wasted. But worse than the assumption that you have nothing better to do than sit around waiting until the doctor is free is the use of the honorific 'Doctor' to refer to the absent medical expert. Let Robin Lakoff explain:

Under few circumstances in this culture are people referred to (not addressed) by title alone .... The only ordinary-world analogue to the receptionist's 'Doctor' is 'Mommy' and 'Daddy' with children ('Hi there, dear. Is Mommy home?') ... 'Doctor' like 'Mommy' presupposes a strongly unequal relationship and thus both justifies the enforced wait and makes objection to it more difficult.

Lakoff is concerned with the politics of language, and shows how people win the power game by hidden means. Here, nothing is said to which exception can actually be taken, and yet the subliminal effect on you as recipient is that you have been insulted. But if you do want to complain, what can you complain about? It's all in your mind, you are responsible for the interpretation. As Lakoff puts it, 'Politics is piled on politics.'

Our concern here is not with the politics of language but with constraints on freedom to say what you mean and what happens when you do. The two concerns are closely intertwined, for what is important is less what was actually said in any exchange, and more *how people remember* what was said. When an exchange is over, it is rare for anyone to remember much detail. What you recall is the overall sense of what happened, why an exchange turned into an argument and how successful you were in getting your own views across.

It is this interpretation which remains with you and which affects your subsequent actions.

Look back at the exchange in the doctor's office. Subjected to the power ploy of the receptionist who adopts the mantle of high priestess to her godlike employer, you remember afterwards the sense of frustration and anger; since the actual words exchanged give little guidance to those not trained in linguistic analysis (or lucky enough to read books like Robin Lakoff's), you are very likely to reconstruct the memory and conclude that it is your doctor's fault that you feel humiliated. Hence the numerous complaints and legal demands for financial compensation directed at doctors in the United States.

The receptionist has won. She has *appeared* to be helpfully doing her job, while at the same time secretly undermining the well-being of those she is supposed to serve.

Others in service jobs develop their own power ploys, and men do it just as much as women when they feel they start with a disadvantage. The electrician who deliberately left the roof insulation piled anyhow and the house strewn with bits of electric cable was getting back at all those employers in the past who had treated him like a servant. The dustmen who scatter rubbish in your garden, the delivery man who leaves a parcel in the rain, the council officer who 'mislays' your application for benefit – all in their different ways are using what power they have to compensate for feeling that they are seen as 'low status' and therefore of no account. We are not yet a 'classless society' here in Britain. But even if we were, service jobs are still service, and even in the classless United States, service is something we require others to give us. Being expected to provide service to others is, as any woman will tell you, a quick road to anger and frustration, for giving service is only pleasant when you give gladly and of your own free will. When you need to earn a living, free will seems to fly out of the window.

18

Facing the Future

Myths are tent pegs which secure the status quo.

(Helena Kennedy)[30]

The young women we met at the beginning of Part Three may not have experienced the contempt and anger that comes the way of the woman in a 'formal' service role. Suzy is an information officer and Maureen works in the editorial department of a women's magazine. Both need to deal with the public, and Suzy provides a service (very efficiently). If they continue to behave to all their contacts as they did with me, they need never meet this anger at all. For they are fulfilling the public's expectations by being helpful and warm and friendly all at the same time.

But unfortunately, even though the women themselves are often unaware of the potentially high levels of anger simmering under the surface, those who deal with them are just waiting for them to make a mistake for it to explode. For there is something inexpressibly infuriating in a woman in a service job being 'unhelpful', 'difficult', 'obstructive'; and if she dares to explain or justify her inability to do what is required, she is in some way proving that women are incompetent, unreliable and should never be put in jobs that demand a modicum of intelligence in the first place. All the unspoken, unacknowledged beliefs about women's failings rise to the surface.

Explosions are not always face to face (or voice to voice over the telephone). Many people – and women especially – save their explosive anger until they get off the phone, and then tell everyone who will listen what 'that stupid bitch' did or did not do. Reputations are shredded this way.

Women have frequently told me things like

'It wasn't a real argument because I didn't want to let myself down and say what I really felt. I would have been embarrassed to say what I was thinking.' (Gayle)

But the damage is done because they then pass on the information that the woman who made them angry is incompetent or unpleasant, and her reputation becomes tarnished by the conviction that she must be 'difficult to get along with'. Men too, who cannot be bothered to deal with an 'obstructive' woman, may react explosively by demanding to be 'put through to the top'. Again, I have been told by many men:

'I won't put up with incompetence. If I am paying for a service, it is on my terms. I always go to the top.' (Ivan)

'Women these days expect to work in a man's world without being equipped. I can't stand being obstructed by some female who doesn't understand the first thing about business.' (Les)

I objected to the tone of this last comment, and Les retorted:

'Women are always whingeing on about being treated as equals. In my experience what they really want is what women have always wanted – a macho male.'

Well, ladies, Les is there to oblige. It is only fair to add, though, that Les is all charm when he pleases, and is the kind of flamboyant entrepreneur we have all seen in glossy magazines with gorgeous women young enough to be his daughter hanging on each arm. So his experience of women may well be limited to those very young women who are turned on by someone else's money and success.

What this brief overview tells us is that there are some men who still think macho is what makes a man, but that even those whose ideas are more up to date are secretly operating with old-fashioned expectations of women. Not just men either. I suspect that most of us, women and men, young and old, to some degree have not thrown off those ancient beliefs that women are gentle, warm, helpful, friendly creatures by nature – and if they behave assertively, coolly and appear to be unhelpful and unfriendly, then they are being obstructive or there is something wrong with them. If they are in any position where they are expected to provide a service, and they appear unable or unwilling to do just this, then they really should not be doing the job – whatever it is – in the first place.

As Andrea, my hairdresser, told me:

'If you want to keep a customer, and she says something you don't like, you keep your mouth shut.'

Anger against women arises, not because they are women, but because they are women failing to behave as they are expected to behave in a job designed to bring out their quintessentially feminine skills.

Women arguing with women as casual acquaintances or as strangers can enjoy exchanging different views, so long as the other woman does not put on airs and claim some kind of expertise. What is expected of a woman in these circumstances is a willingness to listen and to contribute, and any anger or irritation that might arise because she interrupts or fails to listen is very considerably less than the extreme rage that a woman may feel with a woman expected to provide a service.

Men arguing with women as casual acquaintances usually take little notice of what they say anyway, and most arguing with women strangers treated the discussion as unimportant too. Only one of the twelve men arguing with a woman in the Whodunnit experiment had an overtly macho approach, but all did report using 'hard' tactics with women, reflecting an underlying assumption of superiority; none of the men was actually influenced by a female partner, though half went along with her solution, which does suggest they did not really take the whole thing seriously. However, when a man is confronted by a woman who is apparently not convinced that his views are correct in a more formal and therefore more important situation, he is liable to explode. Some men even shake with fury and threaten physical violence.

Women in many jobs where they deal with the public have found they actually need physical protection, and high-status

professionals too find their situation becoming ever more dangerous. The incidence of serious attacks on women doctors, solicitors
and teachers by males has been rising sharply as women become
more numerous in these professions. Female social workers and
psychologists have developed procedures whereby they are never
alone with a male member of the public without some kind of
protection (e.g. a desk) as well as a means of summoning help (e.g.
a panic button).

This anger is *men's* problem. But it is also society's problem, for
it reflects the widespread hidden beliefs that women are not
behaving as women should. Note, people are not angry with
women just because they are women, nor because they are arguing:
they are angry because they are arguing in a situation in which they
are expected to fulfil a different role. They are expected to provide
a service and most especially to be nice, as required by the Division
of Labour which gives them the task of caring for society's
relationships. There is no good reason why women acting outside
the Division of Labour in the course of doing a job should arouse
such rage – but they do.

As Janus looks towards the future, he seems to frown.

Part Four

Playing the Gender Game at Work

Assertiveness is treated as an interpersonal skill which women lack, the acquisition of which will help them to compete on equal terms with men .... The focus rules out questions about the way men relate to women's authority, and the long-term necessity for all women to work with defensive male colleagues.

(Wendy Hollway)[1]

It costs nothing to be gracious and considerate.

(Clara Grantley in *She* magazine)[2]

Argument at work creates as much distress, confusion and anger in people's lives as does argument among intimates, and can be just as important, just as stressful and just as baffling. Argument at work is also necessary. Discussion, debate, dispute, negotiation are all essential elements of working together, and those who do not understand what is going on are at a disadvantage. If you do know 'the rules of the game', you need never be their helpless victim and might even, at times, turn them to your own account.

Work colleagues have to learn to live with each other on a long-term basis (weeks and months, rather than hours as with casual acquaintances and strangers), and the demands of their job usually require them to communicate. Hierarchies are important: arguments that arise between colleagues of equal status, or between boss and subordinate, may have long-term consequences. Politics and power become vital factors.

Does society's growing acceptance of the idea of gender equality mean we find few differences between women and men at work, at least when arguing with each other as equals? Or do the deep-seated beliefs grounded in the Division of Labour also sabotage communications at work?

And there is a further element: argument at work is frequently seen as a game by men, but not by women. In addition to the games they play with colleagues and clients, men are increasingly playing a new one – the Gender Game. And they are establishing the rules.

Games Businessmen Play

For the vast majority of adult American males, anything that involves negotiation is assigned to the *Game Domain* until the negotiation is completed. (Suzette Haden Elgin)[3]

If you listen to men talking on both sides of the Atlantic, you will find they use images of games playing. British men talk of 'being on a sticky wicket', playing with a 'straight bat', even 'bowling a googly' (cricket terms: 'being no-balled' must be symbolic castration?). American men talk of 'throwing a high ball', 'batting to the outfield' and 'getting to first base' (baseball). Both talk of 'level playing fields', 'being on the ball' and 'moving the goalposts' (various kinds of football), while aficionados of chess talk of 'moves' and 'pawns' and 'stalemate', and golfers talk of 'teeing off' and 'birdies' and 'holes in one'.

The key to discovering which game is being played is language. Men themselves may fail to communicate unless they ensure they are thinking in terms of the same game: the rules of tennis or golf are rather different from the rules of football; not to mention the crucial point that football is played by a team, tennis may be played by partners and golf is definitely a one-person performance.

Carrie, a female American college administrator, told me:

'My observation is that there is really a different language. If women are sports fans and speak that language, then they can earn men's respect. This has nothing to do with their skills in business, but it is extraneous stuff that makes a difference.'

So Carrie has noticed that games language is a way of gaining respect, but Elgin's point is something more. Men tend to *be* playing games while they are at work, and these may not always be sports: they may be war games too.

The difficulty most women have is that they tend not to think in terms of games at all, and if they do, they think a game is a *recreation*, it is for *fun*, and so is not important. Wrong, says linguist Suzette Haden Elgin. She argues that women are disadvantaged in the business world because they do not understand the rules by which men operate and which they learned as boys in their all-male culture: all negotiations are games, and games are important. So not only is it crucial to discover what game the other person is thinking of, you had better take that particular game seriously because you can be sure he does.

Women do not compete in games on equal terms with men: in no area of sport are they considered equal, whether their acknowledged physical differences are relevant or not. This may well be yet another reason why women are discounted in business negotiations. They *can* win in such negotiations, but a woman's negotiation skills may frequently be rendered ineffective unless she recognises which game is being played, and whether the men involved are also playing the Gender Game.

What is the Gender Game?

The Gender Game is my term for the various ploys and strategies employed by men who set out to use gender role expectations to their own advantage. This may be done in various ways. Not all the ploys are necessarily disadvantageous to the woman who recognises what is going on. But they are designed to promote the man's future and not the woman's – a factor to be borne in mind by the tender-hearted – and will be turned against the woman if she dares to show she may be a threat. Much of this section will turn out to be an examination of men playing the Gender Game.

Women too sometimes try to play the Gender Game by turning gender role expectations on their head. They are few at the moment, but some exceptionally successful women play their own version of the Gender Game – and win.

Turning stereotypes to your own advantage is precisely the advice that psychologist Glynis Breakwell gives in her book *The Quiet Rebel*.[4] This book might be termed the modern woman's version of Machiavelli's *The Prince*, and is not for the faint-hearted. As she puts it, 'manipulating feelings skilfully' is the key. The woman who wants success in a man's world, according to Breakwell, does not confront. She works quietly, seeing clearly what is going on and turning other people's assumptions to her advantage. She knows when to put on 'the Big Sister Act', 'when to don the character of the Bitch and the ways of the Mother, and with whom'.[5]

> She has to be able to predict what other people will do on the basis of the roles they perform, and ensure that her own freedom of action is not constrained by roles that others try to impose on her. She has to monitor interaction rituals and be willing to disrupt them in order to control roles attributed to her. The way to achieve good working relationships requires three steps: observation, analysis, and only then, action.[6]

'Good relationships' here mean control and manipulation. Working with a woman who is willing and able to control and manipulate can be a devastating experience, for you know that things are happening beneath the surface and it is very difficult to bring them out into the open. From the point of view of the manipulator though, it works: Glynis Breakwell herself has been remarkably successful in her chosen field, becoming in 1994 that most rare of all women academics, a pro-vice-chancellor of a university.

To manipulate is to acknowledge that power lies elsewhere, and can be acquired only surreptitiously. This approach is anathema to those, like me I'm afraid, who prefer to be direct and open. It is also clear acknowledgement that freedom of speech is constrained. If it were not that this approach does work when you are concerned with ends rather than means, I would be inclined to characterise it as reflecting a 'slavegirl mentality': that is, the slave clear-sightedly examines the shackles and tries to turn them to advantage. But Breakwell has shown that the clever manipulator can eventually become the slave-owner, and given the current imbalance of power between women and men, perhaps we should applaud this.

Though Breakwell's language is not that of games playing, her approach may be compared to that of someone playing charades. She talks of 'role-playing' and 'putting on an act' and 'donning the character'. This is the game of a loner, the kind of game many young girls love – play-acting, dressing up, pretending to be someone you are not. So women may play games at work as well, but they are unlikely to be team games, and their language may not reveal as clearly as men which game they are playing.

Most women though are carefully *not* playing games at work, because they want to do their work to the best of their ability and believe they should take their job seriously. They need to learn that games can be very serious, and stakes in the Gender Game are high.

19

Women Who Feel They Are Winning

Jenifer, now 26 years old, joined a small computing company soon after her eighteenth birthday. She had no qualifications, had simply walked out of university (to her mother's consternation) the day she legally came of age, joined a friend in London and found a job. Jenifer had no need for training in that assertiveness we are told women lack: she told the man who interviewed her she would learn whatever skills they needed, in her own time, and he took her on as a clerk. Within two months she had her own desk, her own filing cabinet, her own computer on which she was fast becoming a skilled word processor. They loved her, and she loved them. She arrived at eight in the morning, rarely left for home until six or seven at night. As the company grew – for computing companies were a growth industry even while the economy elsewhere sagged (this was the late 1980s) – Jenifer took on more responsibility, learned more skills. She acquired an assistant. Now she has two. (Both were 18 when taken on, and are learning on the job.) Now Jenifer has a new title, Office Administrator, a part-share in a house and runs a tiny car. Her boss tells her she is an excellent administrator, and promises her further advancement when the company grows.

Jenifer feels successful, and her confident, friendly manner shows this. She is tall, willowy, dresses in a casual smart style, and her smile could soften the hardest heart. But what about argument? She laughed, but would talk only in general terms.

'Oh, yes, I argue with the men in the office all the time. But it's all very friendly, and I usually get what I want. I'm very reasonable and they know it. Of course, some of them try it on, but I tell them, it's time we had more sexual harassment round here, not less. You'd be surprised how quickly they back off then. It's only a game, so I play my part too, and we get on fine.'

Jenifer sees sexual innuendo in the office as a game, just as many men do. She is perfectly happy that her undoubted physical attractions do not go unnoticed, and perfectly confident that she can deal with any unwanted attentions. Like Suzy and Maureen, whom we met at the beginning of Part Three, Jenifer feels that the bad old days are gone and men and women can be friends in the office. Anita, a 24-year-old PA, agrees:

'The thing is to turn it round and say to them the same things they say to you. They just laugh then. It means nothing. Except of course they know I'm not available, so we can get on with the job in a friendly way. There was one man who got aggressive, and he actually chased me round his desk before I could get to the door. I told him straight, Don't you ever do that again or I am going straight to Mr C., he's the boss. That was it. He's careful now.'

Why is it, I asked, that whenever I talk about argument with male colleagues, young women usually bring up the issue of sexual harassment? Anita laughed:

'It's only natural, isn't it? You can't help your hormones.'

This is what men have always claimed in their defence, I pointed out, and added that when sexual harassment leads to court, it is usually presented by the plaintiff as abuse of power. Anita said:

'That's different. That man who chased me round the office was trying to abuse his power, but I stopped him. Most of the time, the fellows in this office are just enjoying being men in the company of women, and so are we women. Don't you like men? I do.'

A lot of issues have been raised in Anita's two short paragraphs: sexual innuendo as natural, stopping abuse of power, hormones, men and women enjoying each other's company, and criticism of bad behaviour interpreted as dislike of all men.

The Gender Game is complicated and difficult to deal with just because relations between women and men *almost always* raise issues of sex. This is especially the case when we are talking of work, where women and men have to meet and work together on a regular, even daily basis, and even more especially when young women are concerned. It *matters* to a man whether the woman with whom he is supposedly discussing a business issue is young, shapely and sexually attractive or middle-aged or old. This does not, of course, mean that every man looks on every woman as a sexual object: but she is seen as primarily a female in relation to him as a male, and so her age and physical attractiveness determine the kind of relationship he can develop with her. Youth and beauty mean sexual attraction to most men, and most of these young and beautiful women are quite happy to be seen as sexually attractive. What they do not want is for that sexual attraction to be translated into action that will cost them their jobs.

Not everyone is as confident as Jenifer and Anita about turning the tables when sexual attentions are unwanted. Deirdre was a 20-year-old student of mechanical engineering when she kept an argument diary for this research. In it she recorded an argument with a fellow student who had put his arms round her and tried to kiss her. She wrote:

'As this happens not infrequently with people I know fairly well, students I meet at lectures mainly, I feel I want to show them I don't like it. As I am trying to be their equal and just a colleague, attentions like this are totally unwanted. People seem to realise how you feel when you object to what they're doing, but don't seem to think before doing it the next time.'

Natural behaviour? What does Deirdre think about it now, eight years after her diary entry? She is now a teacher of physics in a comprehensive school, after six years struggling to be accepted as equal to the similarly qualified mechanical engineers in British Rail. She told me:

'The male students on the mech. eng. course resented us women, there were only three of us and 24 of them. I and another friend were always in the top five or six in exam results,[7] but the other woman on the course was near the bottom on many occasions, and those silly boys would keep on and on, pretending this proved women couldn't do the work. That poor girl, I don't know how she stuck it out. We'd try and help but none of us wanted to be aggressive. Having spent all those years in British Rail, with men trying to use my gender as a weapon against me, I now think all those sexual attentions were another way of trying to get control. Perhaps it might have been better to fight more, except we none of us really knew how. You don't get taught to fight back as a girl, even if you are going into a man's world.

'Things were different at work, but much more difficult. I never had any trouble with the men I had working for me, they were always very nice and helpful, no problems. It was those who were my equals, and just hated to have to deal with a woman. Conflicts were mostly with contractors, where we had to agree, and he would need to win. I got tired and frustrated, and had no sense I could control anything. It was a constant battle. As a teacher, I have a real sense of responsibility, what happens in my classroom is up to me.'

So Deirdre does not think sexual attentions are 'only natural': despite a long struggle to be friends with the men involved, she concludes that sexual attentions both as a student and in her workplace were just one way of 'trying to get control'. She, too, would like control, but over her own destiny, not over other people.

One important difference is the kind of work the women quoted here are involved in. Deirdre tried to move into a predominantly male world, that of applied mechanical engineering. Jenifer is an administrator, Anita a personal assistant, Suzy an information officer and Maureen an editorial assistant: all of these are predominantly female occupations – or in the case of administrators, a growing female occupation. But is it simply a question of numbers in a particular field, or is there something more? What about the difference in *attitude*? Perhaps Deirdre was too diffident; perhaps turning the tables as Jenifer and Anita claim to do is the real solution?

I suggest that the real issue is one of interpretation, and that interpretations are again governed by the Division of Labour. One reason why Jenifer and the others can feel so successful (and perhaps a little smug) is that they are earning a living while doing a job that fits the Division of Labour. It is a woman's task to look after relationships within the social group to which she belongs, make sure everyone within that group is contented and well cared for. Social groupings develop and change, and the increase in women's employment is a reflection of these changes. Women find that more and more they are acceptable and even desirable in a growing number of jobs where their 'womanly skills' are useful. Office administration is one: what does an administrator of a small office do but ensure that everyone has the space and equipment they need to do their job, look after junior staff, and generally minister to the needs of senior executives?

A further point is that we are talking about *young* women. Youth and beauty are important factors in women's apparent success in the marketplace. It is not just that there is a new attitude to women at work (which is a debatable issue anyway), but also that they *are* young and full of vigour and determined to prove they deserve their bosses' confidence. As Jenifer put it, 'I'm lucky to be given the chance to show what I can do. It's now down to me.'

Jenifer does not feel she is being exploited, though she continues to work up to ten hours a day and is willing to spend weekends updating her skills, even when it is supposed to be government policy to encourage training as part of the working week. She has recently taken over responsibilities formerly held by a man, and her desk has been moved from the all-women open office (resembling nothing so much as a typing pool) to a smaller office shared with two male executives, and she no longer does secretarial work: one of her assistants handles that. But she continues to be paid a salary considerably less than any man in the company, and has not been offered the company car the previous administrator had. She now has all the documents at her disposal, and can see the differences, but she does not feel she should point out the discrepancies to her employer. She knows she is young and relatively inexperienced, and she feels lucky. She said:

> 'I don't need to be aggressive about it. They know I'm good, and I'll be promoted to executive level before long. All it takes is hard work and determination.'

What has all this to do with argument? Essentially, it is that a young and attractive woman may find she can achieve a great deal when she chooses to speak up, speak out, take a stand. Assertiveness training has become big business on both sides of the Atlantic, and formerly timid and tentative young women find they can state their own views clearly – and be heard. Employers like young assertive women, willing to take responsibility without the perks, company car and higher pay that men demand: they are good to look at, eager to please and work hard.

So young women tend to believe they have cracked it. They are winning.

And this may be so. Things *may* have changed for this new generation of women making their mark in so many different areas. But the diaries their colleagues kept of arguments with women at the office tell a different story. So do the interviews I conducted with men and women up and down the country.

20

The Male Boss

Hierarchy and Power

Just as in other relationships outside work, attitudes to argument vary greatly depending on who you are and who the other person is. As before, we will examine these different points of view chapter by chapter, discussing concepts relevant to the particular viewpoint.

Let us begin by looking at how the male boss views argument with a subordinate.

Hierarchies dominate the workplace. Men tend to appreciate this crucial fact of life better than women. It makes good sense to them, whereas many women find hierarchies alienating. When women set up in business for themselves, they have often tried to establish co-operatives, in which all participants are theoretically equal. This difference in attitude is fed from two different sources: first, a man can, in principle, see himself climbing the ladder to the top, whereas a woman has traditionally found herself at the very bottom, expected to provide the services which will help the man climb over her to the heights; second, the male culture in which boys learn what is expected of them emphasises power and status, whereas female culture still emphasises relationship and co-operation.[8]

Linguist Deborah Tannen suggests that men look on discussion and argument as 'negotiations in which people try to achieve and maintain the upper hand' whereas women, she says, approach them as 'negotiations for closeness'.[9] We have already seen that a woman may try to achieve the upper hand with another woman if she expects a service from her, and a man may focus on creating a friendly relationship with a man when he enjoys talking to him and status is not important. But at work, status *is* important and closeness is not.

Some women find men's emphasis on status absurd and even comical at times: it is as though they are observing the customs of a strange tribe. Ann, in her very first office job after raising three children, confessed:

> 'I have real problems keeping the contempt off my face when I listen to them. They are like little boys. I got into trouble because I didn't give one of the men his cup of coffee. He knows where the kettle is. What's the problem?'

Ann is at the bottom of the hierarchy, that's the problem – her problem. She laughed and agreed; she had learned that, though she did feel that 'men are such children, playing games all the time'. A dangerous attitude for women to take in a man's world, because men have established the unwritten rules. William told me:

> 'One of the strongest motives in male behaviour is showing that you know the correct form, that you are an insider. Recognising the hierarchy shows you are one of the chosen people, so to speak, you know the shibboleths that puzzle outsiders. There is real vanity in it.'

Women frequently express a wish to change the way things are done in business, to break down hierarchies, create a more co-operative atmosphere. William said:

> 'I don't think I should like that. It would mean a greater emphasis on personal relationships and there are very few people I want to have personal relationships with. Not to mention how phoney it sounds. More informal ways do not in any way imply genuine friendship, when the reality is people are stabbing each other in the back.'

For men have developed a series of strategies which enable them to deal with problems of personal dislike or enmity: they avoid seeing the other person as an individual, but deal with him according to his position in the hierarchy. Most men can call on their experience of team sports, or even gang hierarchies, to understand that they have a specific task to perform within a structure that everyone else understands. Just as every soldier learns on joining the army 'to salute the rank, not the person', so most men in full-time employment are able to accept that the workplace has a social structure into which they must fit if they are to survive, and the first thing they do is learn the rules.

This is the secret behind most men's willing acceptance of hierarchies: by making a distinction between the person and the office he holds, a man can obey the office-holder without feeling in any way inferior to him as a person. Furthermore, he can see clearly where he stands in relation to the others in the workplace, and knows that all subordinates in turn must take orders from him.

Giving Orders to a Woman

Most women in work are low on the hierarchy, and expected to obey orders without question. However, female culture emphasises co-operation and equality. While a woman is unlikely to want 'to cause trouble', she may wish to question her instructions, and she doesn't like being ordered about anyway, she prefers to be *asked*. But from the point of view of the male boss, what happens when a woman queries an order? What happens when he expects prompt obedience because of his position in the hierarchy and she disagrees openly with him?

Anger, that's what happens. Just as we saw that women expected to provide a service to the public incur wrath if they show any signs of not conforming to their expected role, so women in any subordinate role in the workplace seem to be the focus of a great deal of anger. Men report that arguments with female subordinates can fill them with rage.

Mike, 36, is marketing manager for a manufacturer of small consumer electrical goods in the Home Counties. As we will see in Chapter 27, he finds himself engaged in endless battles with other managers on the same level, but he also records disagreements with his boss and disagreements with subordinates. For example, he found that one of his staff (a woman) wanted to change priorities in a series of tasks. When she tried to explain and defend her choice, Mike exploded. He wrote in his diary:

'I am the manager. I say what should be done when.'

Martin, who is manager of a large retail store, recorded a heated argument with Angie, his senior assistant, who tried to persuade him to change his decision not to send her on a training course. His anger reached a high level when she persisted in arguing:

'She was given a chance to put her case. But it is my job to determine how to deploy staff, and she is needed in the shop. Her attitude was unacceptable.'

This led to a series of confrontations, as Angie obviously felt Martin's decision was unfair, particularly when she learned he was sending a more junior member of staff instead. In the end, her boyfriend came to argue with Martin on her behalf. Martin was furious, and had him thrown out.

'My decision was justified, and it was not his place to intervene.'

Indeed not. But we can see that Angie felt unfairly treated, and the more she tried to express this view, the deeper she dug herself in the mire.

Martin and Mike did not want to hear. Nor did Frank bother to listen to his secretary when she argued that his decision to change her working conditions was unfair. In fact, he was not sure whether she actually heard what he said or not:

'She was annoyed! But what I say goes, so she has no choice in the matter.'

Diary accounts tend to be brief, with the male boss firmly circling 4 or 5 for the level of anger he was feeling, and 4 or 5 for the importance he attached to the issue. Interviews on the other hand permit a man to expand and explain why he felt so angry. Arnold, a company secretary in his fifties, told me he was getting more and more annoyed with Glenda, the typist assigned to look after him. Given his position, I was surprised he did not have a secretary. He said:

'She calls herself my secretary, but she's not competent. Unfortunately, I inherited her from my predecessor, and she resists any move to shunt her elsewhere. She's been around too long, she thinks she knows everything, but her work is sloppy and unreliable, and she gets over-emotional and hysterical if I point it out. She brings her family problems into the office, she is grossly overweight and to cap it all she's menopausal. How can a man be expected to work with a woman like that?'

Poor woman, I said. She sounds unhappy.

'What has that to do with it? She's there to do a job, and she does it badly.'

What about argument? He raised his eyes to heaven.

'She's the most bad-tempered, disagreeable harpy it has been my misfortune to come across. I tell you, if she argues with me one more time when I give her instructions, she will have to go. Compensation or no compensation, personnel will have to take it. I do not want that witch in my office any longer.'

Readers will not be surprised to learn that Glenda did lose her job soon after. Now Glenda may have been 'bad-tempered' and 'disagreeable', and she may have been incompetent, and she may have been 'emotional' when her failings were pointed out. We cannot know. But it is worth noting that these are the kind of criticisms frequently made of women, and rarely of men. It is worth noting, too, that her being overweight and 'menopausal' are held against her. Surely having a weight problem is irrelevant to one's skills as a secretary, and what precisely does Arnold mean by 'menopausal'? Does he mean 'too old to be attractive', 'emotional and irrational'? Most *women* will tell you 'menopausal' means the inconvenience of hot flushes and the promise of freedom from the monthly flow – neither of any relevance to one's male boss. But stereotypes tell us that the menopause turns women into witches. Arnold's new secretary is an attractive young woman in her twenties.

Arnold was playing the Gender Game, invoking negative

stereotypes in his campaign to get rid of a woman he disliked. Men in positions of power do not usually need to play this game with subordinates, but may feel the need to do so when the woman is junior in rank but in a different department, for example. Women at all levels are, of course, subordinate to someone unless they are one of that still rare breed, the female chief executive. In Arnold's case, he had clearly been constrained by Glenda's previous history with the company, and was forced to invoke some fairly strong images of unacceptable female behaviour before he could achieve his goal, replacing his predecessor's secretary with his own choice.

A woman subordinate *can* present her point of view without incurring anger, but only when discussion and argument are required as part of the work situation itself. Mike, a marathon arguer whose diary recorded thirty-two arguments in a single week, explains:

> 'This was about a recommendation from my department which I would present at a board meeting. It therefore had to be exactly as I wanted. We went through all the facts, argued respective points and my view was accepted.'

Mike was seeking information as well as discussing the document with a member of his staff. Here the woman is seen as helpful when she argues each point with him, for the purpose of the discussion is to find the best way for Mike to present himself and his department to the board. He didn't feel at all angry because she wasn't setting herself against him, she was using her knowledge and skills to support and promote him (as well as the department and herself).

We can see that these accounts fit perfectly into the Division of Labour schema: women should not argue unless required to do so as a service. Add to the Division of Labour scenario the issue of hierarchy, and we can see that a low-status woman who appears not to acknowledge the status of her male superior by arguing with him almost inevitably incurs anger. All the men quoted here emphasise their coercive power over their insubordinate female subordinates, and coercive power is a key factor within hierarchies. Arnold's need to play the Gender Game came from outside pressure to accept an unwanted subordinate (from the personnel department, presumably), but his assumption of power over his secretary lost her her job.

Psychologist David Kipnis, whom we met in relation to the Whodunnit experiment, says:

> There seems to be an iron law of power: the greater the difference in clout between two people, the greater the likelihood that hard tactics will be used.[10]

That is, the greater the amount of coercive power available to a man – or woman – the more likely it is that he – or she – will use threats and intimidation (which includes expressing anger) to get his/her way. Kipnis found, for example, that women who employ maids use exactly the same hard tactics as men adopt in the workplace. One further complicating – and depressing – aspect of this tendency to abuse power is that the more a person intimidates, the more contemptuous the bully feels of the victim. Our psyches have some kind of balancing mechanism which seems to say: if I behave badly towards P, this must be because P deserves it, because I would not behave badly otherwise. So the anger these women subordinates incur must be their fault.

Dealing with Male Subordinates

When a man has to deal with a male subordinate who argues for a different view, his account is rather different. He may get angry – though the levels are not as high as when the dispute is with a woman – but he also shows a greater need to explain the situation. He still emphasises that ultimately the power of choice lies with him, but coercion is less overt than with a woman. He tries to convince a male subordinate of the rationality of his decision.

Mike, for example, reports an argument with one of his staff about 'pricing of our products':

> 'He wanted to reduce our prices. There is frequent pressure from sales to reduce prices based on insufficient facts. I have to resist this pressure until I am convinced there is a case. He saw that I was right, and he had not got the facts to defend his case.'

Similarly, Gordon, a consultant in software engineering, reported a series of arguments with a member of his staff who was not producing adequate programming for an important contract:

'He does tend to get a bit ratty at times, if I ask him to rethink his work. He finds it difficult to accept that his program isn't working properly, even when it is perfectly clear that it is not. This does annoy me, but I try not to let it get to me too much. The important thing is to get the job done.'

Gordon says he himself hates to be 'bossed around', so he tries to reason with his staff:

'Writing software demands a clear mind and concentration, so bullying doesn't help anyone. Most of my people are very good, and we can talk about differences. It's only this one chap who hates to be told. Unfortunately I'm stuck with him – and he is stuck with me.'

Arguments are seen as part of the job, and pose no problem if the male subordinate is willing to concede that the boss is right in the end. Remember, this is the view of the male boss dealing with disagreement from a male subordinate. For what the subordinate thinks, we must wait until Chapter 23.

Men in charge stress their reasonableness with male staff, and Gordon adds that telling phrase used by so many women when asked about argument with friends: 'talking about differences'. Not that men are claiming to be friends with their staff, but they do talk as though they have established friendly relations. At the same time, they usually add that in the end they are responsible for what is done. They have coercive power, but they do not invoke it as overtly as with women. As Terry, a head of department in a very large comprehensive school, put it:

'I like to maintain a friendly atmosphere, as people are much more willing to co-operate if they like you. This in no way prevents me from making clear how I want the department run. Occasionally I might have a problem with one of the older members of staff who doesn't want to change old ways. But in the end, my view prevails.'

This comment is reminiscent of one made by John Major, shortly after taking office as Britain's Prime Minister. Asked how he reacted to arguments in Cabinet, he replied somewhat ingenuously:

'If you can advance an argument that is credible, if you can sustain the argument and if at the end of the day you can insist that it is done your way then that is perfectly satisfactory. I have had no difficulty in changing policy.'[11]

As a man dealing with men, he is unconsciously led to emphasise his ability to sustain a rational and logical argument, even though in the end he holds the coercive power that ensures his view prevails. (Or he did, until his party began to perceive him as 'weak'.)

The marked difference between how a man in charge reacts to a disagreement from a woman or from a man *may* have something to do with comparative position on the hierarchy. Many of the women are typists and secretaries, and bottom of the heap. But Martin was extremely angry with his second in command, who was a woman, and Mike was enraged by a female member of his executive staff: similar in relationship, one might think, to Gordon and his software team of men, or Terry and male members of his teaching staff, but the levels of anger reported are significantly different.

There *are* male bosses who rant and bully and express rage and anger to their male staff. We know there are because occasionally their antics get them into court and the newspapers. Furthermore, that enormous and growing section of the book trade on how to succeed in the workplace includes numerous volumes on how to cope with awful bosses, bullies being among the worst. But only one of the men in my research gave me a report which might fit this category. This was Oliver, whom we met in the chapter on anger in marriage, an angry and frustrated man working in an insurance office. He reported in his diary a strong argument with a male subordinate about 'the sloppiness of his work':

'I could prove then and there, with copious material for comparison, that his work *was* careless and sloppy. His attitude summed up all I detest in the approach to a job, *any* job. If something has to be done, it should be done to the best of one's ability. His approach was "couldn't really care".'

Oliver added as an afterthought what can be an important factor in attitudes to subordinates – their work can affect your reputation and future too.

'Also (although I honestly think this a less important reason), I am responsible, as his supervisor, for his work, and I did not want people to think I shared his attitude.'

Since some people *are* sloppy and careless in their work, it may simply be that Oliver had got fed up, and is not a bully at all. Certainly there was little evidence from the men in charge that any of them was ever unreasonable with their male subordinates.

21

The Female Boss

Women in Charge of Men: Provoking the Gender Game

To the extent that a woman has power in any organisation, her subordinates naturally have to take notice of what she says. But it is noticeable that if that subordinate is a man, he will question her decisions and argue with her in a way he would not if his boss were a man. Deborah Tannen notes that when a woman takes on a role or job previously held by a man, she begins her work 'with an aura of suspicion about whether she is up to the job'. In what Tannen calls 'a double whammy',[12] co-workers press her to justify her decisions, and this very questioning becomes interpreted as evidence that really she is incompetent. This is the Gender Game in action.

Ros (in her forties) is a publisher who hired Tony (30) as an experienced DTP (Desktop Publishing) operator.

'I know he was anxious to show how creative he could be, and I encouraged him to come up with new ideas .... But he spent so much time arguing that his ideas were better, his quality control slipped badly .... In the end, I had to give him an ultimatum. I know every boss has to take a firm hand sometimes, but it did seem to me he spent much of his time fighting the fact he had a woman boss, and trying to assert his own control. It's very tiring having to deal with that nonsense.'

Agnes agrees. She appointed a new male member of staff to a health service clinic. A series of confrontations ensued.

'He seemed to think that because he was the only man around, he could challenge any decision I came to. Every meeting was a battle, which I'm not used to because we work together and decide together how best to proceed. For some reason he thought this indicated I was weak. He'll learn. In the end I told him straight. Stick to your onions, laddo, you know what you've been hired to do, and you haven't been hired to run this place. Argue? God, that man must be surrounded by lamed donkeys. I can't be doing with this kind of hassle.'

One purpose of the Gender Game as played by the male subordinate is to wear his boss out, undermine her confidence, ensure that everyone realises no woman can be as good as a man in a man's world. Most of the women I interviewed found that their first experience of dealing with male staff was exhausting, and they were inclined to wonder if they were doing things wrong. Further experience, though, showed them that men always do seem to argue more with a woman boss. Never having actually heard the term Gender Game, they nevertheless began to see that they were on the receiving end of a power ploy, and they stopped letting it worry them. Joan is office manager in a medium-sized manufacturing plant, with several male subordinates. She tends to look harassed a great deal of the time, but claims that after years of experience, the men are no real problem:

'There's Ted in the print room, he'll argue as a matter of course whenever you give him a new job. I can't give you an example, there are just so many, I take no notice. When he's had his say, off he goes and the job is done. That's what counts. It's the same with all of them. Lighten up, I tell them. Be glad I'm not giving you your cards.'

So Joan obliquely reminds them of her powers, and the men's attempts at playing the Gender Game lose out to the demands of hierarchy.

Through the Looking-Glass

Various psychological studies have shown that women tend to be more considerate, understanding and generally nicer to their subordinates than do men. Women who have internalised the general assumption that women are caring and nurturing are more likely to bring these attitudes into the workplace than not. Many influential writers and occupational psychologists and pundits in the media agree that women in management have a special nurturing style. Occupational psychologist Beverly Alimo-Metcalfe writes:

> The manager of the future is a listening, sensitive individual with highly developed personal skills with which to manage an increasingly troubled workforce. S/he has a vision, which incorporates an understanding of culture and quality, with the key skill of being able to empower subordinates to take risks in the pursuit of corporate goals. Research demonstrates that women favour these kinds of management styles.[13]

Not everyone agrees that women are good with people, however. A study of 'a mixed group of 711 male and female Chief Executive Officers (CEOs)' in the US and published as an American Management Association Monograph, found that women are 'task-oriented', and emphasise analytical, thinking qualities and personal drive, summed up as 'an individualistic style'.[14] The men, on the other hand, 'value strategic planning, decision-making and working effectively in teams'. Women but not men considered developing political skills essential.

Psychologist Andrew Kakabadse suggests that women CEOs' individualistic work style could 'unwittingly' lead to tensions between executives, and that they need training in self-understanding. If, as women are quoted as saying, they don't want to be 'identified as a corporate animal', this is likely to demotivate the workforce. He writes,

> From the subordinate's viewpoint, the attitude could be, 'If *they* don't care, why should I?'[15]

Note the subtle introduction of the word 'care' where it can be understood as criticising the woman executive. The men are not expected to be 'caring', they talk of 'working in teams'. In malespeak, 'teamwork' is men showing how well they get on with each other, and being 'a corporate animal' shows how much you value (care about?) your job. Valuing 'strategic planning' means showing concern for corporate aims – how could any top executive, female or male, *not* value planning?

My interpretation of these findings is rather different. In my own research, I found that people point out to the investigator those aspects of their approach which they believe they cannot leave unsaid. Thus men, in interviews, talk of the need to take account of people's feelings in negotiations, and very rarely emphasise their ability to think rationally and argue logically. Stereotypes *assume* that men are logical and rational, so they don't need to say so, and this becomes quite clear from their brief and laconic references to facts and evidence: the brevity of their comments surely cannot be taken to mean they don't value facts and evidence, simply that any unadorned mention means they take their importance for granted. Similarly, women rarely talk of being concerned for people's feelings in a work situation, as they seem to assume that this can be understood; they tend to focus on their cool, calm command of the situation, their rationality, and where up against men in any formal situation, their strength of mind and assertiveness. When pushed, men will say they are reasonable and co-operative, while women will say they are cool and unemotional. In other words, they emphasise those areas where they know they are *seen* to have problems.

In the CEO study, women emphasised task attainment and their own analytical powers because they were perfectly aware of the stereotypical assumption that women focus on people and feelings, and are irrational. But precisely because they did *not* focus on people and feelings in their replies, they are then criticised for not being good at getting on with people. Men who know that their upbringing has emphasised individual achievement and competitiveness focus on team spirit, because this is their problem area. And because the researchers are men, and the executives for whom they are writing are mostly men, they are able to interpret what the male CEOs said in the way they intended, while interpreting what the female CEOs said in a way which highlights their difference – and probable inadequacy.

This tendency for the researcher to interpret information

according to a prior mind-set is a crucial point. It is particularly noticeable that it is almost always studies by men that see women as inadequate, and studies by women who see them as offering qualities that men 'need'. While I am all for revaluing what is stereotypically female, in this book I am attempting to reconcile the data, make sense of both points of view. That way, I believe, we will get closer to the truth.

Woman to Woman: Ruling by Consent

Many women pride themselves on *not* using the hard tactics we saw men using with them, and their attitude towards power is more that it is *consensual* rather than coercive. (Remember the brief outline of kinds of power in Part Three.) When it comes to female subordinates, women bosses may get annoyed, but in interview they rarely talk of anger.

Vera is in charge of about twenty people (mostly women) in a private health service provider, and she too appears harassed and stressed. She told me she tries to avoid argument with her staff whenever possible:

'I like to think my staff are happy working for me, and that they can come to me if they have problems. Our bosses are always piling on the work without any warning, and often I feel the pressures are quite unnecessary, so I feel I must protect my staff if I can. I don't think I have arguments – except with people outside the department. I discuss the work with my people and then they know what is needed, and can get on with it.'

Peggy runs a successful boutique in the West Country, with a small staff, all of whom are women:

'I don't have arguments with the staff, they like working here, and we all enjoy working together. Customers are *our* problem. Of course, sometimes there might be a problem about shifts, and I might have to put my foot down if a reasonable discussion doesn't sort it. But they all understand. I am in charge, but I don't push it unless I have to.'

Patricia, who was head of a public relations company until a few years ago, recalls:

'I found that women were not really happy about working for a woman unless they could feel I was on their side. Even joking with them, as the men did, was not the answer. But if I met their complaints and arguments with understanding and sympathy, and avoided any sign of trying to become high and mighty with them, I could have a good fruitful discussion and we'd all be happy.'

This last account may well be the effect of hindsight softening the harsh outlines of reality. Nevertheless, it does appear to be the case that women find they need to use specific strategies to make their hierarchical power acceptable.

Deborah Tannen emphasises the differences in style women and men use to get things done, and this may explain much of the contrast between what women told me in interview, when we could talk about disagreement in general, and their diaries which seemed to report only serious arguments. Tannen shows how women tend to use discussion with their subordinates as a way of ensuring their secretary, PA or other member of staff understands what is required and is willing to carry out the agreed procedure. However, the woman does expect things to be done the way she asks, even if she asks rather than orders. If they are not, and the subordinate argues, she can be very angry.

Lydia is an account executive in a medium-sized advertising agency. Preparing material for a client presentation involves co-operation from a number of people, and she relies on her PA to monitor progress and keep her informed. But she discovered that her PA hated progress-chasing because the creative people in the Design Department would shout at her; so she would pretend all was fine, and hope, and all was fine until one particular day when it wasn't. Lydia explains:

'I was absolutely furious. The client meeting was set up and the ads were not ready, and it was only because I had a sneaking worry about no activity in my office that I managed to pick up on it. Why couldn't she have said something? If she hates chasing people, I'd have thought, she's so good at everything else, I could sort some other way of getting the information. But this really let me down. If she had apologised and appeared to realise what she had done, I could have taken it, but her response to the whole situation was to defend herself by saying progress-chasing was a waste of time. Now I wonder what other areas she's pretending about. You can't have a personal assistant you can't rely on.'

The consensual approach does assume good will and honesty on both sides: if Lydia used this technique and her PA was afraid to confess to wanting to avoid the design people, then Lydia inevitably feels she has been deliberately deceived when the hidden fear comes out. This sense of deception arises whenever a subordinate claims 'I wasn't told to do that' or 'I think it's a waste of time' and leads to high levels of anger, and comments like: 'If she'd only pay attention the first time, there wouldn't *be* any problem. I explained the job quite clearly' (Jan, factory line supervisor).

Phyllis, a canteen manager, was bothered by an unpleasant smell in the kitchens, which persisted even though Pat, the junior, assured her she had scrubbed out the rubbish bins as instructed. Phyllis was understandably angry when she found Pat had lied, and the bins *were* the source of the stench:

'I asked her why she had told me she had cleaned them out properly when this was not true. She said she thought I was too fussy, and she didn't see why she need do it. I pointed out I had thrown good meat out, in case it was the source, because I had trusted her. She just shrugged. I don't understand her attitude, but she'll have to go.'

I think most people would agree that when a woman (or a man) fails to do properly a job for which she (or he) is being paid, and then argues to defend herself (himself), anger is understandable. The sad thing is that some of these disputes are ending with the subordinate finding herself out of a job, because she has failed to understand her responsibility to her immediate boss. Some women do have a problem with following instructions they think are mistaken or unnecessary, especially if the instruction comes from a woman.

This is an example of women going along with the male Gender Game unaware that its purpose is to benefit *men*. It is the reflection of an attitude which says women should provide a service, and men should give the orders. Lots of women believe this too because they have never examined the bases for this belief, and so they resent having to carry out the instructions of a woman. They feel but cannot say (because that would reveal its absurdity): 'Who does she think she is, giving me orders? She thinks she's so wonderful. But I know better.'

Not every woman believes in consensus, of course: indeed, Margaret Thatcher argued, when Britain's Prime Minister, that aiming at consensus is 'wet'. And as one woman financial manager said:

> 'It's pleasant to be liked, but there's a job to do. A woman who doesn't understand that she must do as I say because I say so has no place in my department.'

Women who take this tougher approach may find their subordinates resist unless they have the real clout that comes with being Prime Minister or chief executive of an organisation. Dr Helena Daly, a consultant haematologist at Treliske Hospital in Cornwall, discovered that modelling her behaviour on her male teachers led to disaster. Whereas male doctors could 'bark orders' and expect immediate compliance, she found the nurses simply would not do as she said. Her forceful approach eventually led to her being sacked (in July 1993) on the grounds that she upset nurses by her brusque manner, and was 'rude'. I have never come across a man being fired because he was 'rude' to subordinates, though heaven knows that many men *are* offensive and gratuitously insulting. Dr Daly is not alone: other women have been sacked because of their abrasive manner in a wide variety of occupations, from editor of a provincial newspaper to supervisor on a factory production line. While men can *choose* whether to be authoritarian or not without losing the services of their female staff (even if women don't *like* being ordered about), women in charge of female staff can find themselves more or less forced into adopting a style that reflects underlying assumptions about women's nature if they are to get co-operation. Women expect other women to be considerate of feelings and relationships, whoever they are.

The Female Gender Game 1: 'I'll Be Mother'

Muriel is in her fifties, and runs a hotel in a holiday area. Her work is seasonal, and so she finds she must hire staff for the summer and then lay them off, on a regular basis.

'These days, men down here have such a hard time finding work they are willing to take on jobs they'd have left to their wives in the past. I like to have a mixed staff, so I have been taking on men for the dining room and the kitchen, but it does seem to have created difficulties I could do without. They seem to resent doing what they think is women's work and they seem to resent that they have to do what I say – and they do, let me tell you. I feel worn out sometimes in a way I never used to when the staff were all women. Arguments all the time that I never have with women.

'What I have found is if I treat them all like children with me as the all-embracing Mum, then they are all happy. That's something they can understand, me as a mother figure. So – who cares? If it makes them happy. So long as they do the job, I don't mind acting warm and caring.'

Despite the slightly veiled contempt with which so many people talk of their mothers, women who adopt warm motherly personas are more likely to reach and hang on to powerful positions, whether in business or in government. During the 1970s and early 1980s, the maternal leadership qualities of Golda Meir, who was for so long a leading political figure in Israel, were cited as an inspiration by women in America and in Europe.[16] She was respected, powerful and widely beloved; too old to be a sexual object (she became Prime Minister at 70, saying firmly 'Being seventy is not a sin'),[17] she was widely seen as a mother figure, and even after her death in 1978, her influence lived on. As a candidate for the US Senate told social psychologist, M. Hadley, 'It is when you want to break away from this momma leader model that the problems start.'[18]

It may be objected that Meir's 'motherliness' was just a front, because in reality, in her everyday working life, she was 'domineering'. I would make two comments on this. First, of course her motherly persona was a front, because every politician and every leader – or indeed, every person who attracts any kind of attention – has to develop a public persona, and it might as well be one that works. In a very similar way, Barbara Bush ensured her popularity with the voting public by adopting the persona of 'First Granny' ('She's won the heart of a nation,' wrote journalist Joy Billington).[19] Women as mothers and grandmothers are acceptable in decision-making situations because they are expected to make decisions which are in the best interests of their adopted children. In passing, we may note that Hillary Clinton's big mistake was to aim at a more modern image of the First Lady by presenting herself as a strong woman, equal in intellect to the President, and a reformer in her own right: while feminists applauded, she was widely seen by the voting American public as 'a bossy domineering upstart'.[20] The implications of the Gender Game are that leaders who depend on votes, and bosses who depend on co-operation, have to accommodate the prejudices and assumptions of those whose support they need.

Second, any deviation from the anticipated 'motherly' behaviour is bound to be seen as bossy and domineering. Some women bosses are tough, abrasive and autocratic. Many more, though, are likely to be *seen* in this light because they are simply failing to behave with the expected warmth.

As more women have moved into management positions, the possibility of viewing them all as 'maternal' has receded. Those who in reality are mothers of children tend to make a separation between their maternal behaviour at home and their approach to people at work.[21] And the younger the woman, the less likely it is she wants to be seen as motherly: women in their twenties and thirties want to be appreciated for their skills and competence, not for some stereotypical gender role that they may or may not approve. Nevertheless, when French psychologist Erika Apfelbaum carried out a major study of successful women in France and in the United States in the 1980s, she found that their gender was always a handicap unless they accepted the need to play mother:

> A woman leader is always in a double bind. Although constantly reminded by her entourage of her gender ... she is simultaneously called upon to suppress, minimize or conceal her womanhood, unless she uses it in a maternal way.[22]

Ella, a financial manager, told me:

> 'It was only when I hit my forties that I started to have problems. I was concentrating on my competence, and realised I was coming across as dominant and frightening – not the way to win people over. I did a bit of experimenting, and realised that men had been able to accept me when I was sexy, but age had caught up. All that was left was some older woman image. Motherly seemed to work best. Warm, caring, I'll take care of your problems. They love it. Who cares, if it works?'

So women find themselves playing the Gender Game in spite of themselves, and ask, why should they care if it works? Because work it does.

The Female Gender Game 2: Sex and Power

Some very successful women choose to play a different version of the Gender Game, one that emphasises sex rather than motherhood. Here I do mean sex. When *Fortune* magazine sought out super-successful women ('the ones who blast through glass ceilings, achieve otherworldly feats, and take astronomical risks to boldly go where no man has gone before'), almost the first point it makes is that the chosen seven 'use their sexuality' to gain and keep their power.[23]

Jill Barad, 45, who made Barbie the world's bestselling toy, expected to become CEO of Mattel, and 'decked out in shocking pink from shoes to suit to lipstick', is quoted as saying

'We never gave up our femininity. We didn't become little men. I don't care to get on an equal footing with men.'

She and Linda Marcelli, a flamboyant curly-haired blonde who heads up Merrill Lynch, New York branch, both take advantage of an odd double standard – they will hug and kiss their clients and their colleagues. Men who touch women risk accusations of sexual harassment; women who touch men create warmth and affection, which is, as we have seen, what women are expected to do.

Age does not inevitably lead to loss of charm either. All the women featured were over 40, and Charlotte Beers, CEO of the advertising agency Ogilvy & Mather, was 61, but according to *Fortune*, 'to most men she's beguiling'. One of her clients is quoted as saying:

'I think a lot of male–female business relationships get stilted. What I like so much about Charlotte is that you can have fun with her.'

And another:

'Charlotte, more than anyone in this business, wants to seduce. There's something deep about Charlotte, and also frivolous. She is a woman, a woman, a woman.'

All these successful women faced opposition and discrimination, bosses who labelled them 'weak', men who refused to work for them, clients who discounted their opinions. All were determined to fight back and not give in. Rebecca Mark, 41, CEO of Enron Development which builds power plants all over the world, says (adopting games terminology) women need to 'roll with the punches':

'You can't take things people say personally. If you do, your confidence goes down, your ego gets in the way, and you don't get the work done.'

What is striking about these women is that they *do* get the work done, even against all the odds. This is what makes the powers that be take notice. That, and the fact they don't blend in. Linda Marcelli says:

'In order to lead in a man's world, you can't be plain vanilla.'

And Charlotte Beers believes a leader should inspire, forget how things 'should be done':

'I believe in provocative disruption.'

Their approach may be fun, but sounds exhausting. It also provides ammunition for those men who fear that women have an unfair advantage in the workplace – but does this matter when most of the unfair advantage at the moment is on the other side? Sexual tension exists whenever women and men have to work together, so that emphasising their sexuality is only making overt what is implicit. These women are playing the Gender Game the way men play – for success and power.

Women tend to resent women who play the Gender Game, just as men seem to resent women who try to become 'one of the boys'. Most women want to be rewarded for doing a good job, whatever it may be, and see playing the Gender Game, especially when it involves flaunting one's sexuality, as letting the side down. Most men, however, prefer women who acknowledge sexual difference: they know where they are when a woman is charming, sexy, warm, demonstrative, emotional and personal.

The Thatcher Factor

Margaret Thatcher, Britain's first – and so far only – woman Prime Minister, also played the Gender Game. Her version was distinctive: the strong sensible woman managing the household accounts appealed to Conservative women, and the charming womanly housewife appealed to men. The media talked of her as a bossy schoolmistress, 'handbagging' her opponents, but this was well into her reign as the longest-serving British Prime Minister this century.

She emphasised her femaleness, was always carefully coiffed and manicured, wore strongly coloured suits and costume jewellery, always carried a handbag. In her early speeches, she would talk of being 'a housewife' and 'balancing her housekeeping'. She discovered quickly what psychologists have long known: a lone outsider in any group has greater influence than one of a minority group, so she quickly dispensed with women in her Cabinet. It was to her advantage in all meetings with men – committees, Cabinet, meetings of Heads of State – to be 'a frock sailing in a sea of suits'.[24] It can be a disadvantage too, of course, as all hostility to the outsider is focused on a single person. But played carefully and well, being a lone woman is better than being one of a tiny band of women who are expected to gang up and threaten the majority of men in some unspecific way. Where two or three women are gathered together, they become 'gaggles of women' or 'covens', and are frightening. A lone woman can charm and cajole as well as use the authority of the schoolroom: accounts of those who worked with her suggest Margaret Thatcher did both.

This did not prevent her male colleagues using their own version of the Gender Game, and conflicts in Cabinet were interpreted by them in the usual way: female boss as irrational, emotional and incompetent. As just one example, here is an extract from Alan Clark's *Diaries* of a meeting in 1988, when he was Minister of Trade:

> As the Prime Minister developed her case she, as it were, auto-fed her own indignation. It was a prototypical example of an argument with a woman – no rational sequence, associative, lateral thinking, jumping rails the whole time.[25]

But Thatcher enjoyed argument, it stimulated her, and like the successful American businesswomen quoted above, she saw consensus as a poor substitute for leadership. On her last appearance in parliament as Prime Minister, knowing that she had lost the leadership battle, she could still argue vigorously and say, 'I'm enjoying this.'

When she was finally ousted, many men breathed a sigh of relief that had nothing to do with her policies. She could be restored to her proper place as the wife of her husband. *Today* put it quite clearly:

> She may have lost the highest office in the land, but Mrs Thatcher is at last regaining the greatest prize any woman can have – her femininity.[26]

She was aware of being seen as 'that woman', not just because of her sex but also because she was lower middle class, fighting both gender stereotypes and establishment consensus:

> My experience is that a number of the men I have dealt with in politics demonstrate precisely those characteristics which they attribute to women – vanity and an inability to make tough decisions. There are also certain kinds of men who simply cannot abide working for a woman. They are quite prepared to make every allowance for the 'weaker sex': but if a woman asks no special privileges and expects to be judged solely by what she is and does, this is found gravely and unforgivably disorienting.[27]

Her memoirs impart a hollow ring to her claim that 'the battle for women's rights has largely been won'.[28] Like many successful women, she was not really concerned about women's rights in general, and critics point to her failure to promote women or to offer them a share of her power.

But, I ask – seriously – why should she be *expected* to look out for other women? She's a politician. Politicians have a goal, in her case a vision of what the country might be. Her political vision was of a nation of individuals all out to achieve their own success without hindrance or impediment. And if she set out to put all those elements every civilised nation needs for its survival – water, electricity, telecommunications, transport, coal, oil, gas, steel, health provision, education, provision for the unemployed and the old – into the hands of private individuals, what on earth could persuade her that women needed special help? Women constitute half the population, a population she saw herself as liberating. She is criticised for suggesting that if she could make it, so could others. But this is the logical consequence of her whole approach. She aimed for success in her own way, and would expect others to do the same. This is the attitude of most women who play the Gender Game.

Playing the Gender Game can be effective for a woman because the workplace is still drenched in gender role assumptions. Women bosses may find being mother suits them best, or they may find that flaunting their sexuality serves better; or they may turn being a housewife or a schoolmistress to advantage. Psychologist Helen Haste told a seminar on images of women:

> A maternal voice reduces all men to 5-year-olds. Very effective if you want to get a point across in a meeting.[29]

Many women become aware of gender role assumptions at work, and are annoyed when they discover how often they have to manoeuvre and be warm and flattering for a man to listen. Over coffee one day, I was discussing my research with two women in senior management, both in their forties. Martha, whose ample figure ensures she is never overlooked, said:

> 'I always come on like a cosy mum. Otherwise, men seem to think they can just turn off, and sometimes that can be really seriously annoying.'

Her friend Ros objected:

> 'To hell with that. I've got kids, I don't want a man to be another one. He can damn well listen or take himself off.'

They both laughed, but later Ros said,

> 'It's much easier if you can caress their egos a bit, you know, make them feel you find them sexually attractive, that sort of thing. Even at work, a bit of a flirt, a bit of sexual innuendo helps. While you've got it, use it, say I.'

Which is fine, I suppose, if you've still got it.

I should not be interpreted as *advocating* that women play the Gender Game. I have simply pointed out that in the workplace as it exists at the moment, it is one effective way of dealing with the disadvantages that confront all women when they start to compete with men and try to blur the boundaries in that Division of Labour. Perhaps it depends whether it is important to you to get your point across, or whether it is more important to you to be treated like a rational human being, not sexual object or earth mother.

Indeed, in my view, to be seen entirely in terms of one's gender role is a form of psychological abuse. Must women really be trapped between the Scylla of being seen as sex object and the Charybdis of being mother figure, always seen in terms of their effect on other people and judged by others' reactions rather than their own abilities?

22

The View from Below: Having a Female Boss

Men Coping with the Bitch

> 'She is patronising and indifferent to your needs and opinions. Keep quiet and shut up! Little boys should be seen and not heard.'

Nigel was extremely angry with his female boss, who apparently gave him a bad job appraisal, 'making me appear foolish and very incompetent'. He reacts to his boss's criticism as though she is treating him like a small boy.

Being given a poor appraisal is galling to anyone, but being given a poor appraisal by a woman can lead to a crisis in confidence. In a survey carried out by *New Woman* in June 1990,[30] men were almost unanimous: no self-respecting man would take orders from a woman younger than himself, and some would 'do anything' to avoid working under a woman of any age. One 32-year-old legal executive said: 'Everyone knows men are cleverer, anyway.'

A similar survey of attitudes to women bosses in the *Independent* in 1992 found that prejudice is still thriving.[31] Let us begin with a splendid set of clichés from surveyor Stephen, 58, who has never in fact worked directly for a woman.

> 'What I don't like is when they get promoted on the basis of what they look like. In one company I worked for, the chairman's PA ended up as a director on the board. The story

was they had connecting rooms whenever they went away on business. I mean, obviously she wasn't director material . . . . On the whole, men are fairer than women, more straight. Women are much more bitchy, particularly with regards to other women.'

Financial analyst Brian, 34, makes it clear how a group of men can exclude a woman boss, and reinforce their own assumptions about her probable reactions:

'I work in a team of men, with a woman manager a bit older than me. She finds it hard to understand how we work together, the banter, the names we call each other. She doesn't say anything, but you get the impression she disapproves. She has very fixed ideas – she's not interested in other people's points of view. She'll ask for suggestions, then ignore them. Then it gets confrontational. In the end you have to agree because arguing gets you nowhere.'

Note that 'it gets confrontational': as we saw earlier, many women bosses report that their male subordinates argue about everything. Not only do younger men tend to see argument as a contest they must win, those not reconciled to ideas of equality find having to submit to a woman because she is the boss extremely galling. Rosalind Miles suggests that 'men feel subtly outraged at having to compete with women',[32] and this outrage is undoubtedly enhanced when she proves she is winning by being the boss. This shared sense of justified resentment no doubt fuels the subtle aggression of this 'team of men' as every joke and instance of name-calling reinforces their sense of solidarity against this unwanted outsider.

John, a 30-year-old health service manager, said:

'As I've gained in seniority and competence I've put forward my own views, but professional differences of opinion become conflict. She perceives it as a personal threat and finds it difficult to accept an alternative opinion. She immediately takes on an offended tone of voice and sometimes it ends in tears.'

Does John's boss break down in tears? Or does he just assume she does when she walks away? No woman I ever met said she had broken down in tears at work, though one woman did say she had to take refuge in the Ladies on one occasion because she was afraid she might. No woman in any position of authority is likely, on the balance of probabilities, to start weeping because one of her staff disagrees with her. Perhaps those tears are not literal tears, but an echo of that phrase so often used in our childhood: it will all end in tears. It echoes, too, the cliché that women are always liable to burst into tears, and is yet another move in the Gender Game.

Women bosses are an intrusion. While the Division of Labour permits women in business where they are providing a caring service for those doing the real work, it should exclude women from any situation which requires them to make decisions and especially to assess a man's work. Calling on clichés that belittle women may make coping that much easier: so Nigel summons up images of the cruel mother or schoolmistress for whom 'little boys must be seen and not heard', while John calls on that other cliché that 'women are emotional and tend to burst into tears'. There are plenty more: 'women are unable to take criticism'; 'women are illogical and unable to follow an argument'; 'women use unfair tactics'; 'women nag'.

Seeing any woman in authority in terms of a small set of stereotypes is also part of the Gender Game. There are not many situations in which a male expects to have to do what a woman wants: there's Mother, Big Sister perhaps, Schoolmistress. So having to obey a woman is easily construed as being positioned as a small boy – which is, of course, experienced as an insult. So any woman who attempts to enforce her authority can then be seen as being offensive.

Gavin, a computer operator, wrote:

'She always thinks she knows best, and is never prepared to listen when she's definitely got it wrong. She is the rudest bloody cow I have ever met.'

Gavin's boss *might* have been rude, but in my experience women are likely to be seen as offensive whenever they omit to project themselves as warm, caring and conciliatory. A woman boss is

sume the worst when she isn't clear about something, all she
...s to do is ask. As it was, she had to back down when
...nfronted with the facts.'

...lla, a nursing sister in her forties, was extremely angry after an
...ment about 'classified information':

double-checked the data, pointed same out and the facts were
...disputable. I was right. To have ignored it the consequences
...ould have been very grave. I was very justified.'

...e information being classified, it is impossible to know what this
...ument was really about, but it is clear that Fenella felt her boss
... was completely in the wrong. Women are often disgruntled
...ause they are inclined to think their women bosses may not be
... to their jobs. This is the other side of the assumption that
...men are motherly and caring: as we saw in Part Two, mothers
... not seen as very bright either.
...Not all disputes between women and their female bosses are of
...at order. Women may fear the other is abusing her power. Susan
...ported an argument with her supervisor which she explained in
...rms of 'bloodymindedness', though whose she meant was not
...ear:

'It appeared I was to be exploited. I did not want this to
happen.'

...dith too was extremely angry when she found:

'I had been "inadvertently" omitted from the interviewing
panel. The applicants were to be involved in my department, and
I have always been on the panel before. This is internal policy
and she knew it. I felt justified in arguing. And I won.'

...British newspapers in December 1996 were full of the story of a
...deputy nursing sister at a famous public school reportedly 'flying
...nto a rage' when reprimanded by her superior. Mrs H., the
...enior sister at the school, told a tribunal she had dismissed her
...deputy, Mrs E., because, she claimed, Mrs E. had consistently under-
...mined her authority, refused to recognise her as her superior and

expected to inspire liking and affection – as a mother should.[33]
When one of her subordinates gets upset at her exercise of
authority, it is the woman who is at fault. Both Gavin and Nigel
know this, and turn to the woman's own boss, who in each case is
a man. Gavin gets more satisfaction:

'He sent her a sharp memo, which upset her no end. She was
pretty mad. I thought it was great. One of us is on the way out.'

Nigel, though, found that things did not go well for him: we will
meet him again in the next chapter as he copes with the male as
boss. And Gavin's victory was short-lived, as we will see: women
may be unwelcome in the hierarchy from the point of view of the
subordinate, but those in charge do not want them overturned.

Woman to Woman: Bitch or Human Being?

Though there is a widespread myth that women are bitchy to other
women, this is not the picture I found when women talk about
their women bosses. To give just one example, Karen, a charity
community worker, said:

'I work for a woman boss at the moment. She's older than me, in
her late fifties. It's been very good . . . . All my other experience
has been with male bosses. She's very honest with me; there is
no kind of hidden agenda. She's more truthful as regards the
hierarchy, and more open. With men it's a lot more political.
She'll tell me what I need to know. I trust her. She's also very
loyal – she doesn't join in with any bitching.'

One reader has suggested that perhaps more women in *middle*
management use a considerate, caring style towards their subordinates, whereas women at the very top are just as authoritarian as
male bosses, 'but they get more flak for it'. This may be the case, as
wielding real power can bring its own consequences. However
much a woman like Golda Meir or Margaret Thatcher may wish to
project an image of 'mother' or 'housewife', the realities of
premiership require the kind of decision-making that leads their
subordinates to speak of them as 'domineering'. Furthermore,

power over others can lead to belief in one's own superiority and the others' inadequacy: as Lord Acton wrote, 'Power tends to corrupt.'[34] But the majority of women dealing with subordinates are not in seriously powerful positions: they are supervisors or managers or running small businesses, and most have bosses of their own to whom they are responsible. These are the kinds of bosses who are being talked of here.

One disadvantage the woman boss has is that her considerate and non-bitchy behaviour is simply accepted as what one would expect, and not really noticed unless her subordinates have had previous bad experiences, or some psychologist asks questions. But not every woman boss adopts a 'listening, sensitive' management style, and if she does *not*, she is liable to incur strong criticism. The very fact that she does not behave as a woman is expected to behave leaves her open to accusations of being bitchy, and even of 'being inhuman'. Janice said of her office supervisor:

'She doesn't seem to care about us as people. Shirley, her deputy, always asks after the children. I'd much rather work for her.'

I asked if she would expect a man to ask after the children, but she claimed the men in the office were 'more human – you can talk to them'. She did add:

'It's more of a surprise when a man asks how you are. You expect it of a woman somehow.'

Women bosses are also quite often seen as incompetent by their female subordinates, who talk of them as 'muddled' or say they 'don't give a straight answer'. Ann, talking about the office supervisor, said:

'She seems to find it impossible to make up her mind about anything. I like to know exactly what she wants me to do, but I find she is constantly changing her mind. And then she gets mad with me for not listening.'

Sharon, a PR executive, told me:

'My boss is so overworked, her desk looks like a building site.

But she just doesn't know how to delegate. hold of every last detail, and then when y decision on something, she has to go away an boss. It's a terrible waste of time.'

Sharon eventually decided to go straight to wl were made, and did in fact succeed in getting the changed, so that she now reports direct to the off surprisingly, this led to a confrontation with Ja boss.

'She was hopping mad, but I calmed her down i is no question of my being on the same level as think is what she was worried about. I explaine she was terribly overworked, and that her life v easier if she didn't have to worry about PR too – anyway, and it was only a hierarchy thing. I just to get on with my job.'

'Only a hierarchy thing' *is* the way women often see in the office, improbable though this must seem to aln Lots of women are aware of the realities of power, ar of it themselves. But many others think that being un freely between levels on that staircase of power ju being able to do your work properly. Before you ge woman in your office who ignores all established cor lines, it is worth trying to find out if she understands there in the first place. She may not be seeking power

When talking to me, women tend to emphasise reasonableness and their ability to 'calm her down' whe starts raising a storm. Their diary reports, though, sho can get extremely angry with their female boss. Perh: female bosses are fewer than male ones, there were arguments recorded in diaries, but those there were w heated and angry. Pauline, in middle management, was when her boss queried her holiday dates:

'It's outrageous that she should suggest I am taking than I am entitled to. I don't know why she sho

refused to obey instructions; when she took the matter up with her, Mrs E. had, she alleged, assaulted her.

'She called me a bitch and then brought her arm up. I ducked to try to avoid the blow but she caught me with her fingertips.'

Mrs E. claimed unfair dismissal, and that Mrs H. had wanted to get rid of her. Her representative asked:

'Why would you not accept an apology that she lost her temper?'[35]

Presumably a combined physical and verbal assault requires something more than saying 'I'm sorry'. Such events are fortunately rare.

Rage between women usually seems to arise either when the subordinate has been criticised in her work, or when she simply does not believe her boss should be her boss at all, and perhaps that she could do the job better if only given a chance. Even if this recalls young women's fury at being told what to do by their mothers, there is nothing typically female about thinking you can do better than your boss. Men think that too.

23

The View from Below: Having a Male Boss

Man to Man: 'Your Boss is a Baboon'

Though seeing a male boss as 'a baboon' is not quite as clichéd as seeing a female boss as a bitch, the general attitude it sums up is widely understood. Paul Mungo, the writer of the article[36] from which this title is taken, claims that office politics are based on the animal instinct to struggle for dominance:

> By and large, we are just fairly sophisticated brainy primates with big penises.

No, a woman cannot be a baboon.

> Among baboons the leader is the sleekest and best-groomed. In offices, the boss is the one with the best suit, the silkiest tie . . . . Baboon leaders react vigorously to challenges, demonstrate just who's boss by aggressive behaviour . . . . They are decisive – any decision, not necessarily the correct one, is paramount.

Baboon leaders can't make a mistake, though human bosses obviously can. But if they do, well they always have a subordinate to take the blame. The message of the article is, 'Be glad if your boss is a baboon, it's normal business behaviour. It's time to look for another job if he starts behaving like a human being.' A staggering statement.

Mike's diary does give the impression he is operating in a jungle, and he might well accept an image of his own boss as posturing primate. He reports a series of arguments with his boss during the week, starting on Monday morning with a dispute about a report Mike had written:

'I had included some sensitive financial data in my report to senior management, to make a point about the way our business is run. Boss wanted to conceal the information. He was not prepared to listen.'

Arguments with a subordinate are seen as challenges, to which the boss responds vigorously. Mike's next confrontation was that afternoon, during a 'normal review of business development':

'We argued about customer acceptance of new products. He was so angry he was only interested in shouting and recrimination, so logical argument was pointless.'

Next day, there is another confrontation:

'Sales performance is poor – therefore no matter how efficient our planning, the results did not happen.'

The arguments are strong, sometimes heated, and Mike is very angry each time. He does not get his point across on any occasion. By the end of the week, when Mike is trying to express some fresh ideas about contacting new customers, his boss doesn't want to know:

'He was not interested, was not really listening.'

But Mike continues to present himself as concerned about the business, and even though he was 'very angry' and dealing with a boss who apparently did not listen to him, he did not use the language of outrage some of the women used when reporting arguments with their women bosses. There is a greater acceptance among all the men who sent diaries, or whom I interviewed, that argument is one of the things you expect from your male superior.

Indeed, anger was often not a problem, as subordinates were not always expecting to convince the boss anyway. Colin, a 25-year-old computer programmer, wrote:

'I got the point across only in the sense that he understood my reasons; but he did not accept that they were correct. We agreed to disagree because when the program is written, it will speak for itself. I argued because I felt I had a valid point; and also, if I am correct, it will mean large problems for the practicality of the programs we are currently writing.'

Sometimes the point of the argument is that the subordinate wants something the boss has not yet decided to give: more resources, more staff, special equipment. These negotiations are usually low key, because as Andy, an animal researcher, put it: 'I wanted to do a project using this technique and if he dismissed the procedure he wouldn't help me do it.'

Market forces can have a powerful impact at all levels, so that the boss has a strong incentive to make sure he and his subordinates are working to the same goals. In other fields, like academic research for instance, the man in authority may be expected to give assistance to his researchers without necessarily gaining any clear career benefit himself. In such circumstances, communications can be difficult. Leslie, a researcher in psychology, told me that getting his supervisor to listen was a problem:

'Depends how bored he is, he's often unwilling to put in the necessary commitment.'

Ian, another psychologist, said that arguments in this relationship are difficult to resolve, and he recalled a difference he had with his own supervisor:

'We started with different assumptions. The argument was resolved with a joke. As always, one of us appears to give way. The arguing has stopped, but the argument has not.'

Clearly the academic does not behave aggressively 'like a baboon' when arguing about research. Indeed, even more than in almost any other profession, criticism, challenge and debate are expected among those involved in scientific research, and as Estelle Phillips and D.S. Pugh put it, 'this non-deferential activity is an accepted part of the academic process'.[37] The Canadian psychologist Ben Slugoski, talking about arguing with his superior, told me:

'I would never get angry over academic issues; both stands in the eyes of God are wrong.'

This does not mean that academic arguments do not matter, nor that they never create upset and ill-feeling, nor indeed that superiors do not try to impose their views on their subordinates. Arguments among scientists and academics can be very important and can lead to anger and strong resentment, though this is usually among equals. Many a superior has been known to dominate his researchers, but the subordinate seems to accept this as a way of life and show no anger. John McKinlay, a medical statistician, explains:

'The high-testosterone male attempts to influence and control other people. He likes to win arguments.'

Whether this is because of his testosterone or whether it is because men *expect* to try to dominate is not clear, but men's belief that this is typically male behaviour reinforces that behaviour wherever it can be seen to work.

Being a male boss is certainly easier than being a female one, if what one's subordinates say about their relationships is anything to go by. The only time that a male subordinate in my research showed any sign of outrage and resentment was when his future appeared to be in jeopardy.

The wretched Nigel, whose female supervisor had given him a poor job appraisal, recorded the arguments he had with her superior, and finally with the Head of Department, both male. His first encounter with his supervisor's boss was very distressing:

'He is the boss and a right "know-all". Over-confident and very arrogant. Makes you feel small. He is big-headed and towers over you. He went on about my work programme and the details of my duties. I was very angry, and felt dim and weak-willed.'

This unsatisfactory encounter culminated in a meeting with the Head of Department, but Nigel explained that he couldn't get him to understand:

'His authority and seeing himself as a father figure. He has had different experiences from myself. His approach is narrower than mine whilst I am more open-minded.'

Nigel's diary does not record how this sad affair ended, but it seems pretty clear that his attempts to go over the head of his female boss did not achieve his aim of changing her appraisal. His defensive comments after the last encounter, and his self-serving claim to be more 'open-minded' suggest he was probably given an ultimatum: shape up or get out. There is, in fact, evidence in this diary that the writer is deeply disturbed: this could be because he knows his job is on the line, or because of more long-standing problems. Argument diaries which record everyday conflicts and people's reactions to them could well be used in the diagnosis and treatment of many communication disorders.

Men rarely talk of being friendly with their boss, even though the boss may talk of being on friendly terms with his staff. Being a subordinate is something of which they are constantly aware. Terry, the Head of Department we met in the section on bosses arguing with their subordinates, told me of an argument he had with his own boss, the Head of the school. This was, he said, 'completely absurd':

'I was teaching a particular play at A-level, and it came in a paperback with two other plays not on the syllabus. Apparently a parent complained that one of the other plays contained swearing and the Head wanted me to go through all 22 books inking out all the "fucks". I pointed out that this would simply draw attention to what he wanted to hide, and the chances were much greater that none of the students would even look at the other plays otherwise. They don't usually read *more* than one asks! But the best compromise I could get was that I would go through a "master copy" blacking out all the words he wanted to hide, and some other unfortunate from the office would take my copy and censor the rest of the books. I certainly wasn't prepared to waste my time, and he accepted that. My 6th form thought it a great joke. Of course. The man meant well.'

No, he didn't remember being angry. It was so absurd, he thought it almost amusing. Why did he go along with the censorship? Well, the Head was his boss, and he had the right to issue an order, however ridiculous. Did he act like a baboon, metaphorically beating his chest and strutting to show his power? Terry obviously found the picture hilarious. When he stopped laughing, he explained:

'He's always oversensitive to complaints from parents, however ridiculous. If I were in his shoes, I would act differently. But I would never undermine his authority. He is the Head.'

Which brings us back to the beginning of Chapter 20, where we saw that men understand and accept hierarchies. Terry negotiated a compromise with the Head, but would not actually refuse to do something he thought absurd because he accepts the Head's authority *as* Head. So some men may act like baboons in the jungle, and it seems likely that the pressures of commercial organisations encourage aggressive behaviour. But certainly not every boss behaves that way, it is not a *sine qua non* of being a boss. The important thing is that subordinates accept the authority of the man in charge, even if, as Terry suggests, they are certain they would do the job better.

Keeping Cool: Women and the Male Boss

Most working women have a male boss somewhere in the offing, even if he is not their immediate superior. Most women, too, pride themselves on getting along well with their boss. They claim that they can usually get their male superior to listen to their point of view, and this is because they are careful to keep cool, calm and rational. Valerie persuaded her boss of the validity of her approach, 'By being non-emotional, rational, articulate and confident, and knowing how to show flaws in his arguments.' Valerie is an academic researcher, which may explain why it was acceptable for her to show 'flaws' in her superior's arguments. But women in business use the same kind of explanation. Irene said she was able to convince her superior:

'I had carefully thought out my position and was able to present it calmly and rationally.'

Sharon, who persuaded her male boss to shift the lines of command, told me:

'I was very cool, calm and collected when I approached him because I knew his first reaction might be anger. But when I outlined my reasons, he could see the logic, and accepted what I said.'

Kathryn, a social worker, successfully persuaded her boss that his plans for dealing with a problem family would be less successful than her own ideas:

'I knew where he was coming from so could adapt my argument to his framework. When I translated my ideas into his language, he could see the logic, and agreed to my plan.'

All these women are emphasising their own logic and rationality in a way which none of the women arguing with a female boss ever did. Their assumptions are that when dealing with a man they must be cool, unemotional, and use reason and logic: when dealing with a woman they were much more inclined to talk about their anger and resentment.

Why was this? Do women not feel angry with a male boss? Of course, they do.

Anger does not arise simply because people feel pressured or misunderstood: it can arise out of deep conviction. Fiona is another social worker, whose boss wanted to undertake a project with which she disagreed in principle. In her diary she wrote:

'This argument was temperate but I felt like having a blazing row. He is a supervisor who is not very amenable to argument, particularly from a female! I didn't feel I could push my point too strongly as he is my superior. Also the set-up was rather formal, and it is not the done thing to argue too much. He probably wouldn't have agreed with me anyway. But I couldn't let him get away with the smug statements he was making. I couldn't just sit there and say nothing as I felt incensed.'

However, work pressure and relationships are the usual cause of anger. Rosemary, an office administrator in her twenties, told me she never has arguments with anyone at work, except her boss, who makes her mad.

'He gets so emotional, flies off the handle at the least thing. The problem is, he's short of patience, and gets angry with everyone. It doesn't bother me. I get mad with him for five minutes, I've inadvertently rung one of his bells and he reacts. But it's all over pretty soon. He knows he's impatient. We can live with it.'

Mary, a marketing manager in her mid-thirties, has an 'emotional' boss too.

'He gets upset at the least thing, so one has to be careful, that's all. The thing is he really doesn't like to be taken by surprise. I get angry, he gets angry, but it doesn't go anywhere. I can't say exactly what I think because he won't take it. So if I get angry, I try to keep it to myself.'

Why do these women talk of their bosses being 'emotional'? After all, that is surely a cliché more often applied to women? But as we saw earlier, men tend to get very angry with their argumentative subordinates, and they do not appear to have any compunction about showing it. The women subjected to this anger are more than likely to experience it as an emotional outburst or irrational temper tantrum they must somehow learn to live with.

Self-control is the second major theme found in women's accounts of arguing with their male boss. Even at high levels in the hierarchy, they think before they speak, and if speaking firmly is required, they have made the choice. Andrea, for example, who is a senior lecturer in law in one of Britain's universities, had a strong argument with the head of her department because she was extremely angry about what she saw as a crucial topic: 'communication within the department':

'It was the culmination of a series of non-communication problems which I felt were adversely affecting departmental work. He heard, because I used plain speaking without the usual deference. Whether it has any effect is a different matter.'

Naomi is a high-powered computer consultant, whose subordinate

Gavin we saw in the previous chapter complaining that she was 'rude'. She had to exercise considerable self-control when she received her own boss's memo based on Gavin's complaint.

'I was extremely angry, but knew that I had to keep icy cool if I was going to win this one. Gavin is a very arrogant young man, and quite convinced he is too good to have a woman as boss. I suspect he thought he was going to be able to push me out. But this work is, as I had said, quite inadequate and I was not prepared to tolerate his attitude any longer. I explained quietly and clearly, with evidence. My boss saw my point. Fortunately Gavin has been moved out of my department.'

Many younger men do seem to think they can bypass a woman boss, and get her male boss on their side. This may work on occasions, but the balance of probability is against it. The woman has achieved her position because her boss thinks she can do the job, and though he may be willing to listen to another – junior – man when he complains, and may even believe the complaint at first, he is also amenable to persuasion from the woman whom he appointed. Though it is easy for a man to believe that a woman is 'rude' because this is one of the myths about women's incompetence in the workplace, he can quite easily be persuaded that his original decision to appoint the woman was well founded. Since Naomi was carefully calm and polite, using only rational argument to persuade, her boss became convinced that Gavin would be better placed elsewhere.

Women pride themselves on keeping control of their emotions even in the most trying circumstances. Samantha, a marketing executive, recalls that her boss was surprised by her calm reaction when he informed her she was being made redundant. 'He told me that he was making changes that would make me redundant, and was surprised that I remained cool and unemotional; he told me that Beatrice, a woman on the same level as I was, had broken down in tears when confronted by the same arbitrary changes he was now throwing at me. I asked Beatrice about her reaction later: she said, "Of course I didn't burst into tears. I wouldn't give him the satisfaction."' Someone here is building a myth, and I'd put my money on the male desire to perpetuate these myths as part of the Gender Game.

Women are useful, they work hard and they are reliable. But the Gender Game says they are incompetent, emotional and unreliable: these myths are available just in case.

When Nicola Horlick, a £1-million-a-year City high flyer, hit the front pages over a dispute with her boss in January 1997, she may have thought that the international publicity would force the powers that be at Morgan Grenfell to restore her job. But it was a gamble doomed to fail. Whatever the truth behind the accusations flying back and forth between both sides, the one thing a woman in any position cannot do is give any support to the notion that she might be 'temperamental'. Horlick's skills in the management of £billion funds are not in question; nor is it impossible to imagine that colleagues might have been jealous on learning that her boss had offered her the chance to become managing director of Morgan Grenfell Asset Management, the second most important role in the company. A very high flyer indeed. Knives always come out when top jobs are at stake, and this has nothing to do with gender. But a woman is always vulnerable to gender myths, which will be invoked whenever she gives her enemies an opportunity.

Horlick told the press:

'I feel like I've been stabbed in the back for no reason. That's why I'm so upset.'

So, on the front pages of newspapers in London and elsewhere in Europe, she gave ammunition to those who claimed that she was 'emotional' and 'hysterical'. Her bosses, as well as the media, could then see her only as a woman in a man's world, and her past successes counted for much less than she might have hoped. Her dramatic appeal to the media led some commentators to suggest she had 'put the clock back' for women by her antics. No, she didn't burst into tears, and she was tough, 'bloodied but unbowed', as the *Guardian* put it.[38] But she was not cool, she was not dignified, she was not quiet. These appear to be the only ways women can fight the gender myths effectively.

Being seen as a woman is unavoidable, and she did not help her cause by attacking other women, however much she may believe she is 'different'. In an interview in the *Daily Mail*, she is reported to have said:

> 'The reason why there are so few women at the top is because few want to work hard enough. You cannot blame the City for not promoting women. Most women are not cut out for the job. They let themselves down by being pathetic and crying about their work. They whinge and moan instead of applying themselves.'[39]

Sometimes a woman may feel she can win the Gender Game by siding with men and agreeing with their beliefs about women's shortcomings. This will please the game-players, of course, but will also reinforce their other assumptions about all women, high flyers not excluded.

24

Equals: Men Undermining their Female Colleagues

We have seen that women may have to fight gender role assumptions, but they manage to do so effectively a great deal of the time. And if their male subordinates seem to challenge them more than they would a man, and their female subordinates expect them to be warm and caring, well, they can cope with that too. Susan Douglas, when deputy editor of the *Sunday Times*, told me:

> 'I agree that quite often women are regarded as nurturing and caring and that their intelligence is underplayed and underestimated in the face of the former "more dominant" characteristics. Having said that, I cannot say this attitude has impeded me because one merely has to be forceful about correcting such a blinkered viewpoint when it is encountered. Not always easy, I accept. I'm not suggesting women are regarded as equals or that we have made great progress towards equality in the last few decades. But it is in our own hands much more than ever before to seize opportunities and make our own destinies.'[40]

Many of the women we have met so far would probably agree with her.

However, in my first Diary Study, in which it became clear how important gender is in the psychology of argument, I found significant differences in the reports by women and men of arguments with colleagues.[41] They included the following:

(a) Three out of four arguments reported by men with female

colleagues were said to be unsuccessful (she 'did not hear what was said');

(b) Two-thirds of arguments reported by women with male colleagues were claimed successful (he did hear);

(c) Men reported arguments with female colleagues as 'not important';

(d) Women reported arguments with male colleagues about work as 'very important'.

So though the man does not think his female colleague actually listens to him, typically he does not seem to mind: the argument is unimportant anyway. The woman, on the other hand, does think her male colleague hears what she says, and any argument about work is very important to her. This would suggest that women are winning all the arguments in the workplace, and that men are happily conceding. Does that make sense? To anyone? There must be something else going on, otherwise why would Susan Douglas talk of men's 'blinkered viewpoint'?

Let us examine these diary reports a little more closely, and find out what a woman's colleagues say about her in the context of argument. Though hierarchies are important, most people understand that power can distort judgements, so it is the opinions of colleagues that can make or break a person's reputation at work. After all, the assumption goes, who would know better than someone who works with her (or him) and has (one might suppose) no axe to grind?

Male diarists did not report a large number of arguments with female colleagues, but let us begin by seeing what they have to say.

'She took it personally, whereas I was simply passing on feedback from sources other than myself. This was taken that I was critical of decisions made previously by her.'

Martin, the 45-year-old store manager we met earlier, was recording a 'heated' argument about advertising with his female colleague, the marketing manager. She 'misunderstood', but the argument was not important to Martin. She got aerated, but the heat was not because *he* was angry, it was she who got upset because she was unable to remain detached, view the information objectively.

Mike, whom we have also met before, is himself marketing manager for a manufacturer of small consumer electrical goods. He finds himself engaged in a series of battles with other managers on the same level, mostly men, but he did report a couple with women. One was about 'change of management structure':

> 'Unable to allay other person's doubts. I think the proposed management changes are excellent for me.'

This argument was not important to him either, and he was 'not angry at all'. Why should he be? He was happy about the changes. But men rarely seem to be angry when arguing with female colleagues because the issues are such unimportant ones to them. Mike, however, does record a strong argument with a female colleague and he did feel angry this time, because the issue mattered on this occasion. The argument was about 'paying for research':

> 'I wanted to share some data that had already been collected, but do not see why I should buy it. I was seen as being unreasonable/tight-fisted.'

Here Mike was unable to get what he wanted, but the vast majority of the arguments men recorded with female colleagues were seen as unimportant even though the woman did not accept what they said. Computer programmer Trevor argued 'to support the option I considered best', but it didn't matter. As he put it: 'Different people see problems differently.'

Why are men usually so indifferent to whether or not they have convinced the woman? Interviews with women suggest that arguments may be dismissed as unimportant when the man thinks he can get around the issue anyway. Mike could not lay his hands on the data held by his colleague, and so was angry. But when options for action are discussed, very often women will find that their views have been completely ignored, and their male colleagues are doing what they want to do anyway. Vera, who said she needs to protect her staff from the pressures outside her department, told me:

'I don't always feel we get a fair hearing. I know there are enormous financial constraints at the moment, but I never feel that they take any real notice of what I tell them about workloads, not even when I've gone through the figures and they say they agree with them. Nothing seems to change.'

Did she know why this was, I asked?

'I don't really think men listen. I feel my staff are expected to do too much, and I get worn out just arguing the same thing over and over. They *say* they understand, and agree changes. But nothing happens.'

Vera, who is in her fifties, appears to expect the same good will from her male colleagues that she brings to her work. But she is likely to be disappointed, for most men see argument as a game they must win, one way or another. If the woman produces excellent data which clinches the logic of the argument, then perhaps it is better to agree, and then win by letting the matter drop. Younger women seem to catch on to this ploy quite quickly. Jenifer, the successful administrator we met earlier, told me:

'Some of the men here would love to ignore what I say when it means they actually have to *do* something. But I don't let them get away with it. The number of times I've been told, "Oh no, I wouldn't have agreed to that." Or, "Good heavens, it must have slipped my mind." I write it all down, and copyhold everyone. There's no argument then.'

Anna, 28, who works in university administration, told journalist Hester Lacey:

'You have to be prepared to really use your verbal elbows. Once a man just wandered off when I was trying to sort something out with him – just got bored, and decided he wasn't interested. I tend to back everything up with memos.'[42]

This is a good idea. In my communication workshops for women, I always emphasise that if you reach an agreement with a man at work, *get it down on paper*. That way it is much harder for him to 'forget' the agreement you thought you had come to. I myself have frequently found male colleagues, whom I thought I had convinced of the rational necessity of some particular action, say when reminded later: 'Oh, did we agree to that? I quite forget', or even 'I have no memory of discussing this, but if you say so ... I'm sure you're right.'

These lapses of memory may not necessarily all be deliberate. It is very easy to forget something that was not significant in the first place, and that is the single most salient factor to emerge from the diaries: arguments with women colleagues are 'unimportant', and the diarists are detached.

Mike's argument with a female colleague over her refusal to let him have some data is remarkable on two counts: it is the only argument with a woman at work rated 'important' in the diary corpus; and it is the only account in all my research where a man loses an argument that matters to him with a woman colleague and he does not invoke gender stereotypes.

In interviews, remembering a particular argument does entail a certain level of importance for it to be available for recall, and detachment is replaced by gender thinking. When men recount an argument with a woman colleague, they talk of her failure to keep her own emotions out of the work situation. They say things like:

'I tried to use articulate persuasion, and feel a third party would have been swayed to my side. But she was emotionally involved.' (Darren, 24)

'Her own insecurity in her work meant she didn't listen. She took it personally and felt it was an attack on her work, though I made it clear my argument was purely academic.' (Dhuleep, 35)

'Her problem was she was so busy defending herself, she couldn't hear what I was saying. I was being totally constructive, but everything I said was taken as a personal criticism.' (Matt, 32)

Another older man commented in a letter:

'Men are afraid of provoking women – I speak as one of them. I think we think women are much more likely to "fly off the handle" than men are, that is we think that women are much more inclined to take an argument personally than are men. Of course arguments are not necessarily personal – but easily become so. I have noticed that women regularly construe comments as criticisms.'

How often do we hear that a woman 'should not take things so personally'? Why should this be a telling censure of a woman, when we know that men can be just as upset as any woman when their work is under criticism? Conrad, a company secretary, said:

'It is always difficult when a woman cannot remain cool like a man. Even at my level, one finds that women get emotional and take criticism personally. One does expect it, of course, with secretaries and one takes precautions. But one would hope for less emotion at higher levels.'

Contrast this with a comment by Iain Carruthers-Jones, a psychologist who advises companies on interpersonal behaviour:

Women tend to work more with logic, whereas men tend to be authoritarian. Because they use logic, they stay controlled and calm. I can't recall a woman breaking down in tears in the boardroom, but I have seen men getting rather tremulous and red-faced.[43]

And indeed, Conrad began to get agitated and red in the face as he recalled for me his argument with a woman he thought should consider him her superior. She was in charge of an important department, and had argued that he did not have the right to determine her decisions even when she had consulted him for his views. Conrad's apparent attempts to undermine her surreptitiously by going direct to the president had backfired, and the dispute was now being widely discussed within the company. To my surprise, though his body language said otherwise, he *claimed* he was not angry:

'She has chosen to ignore my instructions. I am not suggesting she has acted improperly, but clearer guidelines need to be set up. I should be able to order her to seek a ruling. It cannot be company policy to allow her ruthless ambition to remain unchecked. She is a very aggressive woman, and my colleagues all find her difficult to get on with.'

Women who insist on their right to independent action in spite of colleagues are frequently seen as 'aggressive' and 'difficult to get on with'. Note, too, that 'ruthless ambition' which so upsets Conrad's desire to be in control. Ambition in a woman is often characterised as 'ruthless' when a man is speaking.

This is yet another aspect of the Gender Game.

Playing Dirty

Going over a woman's head or behind her back in an attempt to curb her powers, or even get her thrown out, is more widespread than we realise. A woman in any position where she must take decisions that affect other people's careers is like an Aunt Sally at the fair: a visible and challenging target – and fair game. The Division of Labour expects men to take decisions that affect others, so when a man is seen to be in the way, the game is War: in Chapter 27, we will find men battling with men, and War is not a clean game with gentlemanly rules either. But the Gender Game provides those who wish to remove an inconvenient woman from their path with a whole set of assumptions that make the task easier: she is clearly incompetent (or she wouldn't have made the disputed decision); she is offensive and rude (however gently she may have put the man down, she has still offended him); her personality does not fit (she should not be a position with power in the first place).

Not that the argument is normally couched in sexist terms. We have moved on in recent years, and 'everyone knows' that sexism in the workplace is out. But you can be fairly sure the Gender Game is being played as soon as a man goes over the woman's head and refuses to accept her competence to do the job, compete as an equal or make decisions that affect others. With another man, he might join battle publicly, or he might seek political allies in a covert manoeuvre to oust the other from power. What he will not try is what he tries with a woman, and that is to get her sacked. I have experienced this version of the Gender Game myself: the men involved might well have been angry had I been a man making the same decision, but their resentment appeared to be exacerbated by my being a woman, and they promptly went over my head and tried to get me removed.

You may think this is paranoia, until you experience it yourself, or see it happen to others. This particularly unpleasant form of the Gender Game often brings victory to the men involved, which is why you hear of it so rarely. Occasionally the circumstances are such that members of the public become incensed, and then you may get a *cause célèbre*. Most women, though, try to keep quiet about such attacks, especially if attempts to oust them are successful: even some well-known names who were willing to talk to me for the sake of my research have asked that I not reveal their experiences. These vicious attacks appear to be a new form of sexual harassment, and create the same sense of powerlessness and shame when the victim does not dare say anything.

A middle-aged woman is unlikely to be viewed as sex object, but can always be undermined by whispers of menopause-induced emotionality and lack of judgement. Professor Wendy Savage[44] and Dr Helena Daly are part of a group of forthright medical women who banded together in 1994 to bring out into the open how frequently female doctors who dare to argue with their colleagues are deliberately targeted by what they call 'whispering campaigns'.[45] Accusations frequently include 'dangerous incompetence' and 'emotional instability', even in at least one case 'madness', and the totally irrelevant charge of lesbianism. Such campaigns are not restricted to the medical profession, but may surface in any occupation where groups of men feel threatened by the incursion of competent female rivals, especially when they start to argue for change.

An attractive younger woman who appears ambitious is likely to be seen as dangerous. Some women do use their sexuality in the fight for power, so that any clever and attractive woman is liable to arouse fear and hostility.

The most obvious inference is that, if at all attractive, any woman who achieves a powerful position must have 'slept her way to the top'. As Rosalind Miles put it in *Women and Power*, 'frequently an unspoken assumption arises that if a woman has both power and sexuality, she must be a whore'.[46] This occurs whether the woman is in the public eye, like MP Ann Clwyd or Green Party founder Petra Kelly, both of whom had to sue various publications for libel, or in business, or any area of human endeavour where sexually attractive women also achieve some power. Journalist Ginny Dougary points out:

> New stereotypes were invented for successful women, in a sort of pre-emptive put-down before women, in any significant numbers, had managed to gain a power base .... Advertising agencies coined a new title for the successful career woman: The Executive Tart.[47]

A BBC film about Britain's first three women editors of national newspapers was given the title: *Killer Bimbos on Fleet Street*. The images evoked by these words have a surprising power to determine how the listener/reader interprets whatever a woman so described may then say.

Marilyn Baxter (when director of planning at Saatchi & Saatchi) told journalist Ginny Dougary:

> 'I don't think about my gender when I'm at work. But at Saatchi's, you are constantly having it pointed out to you that you are a woman. The comment is always, "How typically girly", which is insidiously undermining because it's not just about disagreeing with your point of view.'[48]

French psychologist Erika Apfelbaum found that women always feel vulnerable, however high up the ladder they climb.

> Competence is, for women, an absolute must – an *a priori* untrespassable condition for their access to any prominent position. But this does not preclude the awareness that they are denied entitlement .... It is difficult to get full credibility for one's sayings and decisions, and women must continuously reassess the legitimacy of their decisions because their power base is constantly challenged, often with arguments involving personal innuendo.[49]

25

Equals: Women Reasoning with their Male Colleagues

'Our work involves close co-operation, therefore we often disagree on exactly how the work should be carried out. It's research, and we come from different backgrounds, therefore we have somewhat different views. I often tend to push my point strongly because I feel at an advantage coming from a more academic background. But I give in to some extent because he is more experienced. Also it's necessary to compromise somewhat.'

Harriet expresses clearly the conflicts many women experience when arguing with a colleague. On the one hand, she feels she should 'push her point strongly' because she has good reasons to support the position she is taking; on the other, the situation requires compromise, and since she doesn't feel any pressure to *win*, perhaps the compromise should come from her. Yet again, the one thing she really must do is convince everyone she is good at her job, especially when working with a man who is liable to call on stereotypes given half a chance. But then, he knows things she doesn't, so perhaps she should 'give in'.

One might, of course, argue that this is what happens in all situations where equals need to come to a practical solution. Give and take on both sides, both sides happy – that is what negotiations are all about. Except that there is no sign in any of the reports by men that they feel constrained by the need to agree with a female colleague. Nevertheless, women do report that they argue firmly and rationally with men at work, and that they are usually successful in getting their views across because of their calm, logical deployment of the evidence.

'I was able to express my opinions clearly and pick up weak points in his.' (Jane)

'I felt I had a good argument to support my view, and could produce evidence he did not know. He was prepared to listen, and he could follow my reasoning.' (Irene)

'I was very deliberately calm, and was able to show he had missed something important.' (Valerie)

So these women don't see argument at work as a problem. They believe men are willing to listen to them, and they know they are cool, calm and rational, fulfilling all the requirements of a proper approach to debate. As Beryl points out, the force of argument may not persuade the man to change his stance, but he has been persuaded to consider her argument as a possible view:

'He did listen, though I didn't change his opinion. My arguments were reasonable and he couldn't reject them out of hand.'

So why was it that none of the men talking about argument with their female colleagues seemed to acknowledge that they might have been talking sense? Here are women firmly and consistently stating that they are cool, logical and rational, forcefully countering any 'blinkered view' that they are less intelligent and capable of reason. They see themselves as calm and firm. But as we learned in the previous chapter, men see them as either unimportant and to be ignored, or as emotional and taking things personally.

Many men do have problems listening to a woman expound a rational argument. No, let me express that better. Many men have problems hearing that a woman is actually saying anything sensible when she presents it as a rational and logical argument. This is because gender myths hold that women are incapable of arguing rationally and logically, and if she tries to do so, he spends the time he should be listening actually trying to work out what she *really* means, and whether it is worth his while taking any notice. This does not, of course, apply to all men: in particular, we have seen that it does not apply to a male boss who has a vested interest in finding that his appointee is competent, and so he is more open to logical and unemotional persuasion. But a woman's peers often have more vested interest in finding she is not competent, and seeking ways of undermining her. Gender myths are extremely useful here, and a woman who is becoming a nuisance by persisting in an unwelcome argument is easily interpreted as being emotional and difficult.

These criticisms are not always explicit, but most women have probably been told at some time they are 'over-reacting'. Rebecca recalls:

> 'He wouldn't listen. He just had a fixed idea, kept saying "Whatever you say, your behaviour is different." It got very heated because he seemed to think everything I said was me taking it as very personal.'

My interpretation is that when a woman persists in arguing – when she is firm, and attempts to show that his argument is 'weak' or he has 'missed something' – the man finds anger welling up inside him. But where is this emotion coming from? It can't be from inside him, because he is a cool, rational male, and unlike the male boss, he knows he is not in a position to insist she agree. However, he does 'know' (because everyone knows) that women are emotional and take things personally, as well as being not as good at thinking as men anyway. So all that emotion he is aware of must actually be emanating from *her*. He *projects* his emotional response on to her.

You may feel this is hard to credit, but many psychologists, from William James to the present day, believe that interpreting our own feelings is not as straightforward as you might think. We experience physiological symptoms of arousal as a result of environmental stimuli (e.g. a colleague disagrees with a proposal which we want to defend), and it is this arousal which we call emotion. But the physical symptoms of which we become aware are not distinctive, and determining whether the emotion we are feeling is anger or excitement or happiness depends on other clues. A number of careful experiments by American psychologists S. Schachter and J.E. Singer showed quite clearly that the same physiological symptoms of arousal can be interpreted in completely different ways depending on clues in the environment.[50] After an experimental volunteer had been chemically aroused by injection, a confederate of the experimenters joined him; when the confederate behaved in a light-hearted way, the volunteer experienced the arousal as enjoyment and fun, but experienced it as anger when a stooge was aggressive and disagreeable. These and many other experiments lead psychologists to conclude that we learn to interpret what we are feeling by a combination of what we experience physiologically and what we know is happening in the outside world.[51]

We have seen that men tend to characterise argument with a female colleague as 'not important'. If the disagreement is not important, why on earth should he feel angry? And if it is not anger he is feeling, there must be some other explanation for his symptoms. Gender myths are at hand to provide the answer automatically: women are emotional, and so he must be experiencing the backwash from *her* emotion.

Some readers will understandably resist the conclusions of this section, for my research reveals strong patterns in men's accounts of arguments with women that are seriously disturbing. Despite so many women's conviction that they have the good will of their male colleagues, men's accounts of arguments show that women are not yet being treated as equals. Some men are sexist, and undoubtedly many of us recognise some of the worst examples of the Gender Game. But most women believe that they are able to communicate successfully with their male colleagues, and they find it difficult to credit that the generally good relations they have with men in their everyday lives can be distorted and undermined at work by those ancient beliefs in sexual difference. Many of the men with whom women work today still genuinely believe that women are fundamentally different from them, and so unsuited in crucial ways to positions of power and influence.

These are deep-seated beliefs which we will have to work hard to eliminate, especially since it is often to men's advantage that these myths are perpetuated. After all, once a man has acknowledged that women really are his equals at work, the competition for places on the ladder of advancement is immediately doubled. As we will see in the next chapter on men arguing with other men, competition is a prime motivating force in arguments at work, and warfare the name of the game.

I am not suggesting that the men we have met so far are deliberately playing the Gender Game, because many men really do operate with deep-seated beliefs about differences between women and men. These beliefs are not to be confused with the following outrageous bit of sexism.

Alison, who is 32 and in middle management, told journalist Hester Lacey:

> 'I do disagree with men, and I come out ahead. It's because I say what I think, and if I know I'm right, I will stick to my guns. They hate me for it. Even my female friends have suggested that I could try to be more feminine in the way I go about things, but I hate that woman-thing that everyone has to like you. This isn't just at work. I remember when I was a student, I was winning an argument in a seminar and the lecturer made me hold up my hand. "See, her fourth finger is longer than her index finger – a male characteristic," he said.'[52]

So when a woman argues logically 'like a man', she must be aberrant. It is a neat means of having it both ways to suggest that her argument skills show she is unfeminine, and then to 'prove' it by a physical, genetically determined characteristic that has absolutely nothing to do with sex differences: the lecturer's claim about index fingers has no basis in fact. But the hidden meaning, unexpressed but unmistakable, is that supposed masculine traits of logic and rationality are genetically determined. This is a blatant example of the Gender Game masquerading as science.

Women Do Get Angry

So far, I may have appeared to suggest that women never express anger with their male colleagues, but of course that is not so. The vast majority of the arguments women report with male colleagues emphasise women's cool logic and rationality, and since the men appeared to listen and hear, they say they were not angry. However, some arguments are experienced as much more difficult and the women say they were 'extremely angry', whether or not they got their point across. This does not mean they lost their temper, as most of the time the women report the argument as 'temperate': that is, they circle 2 on the 5-point scale for level of heat generated, and 5 on the scale for how they felt even if they did not express it. Once again, we find women hiding their anger when arguing with a man.

Fenella, the ward sister we met arguing with her female boss, was extremely angry with a male colleague about 'selective admission to skeleton staffed ward of a hospital':

> 'The patient was a "high-dependency"-rated case and there was no trained staff available. It was extremely important, and I had to alert medical staff of the shortage of nurses and that patients are being admitted to an "at-risk" situation.'

Even this brief account allows us to understand, I think, that Fenella felt angry at being asked to accept a situation in which patients might be endangered because trained nurses were not available on the ward. She added that she 'felt justified' in insisting that the patient not be admitted. Nevertheless, this argument was only 'temperate'.

Similarly, Kate, who is a management trainee in a big oil company, was very angry that her male colleague had claimed to have done a job she herself had completed:

> 'It had been irritating me all day, and I was very angry as it was very important to me. No, I didn't really get my point across. Lack of time.'

This argument, too, was only temperate. It is also one of the few that was unsuccessful, as women usually believe they succeed in being heard, and Kate explains this by saying that it was only 'lack of time' that was to blame. Patricia, a psychological researcher in her thirties, is one of the very small minority who did not claim to prevail by logic. She said:

'I was just too angry to express myself clearly.'

Unfortunately, as she took part in my very first investigation, I did not ask her what this was about. However, overall it is only arguments with male colleagues that relate to a sense of injustice which arouse extreme anger in women at work, and it is mainly these that are unsuccessful. Bertha, a cleaner employed by a university, sent in a diary report of an argument with a male colleague:

'He suggested that my workload be increased when another colleague retires. I felt this to be unfair, not only have I enough work of my own to do, it did not come from management.'

This argument became 'heated' (level 4) because she did not succeed in getting her views across, and she became extremely angry (level 5) as the issue was understandably extremely important to her (also level 5).

Even those who avoid arguing if they possibly can may find that a feeling of outrage persuades them to voice an opinion. Rena, who is of Asian ethnic origin and born in Britain, told me that her culture inhibits her from arguing on most occasions as it feels 'wrong':

'But I don't feel it is wrong to argue about injustice. Injustice makes me very angry, and I will argue with anyone then.'

She then told me of an occasion when she was outraged by a male colleague's attitude to another woman who was working with them both on a project. She said:

'When I'm angry I can be more forceful. He had to listen then. He was amazed to hear me tell him his behaviour was disgraceful. I felt justified. And he did accept that her work was valuable, as he should have done in the first place. She's a bit of a feminist, and does come across as aggressive sometimes. He didn't like that.'

An interesting comment which seems to leave women in a double-bind. If they are quiet and unassertive, they are liked by their colleagues, but may find themselves taken advantage of – like Vera, and Kate, or Jenifer and Anna before they learned to record agreements on paper. Or they may stand up for themselves, and find themselves labelled 'emotional' by their male colleagues, and 'aggressive' and 'a bit of a feminist' by their female ones.

Let us now look at what women say about arguments with women equals at work.

26

Equals: Women Discussing Differences with Women

Women's criticism of their female colleagues is remarkably rare in my research findings, and as I came to write this I found myself searching for data that are not there. For 'everyone knows' that women are bitchy about each other, find it hard to get along with other women, and we have already seen that women in a superior/subordinate relationship can have problems. But women working together as equals do not show the pattern of resistance and anger that many myths describe. There is a tendency to explain 'aggressive' behaviour by a woman by claiming 'she's a feminist', leaving the listener to infer that of course the speaker is not a feminist herself. As numerous writers have pointed out, women in the workplace expect to be treated as equals, as their feminist sisters have for so long demanded, but try to avoid the label 'feminist' for themselves as far as possible. Mary (the marketing manager we met with the 'emotional boss') sums up the general attitude:

'I wouldn't want anyone to think of me as a feminist. It's too "in the face". I'm not aggressive at work.'

On the whole, women tell me they do not argue with their female colleagues. Sometimes this is because they just want to avoid ill-feeling, and then they simmer, or pour out their frustration to a willing third party. Jane, a research psychologist, told me:

'I tend to find myself in the middle of two sides. I let each have

284

their say, bitch about the other person, and then I might gently point out some points on the other side. In the end I'm left feeling really sad about why people can't get on.'

This is much like the situation described at the end of Part Three, where women get angry with other women whom they expect to provide a service, and may choose to express their anger to someone else rather than confront them, thereby effectively shredding the other woman's reputation. But contrary to expectations, most women talking about their female colleagues are not hostile or critical or bitchy. They just say that mainly they 'don't argue'. When I expressed scepticism, Mary told me:

'I like to get on with everyone. I really don't argue much at work, just with my boss. The men are always willing to listen to a rational argument, so I have no problems there. And with my female colleagues, we just sit down and discuss any differences we might have. It's not a problem.'

Discussing differences is the constant theme. Rita, who is involved in analysis of market research, reported an argument with a colleague about 'statistics':

'We have a good co-operative working relationship and listen to each other. Even if we don't totally agree, we will try to accommodate each other. I didn't totally get my point across because I was too tired to explain some things clearly, but we agreed to discuss further another time.'

Here both women presumably needed to agree, but the argument was merely 'a mild discussion', and no anger was generated. If Rita's colleague was not fully convinced of her reasoning, Rita blamed herself for not explaining adequately, and promised to try again when she was not feeling so tired. It is probable that her colleague too was not upset, for women claim they can 'talk about differences' without feeling threatened.

Women describe their arguments with other women differently from the way they talk of arguments with men. The latter are all explained in terms of women's ability to marshal the evidence and present it coolly, calmly and logically. Unless, of course, the argument is provoked by a sense of injustice, in which case the woman explains that she was 'justified' in arguing very strongly for what she thinks is right.

Disagreements with women, on the other hand, are described in terms of their relationship. Women appear to take a pride in maintaining good relations with their colleagues, and though they stress their rationality in reports of arguments with men, their ability to sit down and discuss differences amicably is what they emphasise with women. This is yet one more reflection of that underlying Division of Labour we keep coming across.

Isobel, a physiotherapist working in a busy hospital, said:

'We rarely have disagreements because we each recognise that we all have our own skills area, and we complement each other. I wouldn't dream of criticising any of my colleagues about their work. That would be the only thing that would make me angry. If we need to discuss treatment of a patient, we just sit down and talk it over.'

Ros, the publisher we met having problems with a male subordinate, told me of two arguments she had with a woman colleague about 'priorities':

'We certainly had different ideas about which jobs might take priority, but since we knew it had to be sorted, we just got together and talked it through. No, we didn't get upset. What would be the point? We were trying to sort out a practical problem in the best possible way so that no one in either of our departments would be unfairly burdened. In the end, we came up with an excellent compromise, I think we both felt rather pleased with ourselves. You can certainly say that if we hadn't been willing to listen to each other we'd never have come up with this solution. It was what I'd call a creative way through.'

So women 'discuss differences' with their women colleagues, just as they do with their close friends, and at work they say that they 'sit down together' and negotiate. Women's culture of caring for relationships does not appear to prevent them from defending their point of view (as some myths would have it), but it also seems to provide them with a way of resolving such differences as they have in a manner that can satisfy both. They need to get their point across, but they do not necessarily need to 'win'.

Mary Parker Follett, an early investigator into the psychology of negotiation, made a distinction between concentrating on demands and solving the basic problem. She reported an argument she herself had with another woman in a library.[53] She wanted the window open, while the other woman wanted it closed: an incompatible pair of goals, until they discovered, by discussing the matter, that Follett wanted to increase the fresh air, while the other woman was concerned that this created an uncomfortable draught that blew papers around. By identifying their real needs, they discovered that both could be satisfied by opening the window in the next room. This approach is now called 'integrative bargaining'.[54] Women's culture seems to foster an approach which seeks a way for both sides of an argument to feel satisfied wherever possible.

Not that arguments between women are always settled so amicably. Just as with their male colleagues, women may get incensed when they feel they have been treated wrongly or with injustice. Felicity reported an argument because:

> 'Someone asked me to do something at work which it was not my job to do. I pointed this out and she became a bit flustered. I was totally right and she knew it. I had been nervous about pointing it out, but was surprised at my own assertiveness. I don't like being taken advantage of.'

Felicity felt very angry, but kept the argument temperate. Her colleague backed down as she found she had made a mistake. No discussion of differences here, though, as Felicity is 'standing up for her rights'. Defending one's rights can lead to strong argument, especially when both sides feel justice is on their side.

Hilda, a schoolteacher in her late fifties, was extremely angry with three of her colleagues who were planning to take 'one whole day' to attend a meeting of the National Union of Teachers in London. She reported that she got her point across

'Because of my indignation on ethical grounds. My concern was that they should show a proper respect for the school's organisation. I saw it as an infringement of contract, involving imposition on colleagues to do their work for them.'

However, her colleagues were equally convinced that they were justified in taking a day off to attend a union meeting, this too on principle. As Sarah, a younger teacher in her early thirties, explained:

'It is extremely important for us to support our union, as the present government has been whittling away at its bargaining power until there isn't much left. Hilda is right that our being away does put an extra burden on the other staff. In the end, we came to a compromise, because tempers were really fraying. Just one of us went, which meant the workload wasn't too awful. And we did stick to our principles.'

It is interesting to note that even where ethics and injustice are at issue, women seem to be willing to seek accommodation. This is surely one aspect of the Division of Labour which benefits women who work together, for accommodation is not what men seem to think argument at work is really about.

27

Equals: Men Battling with Men

The Gender Game does not arise when men argue with other men at work, because they have no intrinsic problem about a man's proper place in the scheme of things and they *expect* to have to defend their position against other males. But that leaves them free to concentrate on the real issue, which is to ensure that the other man does not steal a march and win the political battle for power or promotion. All of these are military metaphors. Linguist Suzette Haden Elgin believes that games are the metaphor for most dominant adult American males, and that we need to be aware of this because, of course, dominant males are usually those who wield power.[55] Dominant males in Britain and Australia use games metaphors too. For those not in a position to wield much power, however, the struggle to hold one's own and ensure good results to show to one's boss is not so much a game with rules as trench warfare, which no one can win.

Mike, the marketing manager we have met several times, finds himself engaged in a ceaseless series of battles with other men on the same level – the factory manager, the distribution manager, the sales manager.

On Tuesday morning he had a 'strong row' with the factory manager over 'factory production failure'. He writes that he was extremely angry:

'The problem was clearly a factory error so no real defence.'

But the factory manager wasn't taking this lying down, and retaliated by a series of skirmishes with members of the marketing department and a full-scale attack on Mike because 'last minute changes of plans were causing disruption in the factories' on Wednesday. Mike writes:

'I will not have factory manager run this company. I will not stand by and let other dept. heads criticise my staff unfairly. I got my message across because commercial views will overrule factory convenience.'

Mike's words show that this is a power struggle. And just in case there is any suggestion that his people *might* have been even partially at fault, he adds: 'Faults were found in factory communication.'

At the same time he is battling with the sales manager, and reports several strong and even heated arguments about 'poor sales performance'. At various times he asserts:

'I was right.'

'Sales were poor because they were badly planned.'

'Sales manager aware of deficiency but annoyed at being picked up.'

And he explains:

'My job is to keep sales on budget and push etc. sales manager when necessary.'

It is unlikely that the sales manager in question would agree. Part of the problem with a competitive approach to relations between departments is that the success of each department depends to a large extent on realistic co-operation with all others. Marketing and promotion can never succeed without the work of sales people, and sales will never increase without the right products being produced by the factory and delivered by the distribution people to the right place at the right time. All depend on each other, and yet this co-operation is reluctantly given. The standard attitude embraced by Mike and all his colleagues is that only one can win.

Mike makes clear that his co-operation is dependent on his own benefit. He reports another argument, temperate this time, with an administrator about 'issuing reports on time'.

'I was in the wrong with little mitigating defence. This is a regular monthly exchange – I always issue a certain report late because it is tedious, and I do not want it read too far in advance. The administrator wants it earlier.'

When rivalry between departments is not involved, criticism of a man's work by a colleague is taken as a personal attack, and is met by great anger and resentment. Stan reports a strong argument about 'the effectiveness of a computer program I wrote':

'I insisted my program was right and refused to listen to arguments otherwise. Eventually he gave in. I knew I was right and refused to listen to arguments to the contrary.'

In my first study, which involved interviewing research psychologists, one striking finding was that when asked to recall an argument with a colleague, eight of the ten men recalled arguments in which the other had *not* 'heard what they said'. Their explanations were varied: failure was just one of those things, or they didn't really try, or the other man was at fault.[56]

'I was just trying to find out his stance. I'll always argue.' (Mark)

'I had more knowledge than he did, but I didn't really try.' (Homer)

'He didn't know anything about the issue.' (Ian)

'He wasn't interested in my point of view.' (David)

By contrast, most diarists report that the other did *hear*, even if he didn't actually agree. They themselves were successful in getting their point across because of their logic and rationality, or as Jack put it: 'Basically because the facts were in general on my side, or if not, not actively against my suggestions.'

One important difference is that research psychologists are working in an academic environment, in which it is normal to expect that any statement made by one person will be challenged by another. So the fact that the other man isn't interested, or doesn't know anything about the issue, is evidence of failing on his part. Men in other kinds of work, though, need to feel they are in control, and that they are good enough at that quintessentially masculine task of argument for the other man to have to *hear*. Failure on the part of the other man to agree is an expected aspect of male rivalry. As Leslie put it,

> 'I don't always try to convince, just to get my point registered in the other's mind. It's more part of a general campaign, not a battle but a war.'

Men at work often feel they are on a battlefield, or even perhaps conducting guerrilla warfare. Jack writes:

> 'The computer is very important to my work and as such I get very annoyed when it fails to work as I and others expect it to. Thus when the opportunity arises to make sure that others know what problems exist and what I think should be done about them, I say something. It's a continuous campaign of attrition.'

Hank, an American sociologist, combines images of boxing and selling:

> 'It's easier to knock down your opponent when he's made to defend an extreme caricature of his own position. The aim is to sell your argument, and destroy the other. So I didn't give him any credit for any of his points. I wasn't going to lose the fight.'

This aggressive approach must make it difficult to communicate on occasion. Paul reports that, of course, he won the argument:

> 'The simplicity of my case – his was just regurgitation of propaganda.'

And Donald produces a similarly brief and dogmatic explanation of an angry exchange about 'resources':

> 'Because I was right! It was a dispute, not a discussion.'

When men need to come to some agreement about a project on which they are working as a group, personal rivalry may still be involved, but many men in the English-speaking world pride themselves on their ability to co-operate in a team. So when Colin tried unsuccessfully to persuade his colleagues to 'put some colour on to a computer screen background', the argument was important though temperate:

'I was trying to make an improvement (in my view) in the quality of our work. Aesthetic preferences are almost *un*arguable (why *does* someone prefer grey to muted colour?)'

Similarly, Max reports an important but temperate argument with a colleague 'about a work-related issue'. He felt he got his point across because

'There was no substantial counter-argument to the one I mounted. I argued because I felt the resistance coming from my colleague was very irrational and non-productive. The point at issue was small, but the underlying irrational attitude looked dodgy. Consider it a blow against entropy.'

There is an air of detachment about most of the reports of arguments with others in a team when those others are not convinced. The issues are important to the men involved, and though they report that the other 'heard what was said', they also need to explain how it was the other man continued to disagree. This is usually because of some fault in the other person (he was 'irrational') or logic could make no difference anyway ('who can argue about aesthetic preferences?'). When the arguments are successful, the diarist may feel a need to emphasise that agreement was a result of skill and effort. As Vic put it:

'It was hard work as I did not perceive the point of contact immediately.'

Of course, in many cases men at work develop good friendly relations, especially when their co-operation and teamwork develop over a long time. When a man argues with another man, the more they know of each other and the better they like each other, the easier it is for each to risk losing an argument without feeling he has lost face. It helps too if the men can choose those they must work with as a team. Members of the Amadeus String Quartet have been together since 1948, and as First Violinist Norbert Brainin is quoted as saying:

'From the beginning there was the greatest possible sympathy and agreement.'[57]

Their harmonious relationship does not, however, mean they do not need to argue. In an interview with Bernard Levin on BBC TV in 1981, Brainin was asked what happened when members of the quartet had completely different ideas about how to interpret a new piece of music. Brainin replied:

'You argue until you agree. There is no other way. In a quartet there cannot be a majority decision, you cannot force any member to do something.'[58]

It is obvious that a small group of four people making music together would have problems if they did not ultimately come to agreement. However, some men at work will avoid direct confrontation. There is a distinct pattern of competition and even guerrilla warfare in many men's accounts, but what applies to the majority does not necessarily apply to the individual. For some men, negotiation with those they must work with may mean quiet resistance.

What do you do when you need to agree with a colleague about how to approach a situation? I asked Brad, a tall, quiet man who runs a big paper mill for a major conglomerate in America:

'I listen, and then decide.'

So he was thinking of those everyday situations in which he was ultimately boss. What about negotiations and disagreements with people on his level in other parts of the company? Brad found it impossible to say, and when pressed, he joked: 'You're trying to get me into trouble.'

Brad is a successful and powerful man in his community where he is the major employer, but the aggression we have met in some men does not appear to be his way. Some men will avoid unpleasantness if they possibly can. Gerry wrote:

'Sometimes I noticed we were heading to a potential emotional nexus, and quite deliberately I'd do diversionary stuff to avoid that area. This was only when I could definitely see strong negative emotional energy invested and an obvious and justifiably avoidable "lose-lose" situation.'

These men are a minority, but possibly a significant one if they are concerned, as Gerry suggests, with avoiding situations in which both sides to a disagreement lose. However, some men who avoid argument can be dangerous political enemies, using espionage and sabotage. Bill told me what happened when a new man took over the company:

'I asked a colleague what he thought about the changes that were being thrown at us. He said, "I don't know until I talk to Andy" (that's our boss). I thought, how odd not to know what you think until someone's told you what you should think. But I was the naive one. He made sure he found out the politically correct line to take, while I actually said what I really thought. He's on the fast track, I'm losing out. I've noticed recently he'll never actually *say* anything, just jokes with everyone and finds out what they think, and uses it for his own purposes. A real bastard. He's scoring, while all the rest of us are on the sidelines.'

Games metaphors like this are more commonly used when men talk about work in general. In casual conversation, men would say things like:

'My game plan is...' (Mike)

'I found I really was on a sticky wicket. Nothing I could do.' (John)

'I wasn't on the ball...' (Chris)

'That was a bit of an own goal...' (Frank)

These are all images of team games, which may explain why they are not also part of men's explanations for what happened in argument. Being on 'a sticky wicket' or not 'on the ball' are seen as part of the situation, but not as part of the argument itself. When disagreements are the central topic, games where the individual is on his own come to mind: boxing to Hank, above, and chess to Julian. He told me:

'Manoeuvring with colleagues is like playing chess. You don't always go for the direct confrontation at first, you have to get your pieces in position before making an attack.'

Competition is the central meaning of argument between men at work. They may construe disagreements as struggles for power, or as warfare; within teams, there is a conflict between the individual's desire to win and his desire to be a good team player. While not every move in the power struggle is overt, men who are not working together as a team do tend to see themselves in competition with other men, contending with guerrilla attacks, underhand sabotage and manoeuvring for advantage. Work sounds a very uncomfortable place for many men.

28

Arguing with an Audience

Working It Out in Committee

> Chairman of the Committee: 'That's an excellent suggestion, Miss Triggs. Perhaps one of the men here would like to make it.'[59]

Few people who attend committee meetings will fail to recognise the grain of truth in the cartoon quoted above.

Sociologist Cecilia Ridgeway told the American Association for the Advancement of Science in 1993 that if a woman tries to take a lead in a meeting, men will act uncomfortable, look away from her and not pay attention. She interprets this as the woman 'trying to change her status': it backfires.[60] The more a woman tries to speak out, the more difficult it becomes to gain a hearing. Suggestions are met with silence and, if they are good ideas, will surface later as proposed by a man.

Why is this? Are men deliberately excluding women? Are they consciously stealing their ideas, and pretending they are theirs? Though this undoubtedly happens on occasion, I think it very unlikely that so widespread a pattern could arise from purely selfish or malicious motives. This reaction to the competent woman can be found throughout the Western world. It is easy to forget where an idea in your head originally came from, if the motive is powerful enough. And the motive is very powerful indeed. Men's exclusion of women from decision-making where possible, their inability to listen when a woman talks 'like a man', that is, logically and rationally, is an unconscious attempt to protect their view of the world. It is, I believe, each man's instinctive response to a threat to his very sense of himself. We are back to the Division of Labour again, where decision-making is man's prerogative.

Some people suggest the problem is less structural (power being in the hands of men) and more that women's voices are difficult to hear, literally. Caroline, 26, a city solicitor, told journalist Hester Lacey:

> 'Men try to talk over you. In a group meeting, you have to repeat yourself over and over. It's not down to logical skills – you have to stick to your point and not be beaten down, and not let them override you. When I'm trying to be authoritative, I drop the pitch of my voice, because they just don't seem to tune in to a higher voice.'[61]

Anna, the administrator whose colleague just wandered off when she was trying to sort out a problem, said:

> 'I am very careful now to keep very calm, speak slowly – never enter a verbal free-for-all even if all six men in the office are plunging in together, because I know I won't even be heard. Rather than trying to shout above the din, it seems to be more effective to speak more quietly – if people have to strain to hear you, they shut up a bit themselves.'

Yet a male academic told me that women are not listened to in meetings because they tend to speak so quietly no one can hear! There may well be a problem of pitch and 'tuning in': the human brain is designed to filter incoming information so that we pay attention only to what is important. Just as a mother will hear the faintest cries of her new baby that others may not notice, so men in meetings are tuned in to other men because their opinions might be important to them. There is so much going on that tuning out insignificant information helps protect from overload. As we have already seen, what a woman has to say is frequently viewed as unimportant by male colleagues.

I spoke to Lesley Riddoch when she was deputy editor of the *Scotsman*. In editorial conferences she was quite often the only woman out of thirteen people, though occasionally joined by one of two women leader writers. She told me:

'I used to speak out every time I saw a different approach, but they don't want to know. You can see they have a shaped view of the news, they've got the whole thing sorted, and then here is this woman suggesting people do things differently. So often it sounds as though you are suggesting an idealistic approach, when in fact all you are suggesting is that they find other contacts, speak to other people. In theory they should want to find out more, but they like their way, they don't want to have new ideas.'

Being 'idealistic', which means in malespeak 'unrealistic', is yet another criticism thrown at women who come up with ideas that might mean uncomfortable changes, whether these changes are in ways of doing things or ways of thinking. Yet Riddoch did succeed in persuading her boss to accept the revolutionary idea of handing over all editorial decisions to women for a special International Woman's Day edition of the *Scotswoman* on 6 March 1996. Women can have influence, especially with their bosses, who are predisposed to believe in their competence and intelligence. However, this influence tends to be greatly diminished in committee, where women find it difficult to be heard.

Solicitor Caroline added:

'Men think there's no problem. They think the battle is over for women, and that women have won – you don't really talk about it if you want to keep your job.'

Really? Pointing out that men seem unwilling to listen is going to lose you your job? Many women told me things like:

'Men don't want to work with a troublemaker so you learn to keep a low profile and don't complain.' (Ellie, 34, marketing)

'It's better to get along with people. Men don't like it when women whinge about what they think are injustices. I try not to cause trouble.' (Rosemary, administrator)

And worse, in a programme about sexual harassment on British TV, barrister Barbara Hewson said:

'No one wants to work with a troublemaker. If you complain

publicly about harassment, you are saying goodbye to your career.'[62]

Troublemaking is the constant theme. Even Nancy, a mature and wealthy American who comes from a distinguished Republican family and who has been honoured by the party, told me: 'I'm not a troublemaker. I just got rewarded for good work.' Nancy told me that she is 'an ideas person':

> 'I used to give my suggestions to the chairman before the meeting. He would present them as his own. In the end, there didn't seem much point in my actually attending meetings. I would just tell him what I thought, and many of my ideas went through.'

This is a part of being the *éminence grise* or the 'power behind the throne', a role women have played for centuries, but fewer women are content with that today. Since Nancy also claimed never to have experienced any form of prejudice as a woman in the male world of politics, I suggested that this made her exceptional in terms of my research, and could it have something to do with the power that comes from wealth? But she thought not:

> 'That has nothing to do with it. Men get millions from networks, but women don't get near so much. I'm very direct with men, I'm not a pussycat, you know what I mean? But I'm very feminine, I don't turn men off. I don't pester people, I just do my thing. They respect me.'

If a woman is really concerned to influence men, American psychologist Linda Carli found, she must avoid 'coming on like a man'. She needs to hedge her comments around with heart-warming self-deprecatory phrases like 'I'm not really sure, but . . .' or 'I may be wrong', just those phrases that women have mostly learned *not* to use because they make us sound incompetent. Men will agree that a woman who avoids tentative speech patterns sounds more competent, but that apparently has no bearing on the value they attach to her words. To listen, they need to like her and feel unthreatened.

At the 1993 meeting of the American Association for the Advancement of Science, Carli said:

> 'Women who display high-status behavior will be threatening to a male audience unless they also communicate that they have no desire to usurp male status.'[63]

High-status behaviour means talking loudly, rapidly and with conviction, and making frequent eye contact. As we know, many researchers and management advisers believe women should learn to become more assertive, change their style of communication from self-deprecation to sound more knowledgeable and competent. But Carli has found this advice may put women at a further disadvantage if they are concerned to get their ideas across: women who sound 'knowledgeable, competent, confident and intelligent' are seen by men as 'unlikeable, condescending and threatening'.

This is another variation on what we have seen before: women are expected to conform to the Division of Labour, so if they must argue, they should do so in a 'womanly' way. One reader has suggested this contradicts my research – and it does contradict what women generally say they do, which is argue assertively. But if you watch women in action who are effective in argument with men, you will see that they are usually careful to signal their awareness that they are females dealing with males. Self-deprecatory phrases are used by some, but in Britain the most usual approach is a soft, gentle voice, and some of the toughest female negotiators conceal their steel behind a warm and gentle persona. This is a mild form of the Gender Game that most women may find themselves engaging in from time to time. Given the rewards and punishments associated with these supposedly 'masculine' and 'feminine' ways of talking, we should hardly be surprised if linguists like Deborah Tannen in America and Jennifer Coates in Britain have found differences in the ways women and men communicate.[64]

The self-deprecatory phrases and soft gentle voice work less well in a committee situation, and where women have developed these signals when negotiating with colleagues on an individual basis, they may still find they are ignored in meetings. A lone woman or a tiny minority in a large group of men are always seen *as* women, which evokes the solidarity of the male group. Self-deprecation is very likely to be taken at face value. Women may develop different techniques to deal with this. Being a lone woman can, in fact, be turned to advantage, and as we saw, Margaret Thatcher exploited this. But being one of a small minority is usually a disadvantage. Again, a woman's boss is likely to be predisposed in her favour, but male colleagues will probably unite in undermining any woman who appears to be a threat, and she is most likely to be seen as dangerous if she emphasises her competence and forgets to project warmth.

Not all women feel they are talked over or ignored in meetings. Jessica, an American woman who inherited wealth and power, told me she did not understand the main thesis of this book: that women are disadvantaged in many situations because of gender role assumptions. On the whole she has never felt that men do not listen. She said:

> 'I often put proposals to the boards on which I sit [there are many]. These are businessmen, they are used to thinking about ideas. There would be a debate about the pros and cons, but I have never experienced anything like Miss Triggs. In fact, I've almost felt that as a woman, they listened more, were more respectful of me. As a woman I stood out.'

But it turns out that she is probably considerably more politically aware than the women who complain of not being heard. For as we continued to talk, she told me about a particular project in which, as chair of a Community Board, she wanted to appoint a number of school nurses and the administration thought there was not enough money.

> 'It was hard work, a lot of phone calls and manoeuvring, getting the structure right. In the end, we had to go for an open vote, and I carried the ball and had quite a bit of influence on how it was worked out.'

Going for an open vote? She looked startled, as though I am a complete ignoramus, which it turns out I am. I know people lobby behind the scenes, but I did not realise that the properly politically astute get all the discussion done before an issue comes to committee stage. And getting the arguing done behind the scenes very often means that the female members of a committee are not involved anyway. Many a joint decision is agreed in the men's room, and it is often only when a woman is chair of a committee that her views need to be sounded out too.

We might contrast this behind-the-scenes negotiation by men in groups with their attitude to women who try to form alliances. This may simply be for mutual support, but at times may also help them co-ordinate their approach in committee:

> 'Women who get together and try to network within a company find themselves referred to as "the coffee klatsch" or the "knitting club", and individuals are drawn aside and warned not to get involved in "the witches' coven".' (Cathy Cassell, organisational psychologist)[65]

Certainly it is sensible to sound out others before a meeting. Indeed, some successful men would never put forward a new idea before making sure they know how it will be received, and some hesitate to say what they think even when asked. In one of the summer-school classes I have given at Oxford University, we were discussing attitudes to women in the workplace in America in 1996 (all the students were from the US). One successful businessman was mainly silent, even when pressed, but came up to me afterwards and said:

> 'I didn't want to waste class time on my contribution, but in my experience in industry . . .'

He then produced useful, relevant material that would have interested the whole class. When I asked if this was his usual way of putting forward his own views he said:

> 'I'd usually take you aside and see how you react. Not take up meeting time.'

Women are frequently accused of 'wasting meeting time on unimportant matters', and if they do bring up a new point, may be told, 'We don't have time for that now.'

In my experience, too, women can be naive about organisational politics. I recall trying to discuss with one woman how we might handle a crucial debate in committee about the future of a project about which we both held strong convictions. She demurred:

'We shouldn't talk like this. It will look as though we're plotting.'

Properly chastised, I refrained from contacting the other members of the committee I was fairly certain would support the action I proposed. No plotting here. However, as it turned out, our opponents had no such scruples, and lobbied extensively.

But committees have very strange dynamics, and people's actions are guided by intangible unseen influences as well as more obvious pressures. As it happened, this committee was that rarity, an equal balance of women and men. On the day of the meeting, I sat towards one end of the oval table, and the leading opponent (a man) almost diagonally opposite at the other. People drifted in in the usual way, and the table became crowded, for no one had stayed away: the last arrival, a woman, hesitated, did not take the chair saved for her next to my male opponent but walked round the room, found a spare chair and joined us at the other end. I suddenly realised that without any plan, or even conscious intent, all the women were gathered on one side and all the men on the other. The lobbying had led all the committee members to the conclusion that the issue was part of the Gender Game, and they took sides accordingly.

Afterwards, we had coffee together, a larger group than usual, wanting to celebrate a newly discovered solidarity in the face of a united opposition; though one of our number did say she feared it looked as though we had been plotting, which we had carefully refrained from doing. Our celebration was only possible because we were equal in number to the men, and the very strength of our united (unplanned) front was sufficient to persuade one or two of the men that our case was worth supporting. This story may underline just why it is so important to so many men not to allow parity of numbers in decision-making situations.

When the Gender Game is made explicit, many men too would

prefer to have nothing to do with it. Committees, though, are less decision-making arenas than 'potent forms of social control'.[66] When real discussion and disagreement are kept private, there is enormous pressure in committees to maintain a sense of cohesion and to rely on what psychologist Irving Janis calls *group think*. A desire for unanimity prevents proper discussion and realistic appraisal of alternative courses of action. While the concept of group think has been invoked more often to explain how groups of intelligent men could have come up with disastrous decisions such as the Bay of Pigs fiasco,[67] the pressure to agree with what appears to be the majority view can overwhelm individuals even in simple decisions.

One woman provided a detailed account of a board meeting in which invoking the Gender Game led to a surprising outcome. Her professional organisation had been asked to send a representative to sit on a national policy-making committee, and names and CVs of selected candidates had been circulated to board members. The secretary making the request had noted that the current members of the policy committee were mostly white and male, so that they would especially welcome a person of colour and/or a woman who might help balance their perspective. One strong candidate emerged: a woman of Asian origin, with good experience in the appropriate field.

But then a discussion began, and it became clear that some people felt a strong desire to appoint a man who 'is well known to us all'. 'Who has met this woman?' the board was asked. 'So how can we appoint someone we have never met?' One of the few women present pointed out that (a) her referees were well known to the board, (b) needing to know every candidate personally would inevitably mean that the same people were appointed to all posts, and (c) if this was an important point, why not invite her to meet the board? 'But to choose this unknown because she was not white or a man would be to exercise improper discrimination.' The debate became strong, the secretary said a decision had to be made right then, and the chair said it was time for a vote. One man suggested that the vote should be secret, and there was general agreement. The women all looked at each other and shrugged. Another battle lost.

When the votes were counted, the woman candidate had won. This was a surprise to everyone. How did it happen and why did they need a secret vote?

My interpretation is that most professionals really hate to think of themselves as prejudiced in any way. They are often painfully aware of sex and race discrimination, and even if they do not always succeed in rooting out their unconscious assumptions, when issues are brought to their attention they will make every effort to behave appropriately. At the same time, they do not want to be seen as going against the majority view in an issue of no great personal importance: that is, it was of no personal importance to most of the more than twenty men on the board, though it became of great significance to the handful of women – three members plus an assistant taking notes (no vote). The man who proposed a secret ballot knew that he wanted to vote for the strong woman candidate, but did not want to be seen as undermining the usual cosy unanimity of the committee. The discussion had not revealed the extent to which men as well as women supported the female candidate because the Gender Game ('She's not one of us') had been invoked. (The Race Game was also called on, but its rules are different, and it would take us too far afield to discuss that here.)

There are men of good will everywhere. But the pressures on them to conform when decisions are made may overwhelm personal convictions, and women's place in any organisation will depend on the consensual attitude to what is known to its enemies as 'political correctness'.

The Harridan Tendency

'. . . of course, she's a member of the harridan tendency.'

I first came across this phrase on a television news programme some time in 1991, when a Conservative MP was being asked to answer some criticism of policy made by Labour MP Ann Clwyd. Lots of other men seemed to think this was a good way of dismissing what a woman says. Over the next couple of years I noticed that more and more Conservative MPs used this expression when confronted with a comment by a woman with which they disagreed – and then Opposition MPs started to use the phrase too.

'The harridan tendency' seemed to have become a tendency in itself.

What is it about this phrase that makes it so telling? Originally the word came from a French word meaning 'old jade of a horse', and by extension meant 'gaunt' and 'haggard' and 'old'. What is there about calling a woman 'gaunt and haggard and old' that undermines her arguments? Why should calling a woman an ugly old crone be an effective counterblast to her criticisms? Would calling a man gaunt and haggard and old have quite the same effect?

When I analysed the word, its etymological origins and the contexts of its use, I came to the conclusion it is only used of an older woman who demands to be seen as an equal, and it is intended to imply that this particular woman is so old and ugly she could not even sell her sexual favours.

The key to understanding the power of the term 'harridan' is the underlying assumption that a woman's principal function is as sexual object, and once she has lost her charms she is as useless and objectionable as a jaded old horse. Anything she says, whatever the tone or volume of voice, is unpleasing. If a woman is not sexually attractive to men, she can have no value; if a sexually unattractive woman expresses an opinion, the effect is disagreeable, and if she argues she is being quarrelsome. Somehow, linked to the notion of age, decrepitude and ugliness has crept in the notion of a loud and strident voice, a quarrelsome nature, a shrewish and spiteful old witch.

'She's a member of the harridan tendency' is a neat way of insulting and demeaning a woman without laying oneself open to charges of slander. What can the woman do? She knows, and all the listeners know, that the implications are insulting and intended to humiliate. The phrase is designed to evoke all those hidden associations, and if meaning-manipulation experts like politicians use it, you can be sure it does.

Anything the woman now says will be discounted. Men of all political colours can feel a secret sense of relief that here is at least one woman they do not have to take seriously. Women take note that public criticism of a man may lead to being labelled 'harridan' and few want to be associated with any 'tendency'. While extremists of both sexes will have immediately pigeon-holed the unfortunate woman speaker, other listeners will notice the abuse, laugh or not as the case may be, and move on. But what the woman actually said will tend to be forgotten.

Women of all ages are frequently vilified if they choose to express views with which a man disagrees. Most women at some time have been referred to by various animal names – cat, cow, bitch, shrew. Many no doubt will also have been on the receiving end of one of those overtly fearful epithets – 'ball-breaking' and 'castrating' – so often combined, as in 'castrating bitch'.

When you have no basis for an argument, abuse the plaintiff.

This was Marcus Tullius Cicero's advice to would-be orators in Rome. Two thousand years later, the psychological effect remains much the same.

Abuse works well in the public arena – courtroom, parliament, television, newspaper – because the aim of the speaker is not to persuade an opponent to change his or her mind, but to sway an audience to your side. Scoring points is part of the game. When it comes to committees, such abuse is best kept for the corridors and men's room where it can go unrecorded but not unmarked by a potentially receptive audience. Many a woman has erroneously thought that she is treated with respect because she cannot hear the offensive comments made in the privacy of the men's loo.[68]

Labour MP Clare Short told me about her experiences in the House of Commons:

'I'd never experienced anything like it, there was an incredibly strong reaction to me because I'm fairly outspoken. I was an unacceptable harridan .... Being now in a position of seniority and visibility, men around the place don't treat me badly in a personal way any more. Their hostility is played out in the media. It's both media exaggeration and what men say in private, not in front of us. A strong woman shakes men very deeply, it seems to threaten their male culture.'

She sees a double barrier to women being taken seriously:

> 'One is the way women are nurtured and trained not to say what
> they think. Everyone thinks being outspoken and opinionated is
> not feminine. The second is that when a woman is in power, her
> voice is not reported with the same weight as if she were a man.
> The ageing balding male is a power symbol in our society, but
> the ageing woman is a has-been.'

Her generation, 'the luckiest since the war', has seen enormous
changes in attitudes to women, and she confidently expects that the
next stage will be a change in the image of the older woman.

But as we have seen, there is still a long way to go.

When Brenda, a distinguished research scientist, was made chair
of an important policy-making committee, there was a general air
of self-congratulation in the upper reaches of her learned society:
they had acknowledged the scientific achievements of a woman
(academics on both sides of the Atlantic are acutely aware of
demands that they redress the gender imbalance at the highest
levels of all their institutions), *and* they all knew her to be a
beautiful, warm and charming person. But then she acknowledged
publicly that she was ambitious, destroying with one word her
image as delightful woman. Suddenly her colleagues say they
started to hear snide remarks about her 'aggressiveness', her
'ruthless ambition', the 'stridency' with which she conducted
committee meetings and the 'disagreeableness' of her personality.

Brenda told me:

> 'It is always possible that they are right and you are wrong. I
> *would* certainly count disagreeableness as among my traits, if by
> this we mean a tendency to disagree!'

She also prides herself on getting through the agenda of meetings,
and is prepared to accept that this makes her a 'strident chair'.

Brenda is already doing what I have advocated elsewhere: she is
embracing the words used to criticise her, making them her own.[69]
But before we nod sagely to ourselves, slotting away the
information that a woman firmly controlling a committee and
insisting on sticking to the agenda must be strident, let us be clear

what we are doing. Would a man in the same situation be called 'strident'? I doubt it. Certainly I have never come across the term applied to a man in such circumstances. Men who run committees well are called 'firm' and 'strong', good masculine terms which contrast with 'weak' for those more numerous men who are unable to keep committee meetings under control. But Margaret Thatcher, who was strong and firm, was frequently accused of being strident and depicted in cartoons as a witch.

Women need to insist on applying those masculine terms to women, so that eventually they will no longer carry gender assumptions. We know that women can be strong, can be firm, can effectively be in control. Embrace those critical adjectives which flow so freely whenever a woman opens her mouth in a non-supportive role, yes. But let us also try to develop the habit of describing women in ways which support, encourage and praise their freedom of speech and action.

29

Shouting Across the Canyon

Whenever you feel intimidated, remember: an amateur made the
Ark, but a professional made the *Titanic*.

(Verna Wilkins, publisher)

After a series of arguments in which I finally managed to persuade
a colleague that my point of view was important and needed to be
taken into account, I said, wishing to re-establish warmth and
friendliness:

'It's good to know you're there with a sympathetic ear.'

Probably most women would interpret this as it was intended: 'I
know you didn't agree with me at first, but you were willing to
listen and make compromises, and I appreciate that.' But my male
colleague was not at all happy at the suggestion he was so
womanly, and, his voice more angry than it had been during most
of our earlier conflict, hastened to deny what I had meant as a
compliment:

'I'm not sympathetic. I'm a reasonable man, yes, that's it, I'm
reasonable.'

Naturally, I agreed that he was a reasonable man, his hackles
smoothed down, and I noted his exchange as encapsulating many
of the problems women and men have in communicating. As a
woman, I find it baffling that a man should be insulted at being
called sympathetic, which simply means to me, being willing to
listen. As a man, my colleague was offended at a word that in
malespeak is normally applied to a woman: to him, it was as
though I was suggesting he had changed his mind for non-rational
reasons.

Throughout this book, we have seen that women and men interpret disagreements between them differently. In all the various kinds of situation which people can find themselves arguing, how women and men remember what happens depends on who the other people are: whether they like them, are on intimate terms with them or they are casual acquaintances, whether they have to work together and which of them has power, whether there is an audience or the conflict arises just between two individuals, and all of this is permeated by the one difference that can never be avoided – gender.

At work, the gulf between us might be the Grand Canyon. As we have seen, men at work are struggling for power, manoeuvring for advantage over their male colleagues, and understandably perhaps, they do not take kindly to the notion that the competition has immediately doubled if women are acknowledged as equals in all fields. A simple and effective way of undermining half the competition is to play the Gender Game.

While women who argue with male colleagues emphasise their cool, rational approach and their logical deployment of evidence, men tend to ignore what women say as far as possible and, if they cannot, invoke stereotypes.

Even careful explanation of a woman's viewpoint appears easily distorted, whether the words are spoken or written. Journalist Kennedy Wilson, writing in the Glasgow Herald (October 1996), suggested my research had 'caused a flutter in feminist circles' because I had found 'the sexes differ when it comes to logical argument' and so women 'cannot easily win an argument against men'.[70] This led to another male journalist's calling me to find out 'Why women are not good at arguing logically.'[71] Just in case any readers are under the same misapprehension, women are just as good as men at arguing logically. But however logically and calmly a woman does argue, men often choose to take no notice.

Women expend a great deal of effort trying to convince men at work that they are rational beings, while men labour equally hard to convince themselves that women are unsuitable for positions in the workplace where they might pose a threat. Beliefs about essential differences between the sexes can become distorted and transformed into some pretty vicious Gender Games (sexual harassment, trial by gossip, whispering campaigns) precisely because the breakdown in the Division of Labour is leading to women taking jobs formerly taken only by men.

Alisa Cook was appointed a lieutenant in the Royal Artillery: her superiors saw her as exceptionally competent and were able to preen themselves on appointing a woman where no woman had been before. However, her fellow officers were incensed. She told the *Guardian*:

> 'I hadn't realised how much resentment they felt at the fact I was a woman officer in their regiment. One night a brother officer approached me in the mess. He shouted, "You are not fucking wanted here, you should leave".'[72]

She was subjected to a campaign of bullying and sexist taunts: in one particularly aggressive incident, smouldering CS gas canisters were thrown into the room where she was showering. In 1997, she became the first British female army officer to receive from the Ministry of Defence an apology and damages for sexist abuse.

Younger women often say they will turn sexual innuendo back on the men in the office, and some older and successful women effectively use their sex appeal and charm to get their own way. Sexual tension is inevitable wherever women and men must work together and, where it remains at the level of women and men enjoying each other's company, it adds a pleasurable *frisson* to everyday life. But where men feel threatened by the incursion of women, as in the armed forces and all uniformed services, this sexual tension gets transformed into a cruel desire to show that in a traditionally macho world, the female is subject to male power. Sexual abuse and sexual harassment are extreme forms of the Gender Game: when women enter occupations for the first time, harassment is less a 'natural response to hormones' and more a case of men defending their territory.

The Gender Game becomes more subtle as women become more numerous in any field, and the fact that women are in a majority in service jobs like nursing or typing, or on factory production lines in the food and textile industries, may even reinforce old assumptions about women's 'special abilities'. A supposedly genetically determined skill in nurturing seems to have little relevance to how well a woman can type, or file papers, or sort peas on a production line, but women's numerical predominance in these areas has traditionally allowed employers to pay lower wages than would otherwise have been possible if they employed men (women earn around 70 per cent of men's wages on both sides of the Atlantic), while men at work have been able to interpret women's low position in the hierarchy as proof of their inferiority. Thus when a woman in a subordinate position dares to question or challenge a man higher up the tree, she may incur extreme wrath.

As women move into management and climb higher up that hierarchical tree, their enthusiasm and tenacity please their bosses, but worry their male colleagues. For those who really do believe that women are less intelligent, more emotional, incapable of logical thought, women's very existence in the network of those who need to be taken into account in work decisions becomes a source of constant irritation and stress. It is not surprising, then, that many men will ignore what a woman says when they can, for it goes against the grain even to have to *think* about what she says, let alone act on it. Easier by far to agree if she persists, and then forget it, because she is not really important, cannot be because she is a woman. And if a man experiences physiological sensations that might, in other circumstances, be interpreted as anger, this must be the effect of *her* over-emotional response; she is so unimportant in the scheme of things that he, a man, could not be made angry by her.

If a man is so unfortunate as to have a female boss, the sooner he can find some means of shunting her out of the way the better. Sometimes going over her head works, sometimes it does not. Of course, if she runs the business, there is nowhere to go, but she is a woman and easily influenced by a man. So men with a woman boss show a marked tendency to argue, to query decisions, to show unmistakably that they think they could do her job better, and when the woman eventually exercises her authority they are very inclined to invoke stereotypes. Perhaps the most unexpected is that they see her use of hierarchical power as 'being rude'. But a woman exercising power is interpreted as 'bossy' mother or nanny or schoolmarm, which immediately positions the man as a child, and causes offence. If a woman wishes to play mother, it must be a warm, caring mother, not a cruel witch-like mother who tells the child what to do. Or, of course, she may be seen to be 'pretending to be a man', an offence in itself. Gender myths are available to every man who feels intimidated by the presence of women in the workplace.

Women bring their own assumptions into the workplace. They assume that people are there to do a job, and that doing a good job will lead to recognition; they assume that it is better to get on with people than to fight; they assume that good will engenders good will; they assume that if an argument arises, the aim is to find the best solution that suits both, not necessarily to 'win'.

I emphasised at the beginning of this book that I did not ask people reporting on their arguments, 'Did you win?' I asked always, 'Did the other person hear what you said?' However, when male journalists reported my research, their approach was always that 'women can't win'. Perhaps women don't win because they are not *trying* to. But women complain that men tend not to *listen*, and very often they don't.

Women are aware of gender role expectations and say they work very hard to avoid behaving in gender-stereotypic fashion. They avoid being emotional, they stress logic and evidence, remain cool and self-possessed in the face of extreme provocation from angry bosses and hostile colleagues. Mostly they feel they have good relations with everyone at work, and try to negotiate working practices with staff that suit everyone. What makes them angry is to be deceived, or to suffer any kind of injustice. Otherwise, they try to sort out problems without anyone feeling upset or hurt.

The assumptions people bring into the workplace reflect their acculturation into their share of the Division of Labour: getting along with people is traditionally women's task, whereas warfare is the task of men. Furthermore, other people's reactions to them reinforce gender roles. As many women in authority say, they find that 'coming on like a man' is counterproductive because it creates resistance in both male and female subordinates; but if they deliberately behave like a warm, caring mother figure, their subordinates appear happier and will co-operate. Men have greater choice, it appears, when at the top of the hierarchy, but in the meantime their colleagues are manoeuvring for power, and they must guard against appearing 'weak' when on the way up.

Those old gender myths are astonishingly resilient.

Part Five

Building a Golden Bridge

Build your adversary a golden bridge to retreat across.

(Sun Tzu)

Building bridges is our final image. Even in the building of bridges we can discover that Division of Labour which has intervened in all our analyses of argument: traditionally, it is men who build physical bridges across rivers and ravines, and it is women who build psychological bridges between people who disagree within the group. But bridges do more than link two positions separated by distance – they also provide somewhere to go when negotiations get tricky and confrontation seems inevitable. Women and men have been separated for so long by the Division of Labour, both need a golden bridge on which to meet and from which to retreat when the going gets tough.

Bridges take time to build, and construction should begin immediately, from both sides. But psychological bridges require just as much knowledge of materials and resistance and stresses as do physical bridges, and the whole of this book has been an analysis of the kinds of knowledge we need if we are to construct a lasting link between us.

Knowledge is a tricky thing to get to grips with, and this is especially the case when we are talking of psychology. On the one hand, there are objective facts about events and acts: the words written in a diary, for instance, or spoken on a tape-recorder exist outside the writer or speaker, and may be observed in principle by anyone. Thus the words of all the women and men quoted in this book constitute objective facts that we can all examine. On the other hand, there can be reasonable dispute about how we *interpret* objective facts. Thus you may wish to interpret much of the data I have presented in a different way.

How is one to choose between your interpretation and mine? This is where logic and theory come into their own. Choosing between interpretations requires you to answer three questions:

1. Does the objective evidence support or refute the theory?
2. Is the theory logically consistent?
3. Are the conclusions equitable and just?

Scientific proof, especially in psychology, is a misleading fiction: no psychological theory can be proven. But a psychological theory can be shown to provide the best possible interpretation for the evidence on hand. People, as we know, are all different, and though there is a widespread longing for certainties, the best we can say is that *patterns are found* in the data, that some patterns are statistically more probable in some situations than in others, that men tend to behave in one way and women tend to behave in another because we find these patterns occur statistically more frequently in the circumstances analysed. Statistical frequencies and probabilities are objective analyses which may be repeated by other investigators and so may be confirmed or disconfirmed. Where disconfirmation occurs on several occasions, the original calculations may be put in doubt. Analytical evidence in support of a theory is useful, but does not *prove* it is correct: statistical evidence that refutes a theory requires either that the theory is reconstructed to accommodate the damaging evidence, or that it is thrown out altogether.

Analysis may also be qualitative, as in most of this book, and here different interpretations may be in conflict. Though investigators may agree on the patterns in the data, qualitative analysis is essentially subjective: in an attempt to illuminate culture, it relies on shared cultural assumptions to make meanings clear. This is both a weakness and a strength. The weakness is that such analyses are open to the criticism of being 'unscientific' because not based on 'objective' measures which could be made by anyone. The strength is that analyses which use cultural assumptions to illuminate culture are understood by members of that culture in a way that statistics never can be. Thus you will *know* whether what I have said in my commentary on people's statements makes sense in your experience of the society within which you live.

Logical consistency requires that different elements in a theory that is supported by evidence do not contradict each other. You may not agree with all my conclusions, but in order to reject my theory and stick to your own, you need to be able to show that (a) your theory fits the objective evidence better (all quotations in the book fully accounted for) and (b) you are not making contradictory assumptions. For example, you may believe that women are fundamentally less intelligent and more emotional than men because they are born that way, and you have ploughed your way through this book, which claims (among other things) that this is a misconception, with the avowed intent of showing how misguided this female psychologist is. In order to demonstrate my errors, you will need to show how the evidence fits your own theory, and you will need to do this without introducing any suggestion that in some circumstances the women might have been more intelligent or more controlled than the men they were dealing with. This may be difficult in some situations, like the Whodunnit experiment, for example (where people were selected as partners on the basis of age and education level), or women dealing with their bosses at work (where women's self-control contrasts with their bosses' emotional self-indulgence). But you are not entitled to refute one theory with a contradiction in another.

Finally, the conclusions a theory leads to must be equitable and just. This notion of equity does not, of course, apply to theories in the physical sciences like astronomy, say, or chemistry. But I am following philosopher Janet Radcliffe Richards who argues that theories of social relations must include social equity and justice to be acceptable.[1] This book is about women and men arguing in a wide variety of different social relationships, and so equity and justice do need to be considered.

My theory is that the well-established Division of Labour between women and men is sufficient to explain differences in attitude to argument, ways of communicating and use of language; that the Division of Labour is breaking down; that the consequences of this breakdown do lead to injustices; and that understanding what the Division of Labour was for and why it is no longer useful is an essential preliminary to establishing productive communication between us.

30

Trapped between a Hormone and a Hard Social Place

> Women have no need to compete with men; for what they alone
> can do is the more essential. Love, the bearing of children and the
> making of a home are creative activities without which we would
> perish.
>
> (Anthony Storr)[2]

Let us just remind ourselves of why there is this Division of
Labour between women and men. In Part One, Chapter 4, we saw
that there is a deep conflict between two opposing elements in the
human psyche. We have a powerful need to protect our 'in-group'
and defend ourselves from 'outsiders', yet we have a strong desire
for peace and harmony with others. These conflicting needs being
difficult to reconcile in everyday life, Western society has developed the useful separation of responsibilities whereby men deal
with outsiders and decide when hostilities are appropriate while
women take care of relationships within the group.

Remember: the split in the psyche applies to both women and
men. Though culturally, we expect women to be caring and men to
be aggressive, psychologists can show that women are just as
inclined as men to protect the in-group and discriminate against
outsiders, and that men desire friendship and love just as women
do.

Now you may believe that the Division of Labour we have
encountered so often arose precisely because it reflects genetically
determined differences between the sexes. The one difference we
can all agree on is that women bear children, and men do not. It

makes sense to suppose that the human whose task it is to care for a helpless infant for many months would be programmed to be gentle, caring, nurturing – exactly those characteristics needed to promote peace and harmony among all members of a group.

Or at least, it would make sense to think of being 'programmed' if we were like bees or weaver birds. But mammalian brains, and especially human mammalian brains, are far more complex. We do not come fully programmed, but are born with *potential*. This is why we are helpless at birth, and need so long to develop: our brains need to *construct* the world in which we live, so that we can learn to deal with it in everyday life rapidly and without hesitation. The human brain has amazing plasticity.

We all know (or should!) that a baby will learn to speak the language that her or his carers speak. Thus the baby of an English-speaking mother and a French-speaking father brought up (for some reason) in the first three years of life in Japan by a Japanese nurse will speak Japanese. This is because all (or the majority of) the language sounds the infant hears from birth until language is learned are Japanese, not English or French. In other words, the potential for language is built into the newborn brain, but the actual expression of this potential depends on the environment and not the parents' genes. And did you know that even how you *see* the world depends crucially on what you see in those early months of life? If you never see sharp edges, for instance, during the period when neurons are being laid down in the brain to deal with the external physical world, you may never be *able* to see them in future.[3]

This plasticity of the human cortex is even more striking when it comes to social behaviour, and how an adult behaves towards an infant depends crucially on how she or he was cared for in infancy and childhood. Here indeed we have an explanation for many of the ills in our society, and why the findings of psychology are not turned to practical use I shall never understand. Psychologists have known since at least the 1960s that poor parenting in infancy can lead to inability to relate to others in adulthood, to neglect and even to physical abuse of offspring.[4] The so-called maternal instinct in primates and humans is not innate, but depends crucially on experiences laid down in early life. Experiments also show that male monkeys may be gentle with their mates, and with youngsters, but that this too depends on gentle handling in infancy.

We can see why gentleness and nurturing are so important to human society. Without loving care, individuals can grow to adulthood unable to relate to others as human, sexual congress may occur as rape, and when a woman does have a baby, she may have no understanding of how to care for it. A self-perpetuating downward spiral of neglect, cruelty and even death can ensue. By contrast, given what we would call 'normal' care and attention, the human infant grows to adulthood knowing that other people have minds and feelings, and that warmth and friendship can be cultivated with chosen others. The maternal instinct that so many people believe is genetically determined is created most easily by a beneficial spiral of good mothering that moves from generation to generation. Good mothering tends to run in families just because it depends so strongly on experience rather than genes. Good primary care, whoever the carer, teaches the female infant how to care and teaches the male infant the fundamentals of good parenting too.

Why am I emphasising this here? It is because we have seen throughout this book that assumptions about fundamental differences between women and men underlie many of the difficulties we have in communicating with one another. We need to understand the basis of these assumptions, and to realise that human beings have enormous potential for changing their behaviour. If, as I believe, the current Division of Labour has outlived its usefulness, then we need to know that we can change.

31

Power Games

Many Western women are perfectly happy with the notion that they are especially good at feelings, at nurturing relationships. Relationships with other people are important, and being good at understanding others is a virtue. There is no reason why women who feel this is true of them should repudiate it.

What they are not so happy about is the accompanying assumption that if they are good at feelings they must be bad at thinking.

The persistence of this idea that women are irrational, emotional and unable to cope with logical thinking despite massive evidence to the contrary can be explained only by bringing issues of power into the equation.

In Part Three we examined a number of different kinds of power: coercive, consensual, expert, status, wealth. Here I want to present a new model which links the Division of Labour with the three major types of power: coercion, consensus, expertise. (A little thought will show that status and wealth may be subsumed under the other three power types in the analysis I shall give.) The diagram on p.325 shows schematically the relationships between the different elements, and these are explained below.

Starting with biology, we can see that pregnancy and child care provide simple evidence of the usefulness of dividing up tasks among those involved. Nature did it first – only primitive organisms reproduce asexually, and survival in most animal species depends on some form of co-operation between adults in the provision of food and protection from predators. So that the

The Power Gender Model

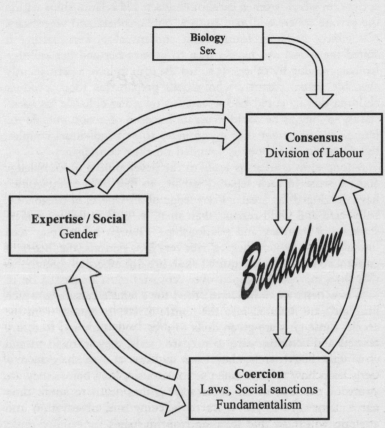

A schematic representation of how the Division of Labour between women and men is maintained by application of power

© Mapstone, 1997
drawn by Michael Abbott

Division of Labour between the sexes we have found in Western society, in which women care for children and relationships within the private sphere and men run the public sphere and wage wars, was almost certainly founded on consensual power sharing. It suited the woman to have a man to protect her and her children from aggression by others. It suited the man to have a permanently available sexual partner, who would prepare his food, produce children that he could know were his own and enhance his social status, so long as he could maintain freedom of action outside the home. To the extent that it continues to suit individual couples, this Division of Labour is founded on their consensus.

A long-term consensus leads to the development of knowledge and expertise in each separate sphere, so that over time, women have developed far greater knowledge of all aspects of pregnancy, baby care and child-rearing than men, as well as deeper under-standing of intimacy and relationships. Though culture may feed into evolution to some degree over very long periods (the theory of cultural co-evolution), acquired skills are not inherited directly, so that the expertise developed over centuries must be passed on to each new generation: hence the need for a female culture in which little girls are initiated into the female mysteries almost from the cradle. Little girls are given dolls to dress and wash and feed, toy tea-sets and cooking ware to prepare meals, they learn to sit and chat with their friends, they learn to listen and to share secrets. Girls learn how to be women unconsciously, long before they are aware of the fact, in the same way as they learn to speak their native language – over years of listening and observation and attempts to imitate and learning from mistakes.

Exactly the same analysis applies to boys, although their initiation into male mysteries may occur in fits and starts. Most women who care for male infants and toddlers 'know' that boys are different from girls, so their function appears to be to discourage little boys from taking part in girlish activities. 'Little boys don't play with dolls', they play with cars and trains, and later on, they play football. But little boys are human and they need their toys to cuddle too – so they are given stuffed animals, and stories about trains that talk. It is no surprise that Winnie the Pooh and Thomas the Tank Engine are so universally beloved, because these are deemed acceptable friends for little boys in the modern version of the male culture. Male culture is, of course, promoted and protected by men. While women tend to teach boys that they are 'not girls' and gradually exclude them from female culture, boys turn to their fathers to learn how to become a man. And if father is at work most of the time, or absent, then they comb comics and television and, increasingly, computer games for information. They learn that to be a man is to fight wars (newscasts, computer games, comics), to play sports, make laws, run the world. They learn that to be male is to be cool, streetwise, tough.

Parents who wish to subvert this acculturation, and teach boys to be gentle and caring and allow girls to be 'tomboys', find that social pressures undermine their efforts at every turn. As soon as children mingle with their peers, long-established custom is reasserted. Little boys who have been taught not to fight are quickly picked on and bullied; by the time he starts primary school, learning to stand up for himself and hit back when physically attacked may be essential for the boy's survival. Though parents may bemoan the fact that their daughters are not interested in the trains or the chemistry set they bought with such good intentions, preferring that etiolated caricature of the female figure, the Barbie doll, it is their sons' urgent need for instruction in fighting with their fists that really creates distress. How are we to learn to live together peaceably if even little boys cannot safely be taught not to hit others because others will almost certainly hit them? This dilemma is a direct consequence of the Division of Labour, and evidence that it no longer serves its original purpose.

The consensus that created the Division of Labour leads to development of separate areas of expertise, which feed back into the consensual division of power. We learn to believe we are better than the other sex at our special skills – and we probably are. It is quite likely that women as a group are better at understanding feelings than are men as a group, for they have invested a great deal of time and energy in learning about feelings. Men as a group are undoubtedly better at warfare, because more experienced in it, have more elaborated concepts about tactics and strategy, concentrate more closely as a group on winning than do women. Men also have considerably more experience running the institutions on which society is founded. Running things, though, which means thinking rationally about needs, determining priorities, planning, juggling time and resources so that essential tasks are done, are all skills women too have developed within their own sphere, and it is precisely here, where male and female expertise overlap, that the consensual share of power is breaking down. When consensus breaks down, coercion is the usual resort of the more powerful partner.

Many analyses by feminist writers have emphasised the institutional controls that men have brought in over the centuries in order to prevent women from escaping their part of the bargain. Controls would not be necessary if women were entirely happy with the set-up, which does suggest that the current Division of Labour has been resisted by large numbers of women for a long time. Though biology and human psychology may have led to an early consensus based on fundamental needs, recorded history of Western society shows regular attempts by women to move out of their restricted sphere, followed by the 'backlash' of control.

During the twentieth century, much of the argument about relations between the sexes has concentrated on woman as home-maker and whether she should 'go out to work'. But as Bonnie Anderson and Judith Zinsser show in their admirable history of women in Europe, until the Industrial Revolution women had always contributed their labour to the production of essential goods. It was during the eighteenth and nineteenth centuries that the increasing wealth of the middle classes took large numbers of women out of the labour force and into the home, isolating them from trade and business, to which they had hitherto always contributed. Unlike their working-class sisters who had to work in factories or mines or basement kitchens in order to survive, many of these women had little to do but look after the children, run the home, and create 'a precious refuge from the cares of the male world of business and industry' for their husbands.[5] The very wealth that allowed the middle-class woman to concentrate on domestic affairs permitted society to exaggerate the traditional differences between the sexes.

> In the new encyclopedias of the eighteenth century, women and men were defined as opposites. Women were emotional; men were rational; women were passive; men were active. Women were gentle; men were aggressive. A woman's virtues were chastity and obedience; a man's courage and honor. Women were meant for the home; men for public life.[6]

Similar changes were occurring in the United States. Psychiatrist Carol Zisowitz Stearns and historian Peter Stearns show that control of anger became an essential theme when the home was seen as a haven from the outside world.[7] On marriage, both women and men were warned: 'Never quarrel . . . it is death to happiness'.[8] But women in particular were firmly admonished to cultivate a gentle spirit, and to avoid any contention, contradiction or dispute with their husbands. A single argument, stories in the ladies' magazines warned, could lead to disaster, separation, even death.

Coercion feeds into expertise, and nineteenth-century woman was taught that she had special virtues simply because she was female. The ideal woman was like Coventry Patmore's Angel in the House who soothed and nurtured, rocking the cradle and ruling the world by her gentle virtue. Some writers came to believe that girls did not feel anger, needing only to be trained in 'cheerfulness': it was boys who needed training in anger control.[9] Women struggled to overcome their rebellious spirits and to be what they too believed they 'ought' to be: quiet, gentle, conciliatory, smoothing over differences, concerned to keep others happy. However, the minatory tone of many writers does suggest that women then, as now, did not adjust to the ruling concepts of ideal womanhood as easily as might have been expected if these ideals had been truly biologically or divinely determined.

To the extent that women accept that they have special qualities that make them more suitable for domestic tasks than men, this leads to a new consensus. Many people do believe that women are 'better' than men, because more caring and more spiritual, and indeed there is a school of radical feminism that claims that men are essentially violent, aggressive and misogynistic, and that women are better off without them: they have broken out of the circle altogether. But for the majority of women, who want to maintain good relationships with the men in their lives, a Division of Labour which accords them high qualities can seem very attractive.

Writer Beatrix Campbell's book on Conservative women shows that many traditional women are very happy with a Division of Labour that gives them autonomy in their separate sphere of caring for people: they find they have considerably more power in intimate and family relationships than they would have if their complementary functions were not attributed value.[10] They do not feel inferior. Within their own female territory they know that it is men who are the weaker sex, are 'like babies' who must be pampered and helped to deal with their unconscious aggressive or sexual urges. They know they are vulnerable to men's uncontrolled impulses, and see themselves as 'more rational, mature, controlled and calm than most men'.[11]

This analysis explains how there can be so many contradictory opinions about the proper place of women and men in society at any one time. Those who find the status quo suits them very well naturally resist any attempt to make changes they fear will disrupt their comfortable way of life, or indeed undermine their under-standing of the way society should be run. By contrast, those who find that the current set-up impedes their freedom of action will try to bring about changes. Given the well-established power imbalance in the public sphere, it is almost always women who attempt to bring about changes and men who attempt to maintain the old way by coercion. This analysis also explains why it is that when women start to make inroads into formerly male fields, men so often invoke aspects of sex and childbirth to keep them under control, this being the single aspect of human biology that differentiates the two sexes.

Vigilant readers will have noted that I have used the term 'sex' in this section almost all the time, rather than the term 'gender' which I used in the rest of the book. This is because the Division of Labour is based on sex, but the consensus which maintained this division *created* gender. As can be seen schematically in the diagram on p.325, breakdown in the consensus leads to coercion; women's vulnerability in pregnancy and child care, which led to the early consensus, is used as a weapon to impose laws, social and religious sanctions, which in turn make living outside the Division of Labour intolerable, if not impossible, and so lead to a new consensus. These coercive measures, which determine gender roles, may also lead to new beliefs about gender skills, which in turn help the new consensus – until more women discover that the restrictions are intolerable and demand more freedom, and the consensus breaks down again, leading to a new cycle.

What appears to be new today, as we approach a new millennium, is that women have discovered that they can realistically aim for power at the top. Though there have been female monarchs throughout history, and Queen Elizabeth I is a glittering symbol of what a woman with determination can do, few were able to act independently of their male consorts or advisers. It is only in the last half of this century that women in any numbers have been able to get into positions where their decisions can make a difference to society. The more women who acquire decision-making power, the harder it is to apply the previous coercive sanctions, and the more likely that the Division of Labour will break down altogether.

In a book about fifteen *Women World Leaders*, American lawyer Laura Liswood noted a 1992 study by the Center for the American Woman and Politics which showed that women in politics *do* affect policy and women's rights. The report also claimed that

> women public officials are changing the way government works. The women legislators were more likely than men to bring citizens into the political process, to favor government in public view rather than government behind closed doors, and to be responsible to groups previously denied full access to the policy-making process.[12]

Attempts at coercion from those who wish to prevent just such influence are well documented: see, for example, Susan Faludi's *Backlash*,[13] or the vicious attacks on Hillary Clinton ever since she entered the White House. Revisions to the old agreement on how to divide up power become less and less easy to negotiate as women discover that power in the outside world is good to have. Increasing numbers of women want control over their future, and they demand a voice – a voice that counts – in how decisions about society are made.

The old Division of Labour is past its prime and failing fast.

32

Calling a Truce

Raising fundamental questions about how society is run may seem to have come a long way from the topic of this book: the psychology of argument. But it is precisely because argument is so central a part of our relations with other people that it involves examining what these relationships mean and, in particular, how gender determines crucial parts of that meaning. Our attitudes to argument are based on cultural assumptions originally held by our parents or other important people in our childhood, and the rapid changes taking place in society today may leave many of us feeling baffled and angry.

Where does this leave us? Precisely where we started, in a society which almost automatically treats women unfairly when it comes to argument. We have seen that assumptions about differences between women and men are so ingrained that when a woman chooses to argue with almost anyone about almost anything, stereotypes are available which allow listeners to discount her views. Men, in particular, tend to fall back on outdated assumptions about women as an effective way of ignoring what a woman says. Women may be unaware of these belittling assumptions, but the research shows that they are often patronisingly indulged when young and beautiful, dismissed as unimportant as they mature, and ignored or offensively abused as they grow old. We could say this verges on being an issue of freedom of speech.

Not every man is guilty of this dismissive behaviour. There are honourable exceptions, both in our personal lives and in the workplace. Some men genuinely acknowledge their female colleagues as equals. Those who choose to appoint a woman to a position which gives her real power may be predisposed to finding their original judgement well founded, and willing to listen to her argument if she is carefully calm, logical and unemotional. But stereotypes are always to hand if she turns out not to be as 'reliable' as hoped. And many men tend to discount what a woman says, and bosses tend to become extremely angry when a female employee dares to argue, thereby subjecting the woman to high levels of rage.

Unsurprisingly, it is in our private lives that the best relationships between men and women are developed. Men in happy long-term relationships with a wife or lover may discover that arguing with a woman can be a positive pleasure when they no longer let assumptions about women in general get in the way. The secret to a good arguing relationship between a man and a woman is forgetting that salient difference – sex/gender – and listening to each other as *people*.

This may not be easy. One of my friends, who generously agreed to read a draft of some chapters, told me she tried relating the findings to her experiences with the new man in her life:

'He does seem to think I'm just being emotional if I try to tell him things. But I find I enjoy him being male, not to say macho, so it's tricky. I shall have to find a new way of talking, and insisting that he listens. I don't want to spoil what we've got.'

What did she mean by 'macho'? She really meant 'sexily masculine'. But need it follow that sexual attraction is diminished by a sense that, *when arguing*, those delicious differences between us that lead to delight in bed are irrelevant? We have seen that we do tend to relate to each other through deep-seated, often unconscious, beliefs about what makes a 'real man' and a 'real woman', and of course it is lovers who are most affected by such concerns.

How then are we to build that golden bridge between us?

Certainly, I am not able to offer a blueprint for its construction, but I hope I have provided enough material for a start to be made. We need to recognise that neither sex nor gender has much to do with intellect, and that the old Division of Labour was based on a convenient separation of functions that suited most people in the past, but which is now breaking down.

We need to understand that the gender roles we have internalised through our upbringing are based, not just upon a simple Division of Labour in the reproduction of our species, but upon a conflict in the psyche of every human being. We need to know, not only intellectually but deep inside, that men need warmth and closeness and women may feel hostility to those who are 'not one of us'. Then we need no longer feel quite as different from each other as our culture has made us. We have more in common as human beings, in the way we think and the way we feel, than we tend to assume when sex intervenes. Couples who live together happily are able to relate to each other as individuals rather than as *representatives* of the other sex. They listen to each other, and care enough about each other to hear what is said.

As I came to write this final chapter, I found myself haunted by an absurd image: Humpty Dumpty as Janus, perched on the parapet of a skeleton bridge, one face glowering grumpily, the other beaming benevolently (but it was quite unclear which face was directed which way). Long lines of porcupines were making their way purposefully towards the bridge from both sides. At the bridge, two porcupines were standing hesitantly, one on either side, as though wondering how safe this uncompleted bridge might be, waving their sharp prickles at each other in a meaningful manner. I assumed that on one side they were all female and on the other side all male, though I couldn't tell. They all looked the same to me.

Notes

(Refer to Bibliography for full scource details where author and date only are cited below.)

What This Book Is About

1. P. G. Wodehouse (1933) *Heavy Weather*. London: Herbert Jenkins. Penguin, 1966, p. 229.
2. F. Nietzsche (1901) *Der Wille zur Macht (The Will to Power)*.
3. Virginia Woolf, 'Professions for Women'. Lecture to the National Society for Women's Service, 21 January 1931. Published posthumously, reprint in Woolf, 1995, pp. 4–5.
4. Mapstone, 1996.
5. G. Wheatcroft (1996) 'An argument for a cool debate between sexes', *Daily Express*, 11 June, p. 8.
6. See, for example, Uta Frith (1989) *Autism: Explaining the Enigma*. Oxford: Blackwell; S. Baron-Cohen, A. M. Leslie and U. Frith (1985) 'Does the autistic child have a theory of mind?', *Cognition*, 21, 37–46.
7. Sir James Mackintosh (1765–1832), quoted in Anon., 1835.

The Research

1. The method of analysis is an extension of Dell Hymes' ethnomethodological analyses of 'communication competence' to explanatory accounts (Hymes, 1972, 1974; see also Rom Harré, 1979; Deborah Schiffrin, 1994: details below). Patterns of 'competent communication' are sought, not in the structure of exchanges, but rather in the content, and how content varies across contexts. Accounts are analysed as intended to provide recognisably meaningful answers to the questions posed, within the context of a research interview by a psychologist.

   Note that this is not a form of conversation analysis (Heritage and Atkinson, 1984) nor the kind of discourse analysis advocated in Jonathan Potter and Margaret Wetherell's (1987) influential book. The focus is not on the dynamics of the interview itself, but rather on the content of what was said: the aim was to seek meaningful patterns in what interviewees chose to say in different contexts. As Schiffrin (1994: 139) puts it in the context of a discussion of ethnography of communication:

> The way we communicate with each other is constrained by culture (simply because it is a part of culture), but it also reveals and sustains culture. From an analytical standpoint, an analysis of the patterns that are formed when we communicate thus contributes to our understanding of culture.

Harré, R. (1979) *Social Being*. Oxford: Blackwell.

Heritage, J. and Atkinson, J. (eds) (1984) *Structure of Social Action: Studies in Conversation Analysis*. Cambridge University Press.

Hymes, D. (1972) 'Models of the interaction of language and social life', in J. Gumperz and D. Hymes (eds), *Directions in Sociolinguistics: The Ethnography of Communication*. New York: Holt, Rinehart & Winston.

Hymes, D. (1974), *Foundations in Sociolinguistics: An Ethnographic Approach*. University of Philadelphia Press.

Potter, J. and Wetherell, M. (1987) *Discourse and Social Psychology*. London: Sage.

Schiffrin, D. (1994) *Approaches to Discourse*. Oxford: Blackwell.

2. Mapstone, 1992a.

Part One: Argument and Humpty Dumpty

1. Quotations are taken from argument diaries.
2. Heider, 1958, p. 195.
3. Ibid., p. 230.
4. For example, Billig, 1985, 1987.
5. See details in Mapstone, 1992a, 1995.
6. For example, Skeat's *Etymological Dictionary* (1879–82, revised 1910) states that 'to argue' means 'to make clear'; *Shorter Oxford English Dictionary* (1972, p. 96) provides as primary meaning for 'argument' 'proof, token' (Meaning 1); *Chambers Twentieth Century English Dictionary* (1972, p. 67) offers 'proof, evidence, reason or series of reasons, exchange of such reasons, debate'; *Collins English Dictionary* (1979, p. 75) gives 'quarrel, altercation' as primary meaning for 'argument' and 'to quarrel, wrangle' as first meaning for 'to argue'.
7. See e.g. Socratic dialogues in Plato's *Meno*, trans. 1956 by W. K. C. Guthrie; or *Gorgias*, trans. 1971 by W. Hamilton; both in Penguin.
8. Strawson, P. F. (1952) *Introduction to Logical Theory*. London: Methuen.

Philosopher A. N. Whitehead, quoted in S. Stebbing (1952) *A Modern Elementary Logic*, 5th edition, revised. London: Methuen, p. 21.

9. A. Flew (1975) *Thinking About Thinking*. London: Fontana, p. 17.

10. J. Piaget (1924) *Le Jugement et le raisonnement chez l'enfant*. Neuchatel and Paris: Delachaux & Niestle, p. 92.

11. Toulmin, 1958, p. 254.

12. M. McConville (1987) 'Silence in court', *New Law Journal*, 138, 1169–70. Quoted in M. King (1988) 'Use of video in child abuse trials', *The Psychologist: Bulletin of the British Psychological Society*, 1, p. 168.

13. Brown, 1965, p. 551.

14. See e.g. G. Paicheler (1977) 'Norms and attitude change II. The phenomenon of bipolarisation,' *European Journal of Social Psychology*, 7, 5–14; G. Paicheler, (1979) 'Polarization of attitudes in homogeneous and heterogeneous groups', *European Journal of Social Psychology*, 9, 85–96.

15. M. Kington (1989) Christmas Quiz, *Independent*, 26 October.

16. I. Lakatos, in I. Lakatos and A. Musgrave (eds) (1970) *Criticism and the Growth of Knowledge*. Cambridge University Press, p. 178.

17. Billig, 1985, 1987.

18. See, for example, P. Du Preez (1980), E. Frazer (1988) and G. M. Gilbert and M. Mulkay (1984). Also J. Potter and S. Reicher (1987) 'Discourses of community and conflict: the organization of social categories in accounts of a "riot"', *British Journal of Social Psychology*, 26, 25–39.

19. Polly Toynbee in *Radio Times*, 28 September to 4 October 1996, p. 14.

20. Tajfel, 1978, 1981.

Part Two: The Porcupine's Dilemma

1. Confucius, quoted in R. Wilhelm (trans.) (1968) *I Ching*, 3rd edition. London: Routledge & Kegan Paul, p. 59.

2. Tysoe, 1992, p. 1.

3. D. H. Lawrence, letter to Dr Trigan Burrow, 3 August 1927, quoted in A. Stibbs (1992) *Like a Fish Needs a Bicycle*. London: Bloomsbury.

4. Many of these interviews have been reported in Mapstone, 1995. Others were carried out between 1987 and 1997. As anonymity was promised, names have been changed, except where first and second names are given.

5. See e.g. Deborah Schiffrin, 1984 'Jewish argument as sociability', *Language in Society*, 13, 311–35.

6. AAUW report, Greenberg-Lake: the Analysis Group, released January 1991, and reported in the *APA Monitor*, American Psychological Association, April 1991, p. 29.

7. Linda T. Sanford and Mary Ellen Donovan, 1984. Quotation taken from 1993 Penguin edition, p. xiii.

8. Sue Lees, 1993.
9. Ibid., p. 77.
10. Ibid., p. 32.
11. Quotes all from L. M. Brown and C. Gilligan (1993) 'Meeting at the crossroads', *Feminism & Psychology*, 3, 13. Other related psychological studies include: Carol Gilligan (1982, 1992) *In a Different Voice*. Cambridge, MA: Harvard University Press; J. B. Miller (1976) *Toward a New Psychology of Women*. Boston: Beacon Press.
12. Quoted in *Daily Mail*, 16 November 1989.
13. Sanford and Donovan, 1984.
14. Dale Spender (1980/1985). Quotation from 2nd edition, p. 112.
15. *Guardian*, 10 August 1995, Society Section, p. 14.
16. Quoted in Sanford and Donovan, 1984, p. 110, from *New York Times Book Review*, 9 January 1983.
17. T. Falbo and L. A. Peplau (1980) 'Power strategies in intimate relationships', *Journal of Personality and Social Psychology*, 38, 618–28.
18. Personal communications.
19. Mike Dickin Shaw, *London Talk Back*, London Broadcasting Corporation, September 1994.
20. D.Phil. thesis, 1992.
21. For example Celia Kitzinger and Adrian Coyle (1995) 'Lesbian and gay couples: speaking of difference', *The Psychologist: Bulletin of the British Psychological Society*, 8, 64–9.
22. Dorothy Parker, 'Somebody's Song', in *Enough Rope* (1926). Reproduced from *The Collected Dorothy Parker* by permission of Gerald Duckworth and Co. Ltd, London; and from *The Portable Dorothy Parker*, Introduction by Brendan Gill, (copyright 1926 renewed copyright 1954 by Dorothy Parker), by permission of Viking Penguin, a division of Penguin USA Inc.
23. Tysoe, 1992, p. 97.
24. Falbo and Peplau, op. cit.
25. John Rowan (1989) 'On being irrational', *Clinical Psychology Forum*, 24, 27–8.
26. Sanford and Donovan, 1984, p. 120.
27. Quote from violent husband used as title for 'Handbook for Victims of Domestic Violence', put out by Plymouth Women's Refuge and Plymouth Guild of Community Services. 1990s.
28. J. Archer and V. Rhodes (1993) 'The grief process and job loss: a cross-sectional study', *British Journal of Psychology*, 84, 395–410.
29. Quoted in Tavris, 1989, p. 221.
30. James Averill, 1982; Carol Tavris, 1989.
31. Tavris, 1989, p. 250.
32. Gray, 1992; p. 152 in paperback edition.

33. J. Veroff, E. Douvan and R. A. Kulka (1981) *The Inner American: A Self Portrait from 1957 to 1976.* Cited in Stearns and Stearns, 1986, p. 211.

34. Stearns and Stearns, 1986.

35. D. Morris quoted in 'Sulkers and screamers', *MS London*, 3 July 1989, p. 18.

36. See e.g. ibid.; *More!* magazine, 'What's a nice couple like you doing in a fight like this?', 11–24 November 1992; *Independent on Sunday*, 'For the kids' sake have a row', 23 March 1997.

37. Review in the *Observer*, 26 February 1995; capitals in original.

38. Barney Hoskyns reviewing Simon Reynolds and Joy Press (1995) *The Sex Revolts: Gender, Rebellion and Rock 'n' Roll.* London: Serpent's Tail.

39. Title of book by Carol Tavris and Carole Wade, 1977/1984.

40. Quoted in R.W. Southern (1970) *Western Society and the Church in the Middle Ages.* Harmondsworth: Penguin, p. 314.

41. Quoted in Joan Smith, 1989, p. 3.

42. Greer, 1970. Quotation from Paladin edition, p. 249.

43. Dinnerstein, 1976.

44. Melanie Klein (1935) *Love, Guilt and Reparation.* London: Hogarth.

45. Jukes, 1993, p. 316.

46. Ibid., p. 64.

47. See, for example, H. E. Gruber and J. J. Voneche (eds) (1977) *The Essential Piaget.* London: Routledge & Kegan Paul; Alice Rossi in Walsh (1987), in a debate on Nancy Chodorow's theory of mothering (Chodorow, 1978). I do not, however, go along with Rossi's suggestion of a biologically based potential in mothers for greater investment in the child than the father, as the well-established Division of Labour is sufficient to explain women's role; Margaret Donaldson (1978) *Children's Minds.* London: Fontana; Annette Karmiloff Smith (1994) *Baby It's You.* (Book accompanying TV series on early development.) London: Ebury Press. Professor Karmiloff Smith was the first developmental psychologist ever to become a Member of the Royal Society.

48. Chodorow, 1978.

49. Ibid., p. 260.

50. Joseph Pleck (1981) also makes this point in *The Myth of Masculinity.* Cambridge, MA: MIT Press.

51. Chodorow, 1978, p. 250.

52. In 1912, Cyril Burt and R. C. Moore published the first paper in Britain showing that objective measures of performance by boys and girls produced no significant differences. See C. Burt and R. C. Moore (1912) 'The mental differences between the sexes', *Journal of Experimental Pedagogy*, 1, 273–84 and 355–88.

53. Halla Beloff (1992) 'Mother, Father and Me: Our IQ', *The Psychologist*, 5, 309–11.

54. John Campion in 'Letters', *The Psychologist*, October 1992, 456.

55. See also: Louise Higgins (1987) 'The unknowing of intelligence', *Guardian*, 10 February; H. W. Hogan (1973) 'IQ: self-estimates of males and females', *Journal of Social Psychology*, 106, 137–8; T. A. Roberts (1991) 'Gender and the influence of evaluations on self-assessment in achievement settings', *Psychological Bulletin*, 109, 297–308.

56. See J.D. Willms and P.D. Kerr (1988) 'Changes in sex differences in Scottish examination results since 1976', *Journal of Early Adolescence*, 7, 85–104; Department of Education in Northern Ireland, *Statistical Bulletin*, December 1991.

57. All unattributed quotes are from interviews, letters and diaries.

58. Payne, 1983; quotations from Virago edition, p. 54.

59. Professor Robert Abelson, Seminar to Department of Experimental Psychology, University of Oxford, Summer 1985.

60. Payne, 1983, p. 382: letter from Ann Scott to Payne.

61. Bly, 1990; quotations are from the Vintage Books edition: this one p. 22.

62. Ibid., p. 227.

63. Ibid., p. 24, my italics.

64. Ibid., p. 11.

65. Ibid., p. 234.

66. In S. French, 1992, pp. 60–61.

67. *The Times*, 14 May 1994: 'The positive force of family feuds'.

68. Philip Larkin (1988) 'This Be the Verse', in *Collected Poems*. London: Faber & Faber, p. 180. First published in *High Windows*, 1974. Reproduced by permission of Faber & Faber, London.

69. S. Calman (1992) 'You're still a child to them', *The Times*, 19 May.

70. Sean French (1994) 'About men, about women,' *Observer*, 27 February.

Part Three: Janus-faced in a 'Post-Feminist' World

1. See *New Larousse Encyclopedia of Mythology*. London: Hamlyn, 1968.

2. George Orwell (1949) *Nineteen Eighty-Four*. London: Secker & Warburg.

3. Ursula K. Le Guin (1974) *The Dispossessed*. London: Panther, p. 44.

4. BBC Southern Counties Radio, 12 September 1994.

5. James Boswell, *Life of Samuel Johnson*, Vol. 1, 31 July 1763.

6. Quoted in L. Peter (ed.) (1978) *Quotations for our Time*. London: Souvenir Press.

7. Oliver Goldsmith, remark quoted in Boswell, op. cit., 26 October 1769.

8. Marc Nicholls (1993) 'What he really tells other men', *Cosmopolitan*, May, p. 55.

9. Quoted in L. Peter, op. cit.

10. Seidler, 1989, p. 126.

11. Henry David Thoreau (1849) 'Wednesday', in *A Week on the Concord and Merrimack Rivers*: see *Concise Oxford Dictionary of Quotations*, 1964.

12. S. Calman (1992) 'I think, he knows, so who wins?', *The Times*, 19 Feb.

13. Trudy Govier (1988) 'Tu quoque, credibility and argument', *Newsletter of the International Society for the Study of Argumentation*, 3, p. 4.

14. Ibid., p. 7.

15. Seidler, 1989, p. 62.

16. Le Guin, op. cit., p. 44.

17. Tannen, 1990. All quotations from Virago 1992 edition. This one p. 169

18. Oscar Wilde (1895) *The Importance of Being Earnest*, Act 1.

19. Miller and Boster, 1988, pp. 283, 285.

20. Ibid., p. 283.

21. Leo Bruce (1945) *Case for Three Detectives*. Harmondsworth: Penguin.

22. For a full account see Mapstone, 1992a.

23. Kipnis, 1976; Kipnis and Schmidt, 1985. See also: D. Kipnis, P. J. Castell, K. Gergen and D. Mauch (1976) 'Metamorphic effects of power', *Journal of Applied Psychology*, 61, 127–35; D. Kipnis, S. Schmidt and I. Wilkinson (1980) 'Intraorganisational influence tactics: explorations in getting one's way', *Journal of Applied Psychology*, 65, 440–52.

24. Rupert Crawshay-Williams (1970) *Russell Remembered*. Oxford: Oxford University Press, pp. 18–19. My thanks to Prof. Edward M. Wise, Wayne State University Law School, Detroit, and Prof. John Slater, University of Toronto, who tracked down this source.

25. Hochschild, 1983.

26. *Independent*, 8 September 1990.

27. Quoted in Rosalind Miles, 1985, Futura edition, p. 31.

28. Personal communication.

29. Lakoff, 1990; incident and analysis on pp. 20–21.

30. Kennedy, 1992.

Part Four: Playing the Gender Game at Work

1. Wendy Hollway (1991) 'The psychologization of feminism or the feminization of psychology?', *Feminism & Psychology*, 1, 35.

2. *She* magazine, February 1993.

3. Suzette Haden Elgin, 1989, p. 54.

4. Glynis Breakwell, 1985.

5. Ibid., p. 35.

6. Ibid., p. 109.

7. Deirdre came second overall in her final exams.

8. See e.g. John Archer and Barbara Lloyd, 1985; Donna Eder, 1990; Marjorie H. Goodwin, 1990; Eleanor Maccoby, 1990.

9. Tannen, 1990.

10. Kipnis and Schmidt, 1985, p. 45.

11. John Major quoted in the *Independent*, 19 June 1991.

12. Tannen, 1994, p. 145. Quotations from Virago 1996 edition.

13. Beverley Alimo-Metcalfe (1992) 'Gender, leadership and assessment'. Paper presented to the conference of the Occupational Psychology Division of the British Psychological Society, Liverpool.

14. C. J. Margerison and A. P. Kakabadse (1984) *How the American Chief Executive Succeeds* (American Management Association Monograph). New York: AMA Membership Publications Division; A. P. Kakabadse (1987) 'Performance and the top executive: gender differences of management style', *The Occupational Psychologist*, 3, 15–17. Leicester: British Psychological Society.

15. Kakabadse, op. cit., p. 16.

16. Erika Apfelbaum (1986) The Henri Tajfel Memorial Lecture: 'Women in leadership positions'. Published in the newsletter of the Social Psychology Section of the British Psychological Society, Spring 1987.

17. Quoted in *Bloomsbury Dictionary of Quotations*, 1987, p. 235. Quotations from paperback 1989 edition.

18. Cited in Apfelbaum, op. cit.

19. Joy Billington (1993) 'The First Granny', *Woman's Journal*, June, p. 62.

20. *Observer*, 26 February 1995.

21. More details in Mapstone, 1992c, 1993a, 1993b.

22. Apfelbaum, op. cit.

23. *Fortune* magazine, 5 August 1996.

24. Joan Smith (1989) on Thatcher.

25. Quoted in the *Guardian*, 25 January 1997.

26. *Today*, 26 November 1990.

27. Margaret Thatcher (1993) *The Downing Street Years*. London: HarperCollins, p. 129.

28. Margaret Thatcher, quoted in Ian Aitken (1982) 'Family life best, says Thatcher', *Guardian*, 27 July.

29. Helen Haste, invited speaker at Images of Women seminar, Oxford University Department of Continuing Education, Summer 1985.

30. 'Does your age work against you?', *New Woman*, June 1990, pp. 86–7.

31. Sarah Hegarty (1992) 'Snakes on the way up the ladder', *Independent*, 2 November.

32. Miles, 1985, p. 225.

33. P. Johnson (1976) 'Women and power: toward a theory of effectiveness', *Journal of Social Issues*, 32, 99–110.

34. Sir J. E. E. Dalberg Acton, Baron Acton. Letter, 3 April 1887, in *Oxford Dictionary of Quotations*, 1964.
35. Report in *Daily Telegraph*, 6 December 1996.
36. *GQ*, October 1994, p. 160.
37. Estelle Phillips and D. S. Pugh (1987) *How to Get a PhD*. Milton Keynes: Open University Press, p. 138.
38. *Guardian*, 18 January 1997.
39. Quoted in 'Talking Dirty', *Guardian*, 6 February 1997.
40. Letter to the author, 2 August 1995.
41. First study, 54 diaries, statistics published in Mapstone, 1992a.
42. Hester Lacey (1996) 'Why women always lose the argument', *Independent on Sunday*, 16 June.
43. Iain Carruthers-Jones (1992), quoted in *Independent*, 2 November.
44. Obstetrician suspended from her job in 1985 and reinstated the following year. See Wendy Savage, 1986.
45. *Daily Telegraph*, 27 May 1994.
46. Quote from Futura edition, 1986, p. 117.
47. Ginny Dougary, 1994, p. xii.
48. Ibid., p. 197.
49. Apfelbaum, op. cit., pp. 11, 12.
50. S. Schachter and J. E. Singer (1962) 'Cognitive, social and physiological determinants of emotional state', *Psychological Review*, 69, 379–99.
51. See, e.g., an excellent discussion in Roger Brown's *Social Psychology* (1965).
52. Lacey in the *Independent on Sunday*, 16 June 1996.
53. H. C. Metcalf and L. Urwicki (eds) (1941) *The Collected Papers of Mary Parker Follett*. London: Pitman.
54. See, for example, Margaret Neale and Max Bazerman (1985), 'Perspectives for understanding negotiation: viewing negotiation as a judgmental process', *Journal of Conflict Resolution*, 29, 33–55; Richard Wendell Fogg (1985), 'Dealing with conflict: a repertoire of creative, peaceful approaches', *Journal of Conflict Resolution*, 29, 330–58; Dean Pruitt and Peter Carnevale (1993), *Negotiation in Social Conflict*. Buckingham: Open University Press.
55. See Elgin, 1989, p. 81.
56. Published in Mapstone, 1995.
57. Brainin quoted in information book accompanying boxed set of Mozart String Quartets produced by Deutsche Grammophon, n.d.
58. *The Levin Interview*, BBC TV 5 September 1987; first broadcast 1981.
59. 'Chairman' – a deliberately sexist term. Cartoon by Riana Duncan, in *Punch*, 8 January 1988.
60. Cecilia Ridgeway (1993) Paper presented to American Association for the Advancement of Science, Boston. Reported in *APA Monitor*, April, p. 19.
61. Lacey, in the *Independent on Sunday*, 16 June 1996.

62. *First Sex*, broadcast 19 July 1995.
63. Linda Carli, address to American Association for the Advancement of Science, Boston, February 1993, reported in *APA Monitor*, April.
64. Coates, 1993.
65. Cathy Cassell, joint presenter with Sue Walsh of 'Internal and external barriers to women's progression at work: integrating clinical and organisational perspectives'. Psychology of Women conference, July 1994.
66. Hedy Brown, 1985, p. 44.
67. Janis, 1982.
68. Based on comments from many male informants.
69. Mapstone, 1990, 1992b, 1992c, 1993a, 1993b.
70. Kennedy Wilson (1996) 'Time to have justice for all', *Herald*, Glasgow, 30 October, p. 20.
71. To protect the innocent, I shall not name the second journalist since he was, after all, basing his query on the account written by the first.
72. *Guardian*, 22 February 1997.

Part Five: Building a Golden Bridge

1. Richards, 1980.
2. Anthony Storr (1968) *Human Aggression*. Harmondsworth: Penguin; quote from Pelican edition, 1970, p. 89.
3. See, for example, D. H. Hubel and T. N. Weisel (1962) 'Receptive fields, binocular interaction and functional architecture in the cat's visual cortex', *Journal of Physiology*, 160, 106; C. Blakemore and G. G. Cooper (1970) 'Development of the brain depends on the visual environment', *Nature*, 258, 477–8.
4. See, for example, the experiments with newborn rhesus monkeys: H. Harlow (1959) 'Love in infant monkeys', *Scientific American*, June; H. Harlow (1962) 'The heterosexual affectional system in monkeys', *American Psychologist*, 17, 1–9.
5. Anderson and Zinsser, 1988, p. 143. All page references are to the Penguin edition, Vol. 2.
6. Ibid.
7. Stearns and Stearns, 1986, 1988.
8. Revd John Brandt, *Marriage and the Home*, Chicago, 1895, cited in Stearns and Stearns, 1986. English writer Sarah Stickney Ellis gave similar warnings in *The Women of England, their Social Duties and Domestic Habits*. London and Paris: Fisher, Son & Co., 1845.
9. Stearns and Stearns, 1986, pp. 76, 77.
10. Campbell, 1987.

11. Haste, 1993, p. 106.
12. Liswood, 1995, Introduction, pp. xi–xii.

   Dr Susan Greenfield, a Lecturer in Synaptic Pharmacology at Oxford University, drew attention in her column in the *Independent on Sunday* ('Under the microscope', 6 July 1997) to research reported by two Swedish scientists in *Nature* (May 1997). Christine Wenneras, microbiologist, and Agnes Wold, immunologist, found that even where a female scientist's published work is frequently cited by others (and is therefore seen to be important), she is rated only slightly above the very worst of her male colleagues by those (men) who judge applications for research funding and promotion. This study should give pause to those who think that old assumptions are dying out. Sweden, after all, was named by the UN as the world's leading country when it comes to equal opportunities.

13. Faludi, 1992.

Bibliography

Abdela, Lesley (1994) *What Women Want.* London: The Body Shop.

Anderson, Bonnie S. and Zinsser, Judith P. (1988) *A History of Their Own: Women in Europe from Prehistory to the Present.* New York: Harper & Row; Penguin, 1990.

Anon. (1835) *Woman: As She Is and As She Ought To Be.* London: James Cochrane.

Archer, John and Lloyd, Barbara (1985) *Sex and Gender.* Cambridge University Press.

Averill, James (1982) *Anger and Aggression: An Essay on Emotion.* New York: Springer Verlag.

Avramides, Anita (ed.) (1995) *Women of Ideas.* London: Duckworth.

Billig, M. (1985) 'Prejudice, categorization and particularization: from a perceptual to a rhetorical approach', *European Journal of Social Psychology,* 15, 79–103.

Billig, Michael (1987) *Arguing and Thinking: A Rhetorical Approach to Social Psychology.* Cambridge University Press.

Bly, Robert (1990) *Iron John: A Book about Men.* New York: Addison Wesley; Vintage Books, 1992.

Breakwell, Glynis (1985) *The Quiet Rebel.* London: Century.

Brown, Hedy (1985) *People, Groups and Society.* Milton Keynes: Open University Press.

Brown, Roger (1965) *Social Psychology.* London: Collier Macmillan.

Campbell, Anne (1993) *Out of Control: Men, Women and Aggression.* New York: Basic Books.

Campbell, Beatrix (1987) *The Iron Ladies: Why Do Women Vote Tory?* London: Virago.

Carnegie, Dale (1936/1981) *How to Win Friends and Influence People*, revised edition. Tadworth, Surrey: World's Work.

Chodorow, Nancy (1978) *The Reproduction of Mothering: Psychoanalysis and the Sociology of Gender.* Berkeley: University of California Press.

348

Clark, Romy, Fairclough, Norman, Ivanic, Roz, McLeod, Nicki, Thomas, Jenny and Meara, Paul (eds) (1990) *Language and Power*. British Association for Applied Linguistics & Centre for Information on Language Teaching and Research.

Coates, Jennifer (1993) *Women, Men and Language*, 2nd edition. Harlow, Essex: Longman.

Danzinger, Kurt (1976) *Interpersonal Communication*. Oxford and New York: Pergamon Press.

Dietz, Mary G. (1977) 'Hannah Arendt and feminist politics', in Mary L. Shanley and Carole Pateman (eds), *Feminist Interpretations and Political Theory*. Oxford: Blackwell/Polity Press.

Dinnerstein, Dorothy (1976) *The Rocking of the Cradle and the Ruling of the World*. New York: Harper & Row.

Dougary, Ginny (1994) *The Executive Tart and Other Myths: Media Women Talk Back*. London: Virago.

Du Preez, Peter (1980) *Social Psychology of Politics: Ideology and the Human Image*. Oxford: Blackwell.

Eder, Donna (1990) 'Serious and playful disputes: variations in conflicts talk among female adolescents', in A. Grimshaw (ed.), *Conflict Talk*. Cambridge University Press.

Elgin, Suzette Haden (1989) *Success with the Gentle Art of Verbal Self-Defense*. Englewood Cliffs, NJ: Prentice-Hall.

Faludi, Susan (1992) *Backlash: The Undeclared War against Women*. London: Chatto & Windus.

Frazer, E. (1988) 'Teenage girls talking about class', *Sociology*, *22*, 343–58.

French, Sean (ed.) (1992) *Fatherhood*. London: Virago.

Gilbert, G. M. and Mulkay, M. (1984) *Opening Pandora's Box: A Sociological Analysis of Scientists' Discourse*. Cambridge University Press.

Goodwin, Marjorie H. (1990) *He Said She Said: Talking as Social Organisation among Black Children*. Bloomington: Indiana University Press.

Gray, John (1992) *Men are from Mars, Women are from Venus*. New York: HarperCollins.

Greer, Germaine (1970) *The Female Eunuch*. London: MacGibbon & Kee; Paladin, 1971.

Griffiths, Sian (ed.) (1996) *Beyond the Glass Ceiling*. Manchester University Press.

Grimshaw, Allen D. (ed.) (1990) *Conflict Talk*. Cambridge University Press.

Haste, Helen (1993) *The Sexual Metaphor*. Hemel Hempstead: Harvester Wheatsheaf.

Heider, Fritz (1958) *The Psychology of Interpersonal Relations*. Hillsdale, NJ: Lawrence Erlbaum.

Hen Co-op (1993) *Growing Old Disgracefully*. London: Piatkus.

349

Hochschild, Arlie R. (1983) *The Managed Heart*. Berkeley: University of California Press.

Hochschild, Arlie and Machung, Anne (1990) *The Second Shift*. London: Piatkus.

hooks, bell (1989) *Talking Back: Thinking Feminist, Thinking Black*. Boston: South End Press.

Janis, Irving (1982) *Victims of Group Think*, 2nd edition. Boston: Houghton Mifflin.

Jukes, Adam (1993) *Why Men Hate Women*. London: Free Association Books.

Kennedy, Helena (1992) *Eve Was Framed*. London: Chatto & Windus.

Kinnock, Glenys and Millar, Fiona (1993) *By Faith & Daring: Interviews with Remarkable Women*. London: Virago.

Kipnis, David (1976) *The Power Holder*. University of Chicago Press.

Kipnis, David and Schmidt, Stuart (1985) 'The language of persuasion', *Psychology Today*, 4, 40–46.

Kuhn, Deanna (1991) *The Skills of Argument*. Cambridge University Press.

Lakoff, Robin (1990) *Talking Power: the Politics of Language*. New York: Basic Books.

Lees, Sue (1993) *Sugar and Spice: Sexuality and Adolescent Girls*. Harmondsworth: Penguin.

Liswood, Laura A. (1995) *Women World Leaders*. London: HarperCollins.

Maccoby, Eleanor (1990) 'Gender and relationships: a developmental account', *American Psychologist*, 45, 513–20.

Miles, Rosalind (1985) *Women and Power*. London: Macdonald; Futura, 1986.

Miller, Gerald R. and Boster, Frank (1988) 'Persuasion in personal relationships', in S. Duck (ed.), *Handbook of Personal Relationships*. Chichester and New York: Wiley.

Okin, Susan Moller (1979) *Women in Western Political Thought*. Princeton University Press; Virago, 1980.

Payne, Karen (ed.) (1983) *Between Ourselves: Letters between Mothers and Daughters*. London: Michael Joseph; Virago, 1994.

Pruitt, Dean G. and Carnevale, Peter J. (1993) *Negotiation in Social Conflict*. Buckingham: Open University Press.

Richards, Janet Radcliffe (1980) *The Sceptical Feminist*. London: Routledge & Kegan Paul; Penguin, 1982.

Sanford, Linda T. and Donovan, Mary Ellen (1984) *Women and Self-Esteem: Understanding and Improving the Way we Think and Feel about Ourselves*. Anchor Press/Doubleday; Penguin, 1985.

Savage, Wendy (1986) *A Savage Enquiry: Who Controls Childbirth?* London: Virago.

Seidler, Victor (1989) *Rediscovering Masculinity: Reason, Language and Sexuality*. London: Routledge.

Smith, Joan (1989) *Misogynies*. London: Faber.

Spender, Dale (1980/1985) *Man Made Language*, 2nd edition. London, Boston and Henley: Routledge & Kegan Paul.

Stearns, Carol Z. and Stearns, Peter N. (1986) *Anger: The Struggle for Emotional Control in America's History*. University of Chicago Press.

Stearns, Carol Z. and Stearns, Peter N. (eds) (1988) *Emotion and Social Change: Towards a New Psychohistory*. New York: Holmes & Meier.

Tajfel, Henri (1978) *Differentiation between Social Groups: Studies in the Social Psychology of Intergroup Relations*. London: Academic Press.

Tajfel, Henri (1981) *Human Groups and Social Categories*. Cambridge University Press.

Tannen, Deborah (1990) *You Just Don't Understand*. New York: William Morrow. (1991/1992) London: Virago.

Tannen, Deborah (1994) *Talking from 9 to 5*. New York: William Morrow. (1995/1996) London: Virago.

Tavris, Carol (1989) *Anger: The Misunderstood Emotion*, 2nd edition. New York: Simon & Schuster/Touchstone.

Tavris, Carol (1992) *The Mismeasure of Woman*. New York: Simon & Schuster/Touchstone.

Tavris, Carol and Wade, Carole (1977/1984) *The Longest War: Sex Differences in Perspective*. San Diego: Harcourt Brace Jovanovich.

Toulmin, Stephen (1958) *The Uses of Argument*. Cambridge University Press.

Tysoe, Maryon (1992) *Love Isn't Quite Enough: The Psychology of Male–Female Relationships*. London: Fontana.

Tysoe, Maryon (1995) *The Good Relationship Guide*. London: Piatkus.

Vallely, Bernadette (ed.) (1996) *What Women Want*. London: Virago.

Walsh, Mary Roth (ed.) (1987) *The Psychology of Women: Ongoing Debates*. New Haven, CT: Yale University Press.

White, Kate (1995) *Why Good Girls Don't Get Ahead, But Gutsy Girls Do*. London: Century.

Woolf, Virginia (1995) 'Professions for women', in R. Bowlby (ed.), *Killing the Angel in the House: Seven Essays*. Harmondsworth: Penguin.

Related Publications by the Author

Mapstone, Elizabeth (1988a) 'A new acid test?' Editorial, *The Psychologist: Bulletin of the British Psychological Society*, 1(10), 387.

Mapstone, Elizabeth (1988b) 'Defending freedom of speech'. Editorial, *The Psychologist: Bulletin of the British Psychological Society*, 1(11), 427.

Mapstone, Elizabeth (1989) 'Secrets, security and freedom'. Editorial, *The Psychologist: Bulletin of the British Psychological Society*, 2(3), 91.

Mapstone, Elizabeth (1990) 'Rational men and disagreeable women'. Paper presented to a symposium on Gender Relations, British Psychological Society London Conference, City University.

Mapstone, Elizabeth (1991) 'Special issue on animal experimentation'. Editorial, *The Psychologist: Bulletin of the British Psychological Society*, 4(5), 195.

Mapstone, E. R. (1992a) 'Rational men and disagreeable women: the social construction of argument'. DPhil thesis, University of Oxford.

Mapstone, Elizabeth (1992b) 'Disagreeable women and rational men: stereotypes in diary accounts of argument'. Paper presented to the 25th International Congress of Psychology, Brussels, 24 July.

Mapstone, Elizabeth (1992c) 'Stereotypes in human relations'. Keynote paper in forum on relationships between women and men. Nuffield College, Oxford, 17 November.

Mapstone, Elizabeth (1993a) 'On disagreeing and being disagreeable: gender stereotypes in argument diaries'. Paper presented to the Annual Conference of the Psychology of Women Section, British Psychological Society, Sussex University, July.

Mapstone, Elizabeth (1993b) 'Against separatism', in Sue Wilkinson and Celia Kitzinger (eds), *Heterosexuality*. London: Sage.

Mapstone, Elizabeth (1995) 'Rational men and conciliatory women: graduate psychologists construct accounts of argument', *Feminism & Psychology*, 5(1), 61–83.

Mapstone, E. R. (1996) 'Division of labour in the social construction of argument', *British Journal of Social Psychology*, 35, 219–31.

Index

Abelson, Robert 103
abuse/abusive husbands 67–8,
  69–70, 70–6
adolescent boys: and fathers 52,
  110, 111–12, 117; and mothers
  117
adolescent girls: and fathers
  113–14; and fear of argument
  42–3; and mothers 117; and sex
  43
affiliation, ideology of 32–3
age: and argument 44–5, 46–7,
  48–9, 306–10
Alimo-Metcalfe, Beverly 233
Amadeus String Quartet 293–4
ambition, female 273, 309
American Association for the
  Advancement of Science 297,
  301
American Association of
  University Women: survey 42
American Management
  Association: Monograph 233,
  234
Anderson, Bonnie S., and Zinsser,
  Judith P.: *A History of Their
  Own* ... 328–9
anger 69; at belittlement 75–7;
  expressing 80–2; fear of 72, 73,

79; and gender 146–7; hiding
  43–4, 46, 81, 82–3; normal
  77–82; as weapon 185; *see also*
  violence
Apfelbaum, Erika 241, 275–6
Archer, John 76
argument 16–19;
  as defined by men 20–1; as
  defined by women 24–6, 27;
  and Division of Labour 32–5;
  as a game 134, 211–12, 270;
  ideologies of 27–31, 32; and
  memory 1–2, 190, 204, 270–1;
  psychology of 150–1, 267–8
Aristotle 28
assertiveness 210, 220
Astley, Gordon 127–8, 132
authoritarianism 238–9

Barad, Jill 241–2
Barbie dolls 241, 327
Baxter, Marilyn 275
BBC TV: *Killer Bimbos on Fleet
  Street* 275; *Living with the
  Enemy* 112
Beatrice and Benedick 37
Beers, Charlotte 242, 243
Beloff, Halla 95–96
Bernard of Clairvaux, St 90
Bill, The 186